Easy Web Development with WaveMaker

A practical, hands-on guide for amateur developers to design, develop, and deploy web and mobile applications using WaveMaker

Edward Callahan

BIRMINGHAM - MUMBAI

Easy Web Development with WaveMaker

First published: July 2013

Production Reference: 1190713

Published by Packt Publishing Ltd.
Livery Place
35 Livery Street
Birmingham B3 2PB, UK.

ISBN 978-1-78216-178-3

www.packtpub.com

Cover Image by Aashish Variava (aashishvariava@hotmail.com)

Credits

Author
Edward Callahan

Reviewers
Michael Simcich
Michael Kantor
Arjunkumar Krishnamoorthy
Jörg Lew
Eliecer Daza Parra
Giuseppe Luigi Punzi

Acquisition Editors
Rukhsana Khambatta
Rubal Kaur

Lead Technical Editor
Anila Vincent

Technical Editors
Sanhita Sawant
Hardik B. Soni
Dennis John

Project Coordinator
Hardik Patel

Proofreader
Paul Hindle

Indexer
Tejal R. Soni

Graphics
Ronak Dhruv

Production Coordinator
Pooja Chiplunkar

Cover Work
Pooja Chiplunkar

About the Author

Edward Callahan is an accomplished open source software engineer and consultant living in the San Francisco Bay Area. Currently with Typesafe, Edward was the Scrum Master and a core contributor to the WaveMaker project in VMware's SpringSource division. He led the formation of the WaveMaker developer community and has written countless forum posts, examples, and wiki articles about its development. Prior to joining WaveMaker, he was a Senior Manager of technical support for Progress Software's Enterprise Infrastructure Division. He completed his education at Worcester Polytechnic Institute and Northeastern University.

Acknowledgement

It has been said that an open source project isn't a "real" project until there has been a book written about it. This book is the result of a collective effort by many, many people, without which there would be no WaveMaker to write about.

First and foremost, I want to thank my family; my incredibly supportive wife Tamara and my darling girls, Lauren and Olivia. Their love, understanding, and patience throughout this process has been simply wonderful.

I would also like to thank the WaveMaker team, and in particular Chris Keene, Derek Henninger, and Michael Kantor. The collective energy and drive of the team we formed at WaveMaker is the stuff that empowers us to move mountains, build villages, and change the world.

Finally, a gigantic thank you to the WaveMaker community. If it were not for the participation and contributions of community members; folks like Manuel, Stefano, Thomas, Gary, Jose, Lenny, Jeff, and Niek to name but a few, WaveMaker would never have matured into the awesome little IDE it has become. Working incredibly hard truly can be fun when collaborating with a global group of guys and gals like those of the WaveMaker community.

About the Reviewers

Michael Kantor was a Lead Developer on the WaveMaker JavaScript framework for four years, during which time he evolved both the JavaScript framework and WaveMaker Studio's UI capabilities. In particular, he comes from a background in mobile applications, and implemented much of the mobile support in WaveMaker in his copious free time. He is now building JavaScript frameworks at `www.servicemax.com` (sadly, not an open source framework).

Arjunkumar Krishnamoorthy is a Lead Engineer with Causeway Technologies in Bangalore, India. He is well versed in Java, JavaScript, Node.js, Backbone.js, and others. Arjun has also contributed to open source projects. He is passionate about programming, research, and open source technologies.

Jörg Lew works as a Senior Consultant at VMware, focusing on automation and integration of datacenters. He used WaveMaker in several customer projects, especially to build web-based frontends for automation solutions based on VMware vCenter™ Orchestrator. You can find some of these stories published on his blog, `www.vcoportal.de`. In his spare time, he lectures on Internet Technology and Java Development at the University of Applied Sciences in Kempten, Germany.

Jörg lives in the beautiful area of Allgaeu in the south of Germany.

Eliecer Daza Parra has been a web developer since 2005. He has ample experience in Java, Python, PHP, and jQuery. He has been working with WaveMaker for over 10 years since the release of its third version. He has more than 8 years of experience as a Java developer. He has been a developer of software for information management and customer relationship management (CMR), health promoting enterprises (EPS), public transportation, and education companies in both the private and public sectors. For the past two years, Eliecer has been working as a Python developer.

Among his main areas of interest are the development of Linux, Python, Android, and Google services. He has a huge interest in nurturing blog spaces about Linux administration and programming.

My heartfelt appreciation to God, my beloved mother and friends, my family, and July.

Giuseppe Luigi Punzi has more than 15 years of experience as a professional developer, having skills in Object Pascal, Oval, OPL, Visual Basic, .NET, Java, and others languages/platforms.

He has a passion for new technologies and methodologies, and is an active WaveMaker community member.

He is a cofounder and consultant in *Komenco IT Solutions*. Apart from other services, his company is specialized in outsourcing and custom-made software.

www.PacktPub.com

Support files, eBooks, discount offers and more

You might want to visit www.PacktPub.com for support files and downloads related to your book.

Did you know that Packt offers eBook versions of every book published, with PDF and ePub files available? You can upgrade to the eBook version at www.PacktPub.com and as a print book customer, you are entitled to a discount on the eBook copy. Get in touch with us at service@packtpub.com for more details.

At www.PacktPub.com, you can also read a collection of free technical articles, sign up for a range of free newsletters and receive exclusive discounts and offers on Packt books and eBooks.

http://PacktLib.PacktPub.com

Do you need instant solutions to your IT questions? PacktLib is Packt's online digital book library. Here, you can access, read and search across Packt's entire library of books.

Why Subscribe?

- Fully searchable across every book published by Packt
- Copy and paste, print and bookmark content
- On demand and accessible via web browser

Free Access for Packt account holders

If you have an account with Packt at www.PacktPub.com, you can use this to access PacktLib today and view nine entirely free books. Simply use your login credentials for immediate access.

Table of Contents

Preface

This book describes an easier way to build custom, modern web applications using WaveMaker Studio, the web development tool for non-professional developers. WaveMaker runs in a browser and provides an intuitive visual development interface. The resultant applications use proven open source libraries, including the Spring framework and the Dojo Toolkit with the Model-view-controller (MVC) pattern. This is professional-grade development made easy.

In this book, we will walk through the entire development process. We will start with using the Studio and planning the application. We will then cover using JavaScript, Java, CSS, relational databases, and web services to provision functionalities and enhance the user experience. We shall conclude with deployment and debugging. By the end of this book, readers will be equipped to experience the joy of having designed, developed, and deployed a web application.

Communities are a wonderful resource for users of open source projects, as the collective wisdom of a community always outpowers the knowledge of any single individual. Readers are encouraged to participate in the WaveMaker developer community at http://dev.wavemaker.com. There, you will not only find documentations and examples, but also a fantastic group of users, new and old, with whom you can discuss, share, and collaborate.

What this book covers

Chapter 1, Getting Started with WaveMaker, covers setting up WaveMaker and the example project workspace. It also explores an example application from a user's perspective.

Chapter 2, Digging into the Architecture, explains the application architecture, covering the client, server, and communication between the two.

Chapter 3, Using Studio, walks through every aspect of using Studio, from visually assembling the application to using the binding dialog and code editors.

Chapter 4, Designing a Well-performing Application, covers how to design your application so it performs well and is easy to use.

Chapter 5, Navigating towards Reusability, explains the numerous navigation techniques, such as pages and dialogs, available to developers to create reusable components and a customized user experience.

Chapter 6, Styling the Application, covers using CSS with the WaveMaker framework to style applications.

Chapter 7, Working with Databases, covers everything you need to know about working with relational databases in WaveMaker.

Chapter 8, Utilizing Web Services, explains how to consume web services in your applications.

Chapter 9, Custom Java Services, covers everything you need to know to utilize Java for custom server-side functionality.

Chapter 10, Customizing the User Interface with JavaScript, explains how to customize applications using JavaScript while leveraging the WaveMaker client framework.

Chapter 11, Mastering Client Customization, explores advanced client customization techniques such as custom formatters, custom grid columns, and dynamic page content.

Chapter 12, Securing Applications, covers the WaveMaker security model and explains how to secure your application. It also introduces customization of the security configuration for advanced cases.

Chapter 13, Deploying Applications, explores the deployment process while reviewing your deployment options.

Chapter 14, Mobile Deployment, introduces building a native mobile application from your WaveMaker application using PhoneGap.

Chapter 15, Debugging, covers how to troubleshoot and debug applications, from logging to debugging with browser and Java tools.

What you need for this book

Readers should have WaveMaker 6.5 and a web browser installed on their computer. In this book, we will demonstrate using Google's Chrome browser and its Developer Tools, but comparable web developer tools such as Firebug for Firefox can be used as well.

Optionally, more experienced readers may wish to have a GitHub client and a code editor or IDE tool such as Eclipse available. These are not required.

Who this book is for

This book is primarily for business developers—tech-savvy users who want to build modern, responsive web applications that connect to databases, REST, and Java services. This book is also for the rapidly growing group of amateur developers who are also known as citizen developers.

No specific technical background is assumed. However, we will be interacting with numerous technologies throughout the course of this book. The more of those technologies you are familiar with, the easier you will find this book. As we cannot explain every technology utilized, links to those projects are provided for further reading if needed. If you are already familiar with some of these areas, or you have some development experience, you will be able to move through this book more quickly than those just starting out with web development.

This book is also good for experienced developers who are interested in using WaveMaker as a tool to build AJAX browser clients to their web and Java services.

Conventions

In this book, you will find a number of styles of text that distinguish between different kinds of information. Here are some examples of these styles, and an explanation of their meaning.

Code words in text are shown as follows: "Being a Java application, we have a WEB-INF folder, which contains our web.xml as well as our classes and lib folders."

A block of code is set as follows:

```
<div id="_wm_loading" style="z-index: 100;">
<table style='width:100%;height: 100%;'><tr><td align='center'><img
alt="Loading" src="/wavemaker/lib/boot/images/loader.gif"
/>  Loading...</td></tr></table>
</div>
```

When we wish to draw your attention to a particular part of a code block, the relevant lines or items are set in bold:

```
ClassPanel: ["wm.Panel", {"_classes":{"domNode":["CustomRedTextHorizGr
adientPanel"]},"height":"125px","horizontalAlign":"left","verticalAlig
n":"top","width":"100%"}, {}, {
```

Any command-line input or output is written as follows:

```
c:\Java\jdk1.6.0_45\bin\javaw.exe -Xms256m -Xmx512m -XX:MaxPermSize=256m
-jar "C:\Program Files\WaveMaker\6.5.3.Release\launcher\launcher.jar"
```

New terms and **important words** are shown in bold. Words that you see on the screen, in menus or dialog boxes for example, appear in the text like this: "Click on the **Test Connection** button to verify your settings. Once the connection tests successfully, save the properties by clicking on the **Save** button".

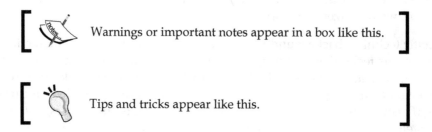

Warnings or important notes appear in a box like this.

Tips and tricks appear like this.

Reader feedback

Feedback from our readers is always welcome. Let us know what you think about this book—what you liked or may have disliked. Reader feedback is important for us to develop titles that you really get the most out of.

To send us general feedback, simply send an e-mail to feedback@packtpub.com, and mention the book title via the subject of your message.

If there is a topic that you have expertise in and you are interested in either writing or contributing to a book, see our author guide on www.packtpub.com/authors.

Customer support

Now that you are the proud owner of a Packt book, we have a number of things to help you to get the most from your purchase.

Downloading the example code

You can download the example code files for all Packt books you have purchased from your account at http://www.packtpub.com. If you purchased this book elsewhere, you can visit http://www.packtpub.com/support and register to have the files e-mailed directly to you.

The example code for this book is also available on GitHub at https://github.com/edwardcallahan/Easy-Web-Samples. The example code has been published under Apache 2.0 license.

Errata

Although we have taken every care to ensure the accuracy of our content, mistakes do happen. If you find a mistake in one of our books—maybe a mistake in the text or the code—we would be grateful if you would report this to us. By doing so, you can save other readers from frustration and help us improve subsequent versions of this book. If you find any errata, please report them by visiting http://www.packtpub.com/submit-errata, selecting your book, clicking on the **errata submission form** link, and entering the details of your errata. Once your errata are verified, your submission will be accepted and the errata will be uploaded on our website, or added to any list of existing errata, under the Errata section of that title. Any existing errata can be viewed by selecting your title from http://www.packtpub.com/support.

Piracy

Piracy of copyright material on the Internet is an ongoing problem across all media. At Packt, we take the protection of our copyright and licenses very seriously. If you come across any illegal copies of our works, in any form, on the Internet, please provide us with the location address or website name immediately so that we can pursue a remedy.

Please contact us at copyright@packtpub.com with a link to the suspected pirated material.

We appreciate your help in protecting our authors, and our ability to bring you valuable content.

Questions

You can contact us at questions@packtpub.com if you are having a problem with any aspect of the book, and we will do our best to address it.

1
Getting Started with WaveMaker

WaveMaker Studio is an open source project that enables web application development by non-professional developers. WaveMaker is not a programming language; instead, it is a tool that makes it easy to build web applications in leading languages. As you visually assemble components in your browser, WaveMaker constructs an industrial strength application using leading open source libraries, such as the Spring Framework and the Dojo Toolkit. The result is a standards-based web application that can be built by a beginner and maintained by an expert.

We'll prepare for our journey by setting up our workspace. First, we will need to get ourselves a copy of WaveMaker Studio and the required examples. This book includes eight example applications. Viewing the sample projects in the Studio, as a developer, is a great way to better understand how these applications were built. With the example source code in hand, we will take one of the example applications out for a spin. This will provide us with a tangible understanding of our destination and a look at what we are able to create using WaveMaker. We'll end our introduction with a quick look under the covers of the sample. By examining the sample from a developer's point of view, we'll get our first feel for how things work under the pretty user interface.

In this chapter, we will:

- Set you up with your own WaveMaker Studio
- Configure your workspace to run the examples
- Tour a simple sample WaveMaker project
- Peek under the covers of the sample application

Setting up your workspace

In order to build and deploy applications of your own, you'll need WaveMaker Studio. Even if you are not ready to build your own application and just want to examine the sample applications from a developers point of view, you'll want to view the project from within the Studio. So, we shall begin with setting up WaveMaker Studio.

Getting the right version

This book is about WaveMaker Version 6.5. WaveMaker is an active open source project with on-going development. The first 6.5 Version of WaveMaker, 6.5.0, was released in October 2012. Patch releases, such as 6.5.1, have followed. In time, newer versions such as 6.6.0 will also be released. For best compatibility with this book and its sample projects, you will want to use the latest release version of 6.5 available, currently 6.5.3. Newer versions of the Studio will generally open and run the sample projects, but the constant evolution of the project will result in changes that may render some things discussed in this book obsolete or incorrect. Instructions provided in this book are for Version 6.5 and may not exactly match how things are done with newer versions.

Now that we know what version we will be using, we will review our browser and installation options. There are two common ways to run the Studio: installing a release package or, for advanced users, building from source. First, let's ensure we're using a good browser.

Being browser smart

The reality is that not all browsers are created equal. Things such as rendering speed, developer support, and support of HTML5 features can vary widely among browsers. While there are many browsers out there, more than many people even realize, we shall concern ourselves only with the most common ones. Of those, we can generally categorize them into three families based on their underlying layout engines. Here, the "big three" for both desktops and mobile are—Gecko: used by the Mozilla Foundation for Firefox, WebKit or Webkit forks: used by Apple's Safari and Google's Chrome and Trident: used by Microsoft's Internet Explorer.

WaveMaker applications make heavy use of JavaScript in the browser. Therefore, the faster a browser can parse and run JavaScript, the faster a WaveMaker application will generally run in that browser. Deployed WaveMaker applications will run in the most common browsers. For older versions of Internet Explorer that lack HTML5 support and have rather slow JavaScript engines, we can use plugins such as Google Chrome Frame. Chrome Frame enables our JavaScript application to run in the Chrome V8 engine even when the application is loaded from an older version of Internet Explorer. You can learn more about Chrome Frame at `https://developers.google.com/chrome/chrome-frame`.

 In June 2013, Google announced the retirement of Chrome Frame.

We may not get to dictate what browser our users use to run our application, but we do get to choose what browser we primarily develop in. Here too, some browsers are better than others. As such, Chrome and Safari are the preferred development browsers by most WaveMaker developers today. In this book, we'll be using Google Chrome, as it is fast, has excellent developer support, and is available on all major platforms. You are welcome to use other browsers; however, we will only using Chrome in this book.

WaveMaker applications work in the most popular modern browsers. However, those browsers may interpret your Cascading Style Sheets (CSS), JavaScript, or resultant HTML differently, and you'll want to test your application in the browsers your users will be using before you declare victory. This testing may require using another system or a virtual machine (VM). Someone developing on OS X, for example, might use a VM running Windows in order to test with Internet Explorer. WaveMaker handles most of all the cross-browser issues for you, and your application may "just work" in other browsers. However, you'll still want to test it.

 If something isn't working right, clear the browser cache to ensure the correct file loading. We'll discuss why in *Chapter 15, Debugging*.

As a general rule, the more customization you do, the more cross-browser testing you'll want to do. I suggest you first get your application working in a developer-friendly browser to flush out the general issues. Then, cross-test in other supported browsers to get the browse-specific issues before declaring the application as done.

Installing locally using a release package

Installing a release package is the easy way to install the Studio. WaveMaker 6.5 is distributed as an installation EXE for Windows, a DMG disk image for Mac OS X, and as RPM and DEB packages for Linux. You will need administrator or root access to install WaveMaker. You will also need the Java command available to run the embedded Tomcat. WaveMaker 6.5.3 ships its own compiler, the same one used by eclipse for JDK 6 compilation, but you still need a JRE to run the embedded Tomcat.

You can install the Studio on your local machine or on a remote host on the network. If you install on a remote host, you only need to point your browser at the remote host instead of the local host.

The installation packages for the latest stable release can be downloaded from the WaveMaker site, `http://www.wavemaker.com/downloads/`. For installation packages of older releases, such as downloading Version 6.5.x when it is no longer the latest version, visit `http://dev.wavemaker.com/wiki/bin/wmdoc/Releases`.

The release packages are available for Windows, OS X, and Linux. For more information about installing WaveMaker on your platform of choice including overcoming installation issues, see the install guide in the documentation located at `http://dev.wavemaker.com/wiki/bin/wmdoc_6.5/WMInstallGuide`.

The first thing you need to do after installing a release package is install the dependency bundle. These are files that are required to run the Studio, but cannot be distributed with WaveMaker Studio. WaveMaker is distributed under the Apache 2.0 license. A few libraries used by the Studio, such as the Ace editor, are licensed under the **General Public License (GPL)**. The Apache license is not compatible with most GPLs. Therefore, you must download the GPL libraries separately. To make this as simple as possible, the Studio configuration tool will help you download a pre-packaged bundle of libraries with the correct versions needed. A few other libraries used by WaveMaker, such as the JAR file `wsdl4j` used for web services, have incompatible licenses. You will be prompted to download and install these libraries if you perform an action that requires an additional library.

 If you experience difficulties running the Studio, the debugging process is described in *Chapter 15, Debugging*. Studio is a WaveMaker application, and the processes are quite similar as a result.

Building a Studio from GitHub

Building your own Studio from sources takes the most effort to set up, but provides the most flexibility and control over the development environment. It is also the first step should you wish to get involved in open source software and contribute to the development of WaveMaker. This configuration is recommended for advanced users. If you are not comfortable building source code using Maven, use the installed version described previously instead.

To build your own Studio, you will need the following:

- A Java 6 JDK

The following are optional, but highly recommended:

- Tomcat 6, for running your Studio
- A git client, to keep your version up to date

To clone the repository, use the following `git clone` command:

```
git clone https://github.com/SpringSource/wavemaker.git
```

You will want to use the 6.5.X branch:

```
https://github.com/SpringSource/wavemaker/tree/6.5.X.
```

Use the `git checkout` command:

```
git checkout 6.5.X
```

The preceding `git checkout` command is used to switch your local copy to the 6.5.X branch. The 6.5.X branch is stable and contains any updates made to 6.5 since the 6.5.3 release. Tags for specific releases, such as 6.5.2, also exist should you want the source for a specific release version.

The master branch, on the other hand, is a work in progress for the next version, and may not be completely stable at any given moment. You generally will not want to use the master branch unless you know what you are doing and are comfortable dealing with the possible consequences. With that said, the master branch is an easy way to see the newest features and fixes in the WaveMaker project.

If you don't have or don't want to use a `git` client, you can download the source code as a `.zip` or `.tar.gz` file directly from GitHub. Using the `git` client has the advantage of being able to pull updates without having to download the whole source tree, and easily you can switch branches. Downloading as a bundle is an easy way to access the source code. If you just want to browse the source code without downloading it all, you can do so via the GitHub site, `https://github.com/SpringSource/wavemaker`.

The project README explains how to clone, build, and deploy WaveMaker. It is available at `https://github.com/SpringSource/wavemaker/blob/master/README.md`.

> The `inplace` deployment to your own Tomcat lets you use your Tomcat installation. Using the `inplace` target option with a `git` clone workspace is the easiest way to update Studio without building an installation package. To use this feature, you will need the manager app enabled with accounts that match those in `/wavemaker-tools/src/main/resources/com/wavemaker/tools/project/app-deploy.xml`.

Setting up the examples

Now that you've got a Studio in your browser, let's get the examples set up so you can view them in the Studio. The examples are stored on the code sharing site GitHub. If you aren't familiar with GitHub or otherwise don't have a `git` client, don't worry. GitHub lets you download and unpack the repository as a `.zip` file from their site by visiting the following URL:

`https://github.com/edwardcallahan/Easy-Web-Samples/archive/master.zip`.

If you do have a `git` client installed, the easiest way to get the examples is to clone the example repository using git clone, as shown in the following command:

`git clone https://github.com/edwardcallahan/Easy-Web-Samples.git`

However, when you get the example projects, they will need to be copied to a folder on the host running the WaveMaker Studio Tomcat server. Either copy the projects into your Studio's project folder or update the project folder. To do that, go to the **WaveMaker File** menu and select the **Preferences...** menu item to set your **WaveMaker Folder** to the **Easy-Web-Samples** directory.

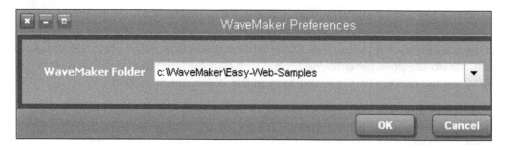

You should now see the sample projects listed in the open project dialog. Each project in the bundle also contains a project export in its export folder. Use the Studio file menu to import each project export individually.

Some of the sample projects use a MySQL database and others use an embedded HSQLDB database. HSQLDB examples require no configuration. If a project uses a MySQL database, a database export is included with the project in the `src` directory. The free community edition is fine as no enterprise version features are used. You'll need to be able to access a MySQL server to import these exports. Setting up MySQL is not required to run those examples, but the examples are more fun with data.

Importing the database

If you want to use the database, you'll need to import the database export file named `custpurchase.sql` in the project `src` folder. One way to import the database export is to connect to your MySQL server using the `mysql` command line client. As the export creates the database for us, we only need to source the file. The easiest way to do this is to start the `mysql` client from the directory containing the export file. Then, from within the `mysql` client, use `mysql> source custpuchase.sql` to load the database schema and data from the file.

We'll cover working with databases in *Chapter 7, Working with Databases*, but examples are better with data, so let's configure our Java Database Connectivity (JDBC) connection to the database using the following steps:

1. Open the **Services** tab with the project open in the Studio.
2. Select the **custpurchaseDB** service from the service tree.
3. Open the database connections dialog by clicking on the wrench button.

In the database connection settings dialog, update the **Username**, **Password**, and **Host** fields to use the same connection you used to create the database in MySQL. Should your MySQL server not be running on port 3306, enter the correct port number as well. No other fields require review for this. The connection URL will be updated based on your other entries. Click on the **Test Connection** button to verify your settings. Once the connection tests successfully, save the properties by clicking on the **Save** button.

Introducing CRM Simple

Simple CRM is precisely what its name implies; a simple customer relationship management (CRM) example application. We have exactly what you'd expect in a basic sample of a CRM application; customers, orders, and ordered items. It is a database-driven application, where the schema consists of five tables and includes one-to-many and many-to-many relationships.

Open the project named CRM_Simple in the Studio and run the app. The **Run** button in the top menu bar deploys the application and opens a new browser window.

If there are no problems and the database connection is good, the new application is loaded in the new window with the customer list populated. The WaveMaker launcher process sends the Studio URL to the default browser on the system. You can specify a specific browser in the preferences accessed by the **Advanced Options** button when the Studio has been stopped.

Or, if you prefer, simply copy the URL of the application from the launched windows into the desired browser; in this case, we'll be using Google Chrome.

The first thing we are likely to notice is the size of the layout. The layout of this particular application targets a tablet. If you are using the application from a touch input device, the lists are scrolled with a flick of the finger, as we would expect. If, on the other hand, you load the application in a desktop browser, scroll bars appear where needed, and you can use your mouse to scroll through the list.

At the top of the customer area is a search box. There's some placeholder text informing us that we can search using any part of a company name. Typing `city`, for example, immediately returns us both "City Light Books" and "Fog City books." It does this even though only City Light Books begins with the word city, and both entries capitalize "city." The X icon at the right end of the search editor clears out our search and resets our results with a single action.

As we select different customers from the list of companies, the details near the top of the screen, including the companies' contact picture, refreshes to the selected customer. The companies Twitter ID is presented as a link, should we wish to send the customer a quick message via Twitter. At the same time, the list of orders to the right is updated. As we make our selections, the lists highlight the currently selected items, lest we forget which customer or order we have chosen. Likewise, when we select an order presented by order date, we are presented with the line items of the chosen order.

Now let's begin to enter a new customer by clicking on the **New Customer** button. We are presented with a straightforward form. The `company name`, `address`, `city`, `state`, and `zip code` fields are required, as suggested by the red asterisk next to the labels. As we would expect from a modern application, validation helps the user complete the form successfully by ensuring the user has entered acceptable data, such as ensuring a phone number has the correct number of digits. When you enter values for all the required fields, the **Save** button becomes enabled. Click on or otherwise point at an element and that element is given the focus of the application. It becomes the active element that receives input. Moving focus away from that element triggers the blur event for the node. If we trigger the blur event for any required editor in the form without entering a value, validation displays both a warning icon and a friendly pop-up message.

Clicking on the **Inventory** button navigates us to the list of items in our fictitious book supplier inventory. Again, highlighting provides feedback on the selection we have made. Here we have another form which we can update an existing item, create a new item, or delete an existing entry. When taking a new order, the date editor opens a calendar date picker, just as we'd expect. The **Companies** button quickly navigates us back to our customer view, ready to look up another.

Not a bad little application, eh? We've seen styled widgets, such as the search editor, combined with rich editor validation and in-form assistance assembled to present intuitive database forms and navigations. Would you call it "pixel perfect" or so compelling that you expect it to race to the top of app store downloads? No, probably not. Is it usable and functional? It certainly is. Does it solve a problem or deliver a business solution, however fictitious the business may be? Yes, yes it does.

Now consider that almost no code was used to create this application. Oh sure, there's plenty of Java and JavaScript being executed, but the vast majority of the effort in building a simple application such as this is done visually. The developer need only select values, tick on and off desired behaviors, and connect events with responses. Many WaveMaker users use some JavaScript code to get the exact behaviors they want in the browser. Java can also be used for custom server-side services. This application does use a data expression analogous to a formula in a spreadsheet cell to sum order totals. However, such expressions are no more complicated than macros in a Microsoft Office document.

In this one example, we get a hint of the professional grade aspects of our application. Because the data access layer is built using popular open source frameworks, the level of customization shown does not require us to code those features ourselves.

Exploring the sample application

Let's continue exploring the application in the Studio. Don't worry if you don't yet understand everything you are about to see. We will explain all of this in detail in future chapters. For now, we just want to explore the application and have a bit of fun.

Studio provides us with a visually-oriented way to view the application's construction. Selecting the **Canvas** tab brings us to the visual layout of the application. In the canvas area and the model tree, we can see all the visual components or widgets that are on this page of the application. Selecting a component, such as an **editor** or **service variable**, either by clicking on it in the canvas area or from the model tree, shows its properties in the property editors on the right. For example, select the title label at the top named **labelTitle**. It's the label that says **CRM Simple** with a blue background. Once selected, on the right you'll see a caption property with the value **CRM Simple**. If you change the value of the caption property, the title shown in the label will also change as soon as you blur the property editor. We'll discuss using the Studio in detail in *Chapter 3, Using Studio*.

Let's interact with the application at a different level. Open the developer tools built into Chrome. The developer tools can be accessed by clicking on the Chrome menu in the upper-right corner, choose tools, then developer tools. Alternatively, you can use the keyboard shortcut to open the developer tools. On Windows and Linux, use *Ctrl + Shift + J*. On OS X, press *command + option + J*. We can do many interesting things here in the developer tools. We'll be using the developer tools as our JavaScript debugger in *Chapter 15, Debugging*.

Ensure you have the console open. You should see an arrow **>** symbol, next to which you can enter commands. If you know the JavaScript console, you know how we can execute JavaScript here. We could enter the classic `alert("Hello Wavy World")` for example to raise an alert dialog. This means from here we can also access the components and the HTML elements, or DOM nodes, of the application. In the case of a WaveMaker application, entering `app` at the console prompt will return the application object. Entering `app.theme` will return the string name of the theme used by this application, `wm_coolblue` in the case of CRM Simple. We'll discuss theming in *Chapter 6, Styling the Application*, as part of CSS and styling.

In Studio, we saw how easy it was to change the caption of the title label. We can also change the title from the console. Enter `main.labelTitle.setCaption ("Hello Web");` the title of the app is now Hello Web. We'll be working with applications in this context on and off while working with WaveMaker. In *Chapter 10, Customizing the User Interface with JavaScript* and *Chapter 11, Mastering Client Customization*, we'll focus on using JavaScript to customize our application.

Finally, let's take a look at our application from the file system. Open the `CRM_Simple` project folder in a file system tool such as Finder or Explorer. If you are using the Studio on a remote server, use **Source**, **Resources**, and select **Project** from **Folder Shortcuts** to view the remote file system. Within the services folder, we see our `custpurchaseDB` service, in which we will find all the generated source code for our project including the Hibernate mapping for our database schema. We'll discuss how this service came to be in *Chapter 7, Working with Databases*.

Under webapproot, we see the top level of our deployed application, including `index.html`. Under the pages folder, we see a folder for each page in our project. Being a Java application, we have a `WEB-INF` folder, which contains our `web.xml` as well as our classes and `lib` folders. Don't worry if this doesn't make sense yet, we'll learn about this soon enough.

There is a lot we can learn by looking at the project on the file system. Touring the file system is always on the day one agenda when training teams on WaveMaker. We'll continue our tour of the project from the file system as we dig into the application architecture in the next chapter.

Summary

We have examined a simple CRM sample application built using WaveMaker. While the scope of the application may have been limited, it still provided us with a robust user interface. We have secured access to a copy of WaveMaker Studio and the example application. We have chosen Google Chrome as our development browser and even started looking at how the sample application is put together.

In the next chapter, we'll continue into the application architecture. We'll look at the JavaScript client and how it is put together, including its use of the Dojo Toolkit. We shall also look at the Java server side of the application and how it works. No understanding of a web application would be complete without looking at the asynchronous transfer of data between browser and server. We'll also look at how types work in WaveMaker.

2
Digging into the Architecture

Now that we've seen the end result, let's take a look at how it is all put together. In this chapter, we will examine the WaveMaker application architecture. We will learn about the client, the server, how they are constructed, and some of the core features available to us in each. We'll examine the HTTP requests made to the server and examine the JSON request of a database read call. We'll also learn about typing in WaveMaker. We'll finish this chapter with a tour of the Studio WaveMaker application. By the end of this chapter, you will have learned about:

- The client framework
- The server architecture
- Communications between client and server
- Types
- Application file structure

The big picture

A very short description of a WaveMaker application could be: a Spring MVC server running in a Java container, such as Tomcat, serving file and JSON requests for a Dojo Toolkit-based JavaScript browser client. Unfortunately, such "elevator" descriptions can create more questions than they answer.

For starters, although we will often refer to it as "the server," the WaveMaker server might be more aptly called an application server in most architectures. Sure, it is possible to have a useful application without additional servers or services beyond the WaveMaker server, but this is not typical. We could have a rich user interface to read against some in memory data set, for example. Far more commonly, the Java services running in the WaveMaker server are calling off to other servers or services, such as relational databases and RESTful web services. This means the WaveMaker server is often the middle or application tier server of a multi-tier application's architecture.

Yet at the same time, the WaveMaker server can be eliminated completely. Applications can be packaged for uploading to PhoneGap build, `http://build.phonegap.com/`, directly from WaveMaker Studio. Both PhoneGap and the associated Apache project Cordova, `http://cordova.apache.org`, provide APIs to enable JavaScript to access native device functionality, such as capturing images with the camera and obtaining GPS location information. Packaged up and installed as a native application, the JavaScript files are loaded from the devices, file system instead of being downloaded from a server via HTTP. This means there is no origin domain to be constrained by. If the application only uses web services, or otherwise doesn't need additional services, such as database access, the WaveMaker server is neither used nor needed.

Just because an application isn't installed on a mobile device from an app store doesn't mean we can't run it on a mobile device. Browsers on mobile devices are more capable than ever before. This means our client could be any device with a modern browser.

You must also consider licensing in light of the bigger picture. WaveMaker, WaveMaker Studio, and the applications create with the Studio are released under the Apache 2.0 license, `http://www.apache.org/licenses/LICENSE-2.0`. The WaveMaker project was first released by WaveMaker Software in 2007. In March 2011, VMware (`http://vmware.com`) acquired the WaveMaker project. It was under VMware that WaveMaker 6.5 was released. In April 2013, Pramati Technlogies (`http://pramati.com`) acquired the assets of WaveMaker for its CloudJee (`http://cloudjee.com`) platform. WaveMaker continues to be developed and released by Pramati Technologies.

Now that we understand where our client and server sit in the larger world, we will be primarily focused within and between those two parts. The overall picture of the client and server looks as shown in the following diagram:

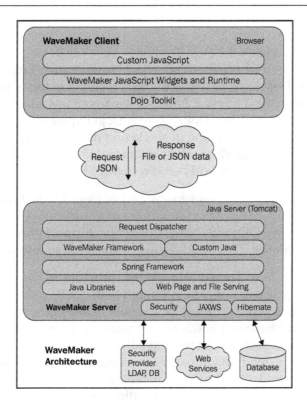

We will examine each piece of this diagram in detail during the course of this book. We shall start with the JavaScript client.

Getting comfortable with the JavaScript client

The client is a JavaScript client that runs in a modern browser. This means that most of the client, the HTML and DOM nodes that the browser interfaces with specifically, are created by JavaScript at runtime. The application is styled using CSS, and we can use HTML in our applications. However, we don't use HTML to define buttons and forms. Instead, we define components, such as widgets, and set their properties. These component class names and properties are used as arguments to functions that create DOM nodes for us.

Dojo Toolkit

To do this, WaveMaker uses the Dojo Toolkit, http://dojotoolkit.org/. Dojo, as it is generally referred to, is a modular, cross-browser, JavaScript framework with three sections. Dojo Core provides the base toolkit. On top of which are Dojo's visual widgets called Dijits. Finally, DojoX contains additional extensions such as charts and a color picker. DojoCampus' Dojo Explorer, http://dojocampus.com/explorer/, has a good selection of single unit demos across the toolkit, many with source code. Dojo allows developers to define widgets using HTML or JavaScript. WaveMaker users will better recognize the JavaScript approach.

Specifically, WaveMaker 6.5.X uses version 1.6.1 of Dojo. Of the browsers supported by Dojo 1.6.1, http://dojotoolkit.org/reference-guide/1.8/releasenotes/1.6.html, Opera's "Dojo Core only" support prevents it from being supported by WaveMaker. This could change with Opera's move to WebKit.

Building on top of the Dojo Toolkit, WaveMaker provides its own collections of widgets and underlying components. Although both can be called components, the name component is generally used for the non-visible parts, such as service calls to the server and the event notification system. Widgets, such as the Dijits, are visible components such as buttons and editors. Many, but not all, of the WaveMaker widgets extend functionality from Dojo widgets. When they do extend Dijits, WaveMaker widgets often add numerous functions and behaviors that are not part of Dojo. Examples include controlling the read-only state, formatting display values for currency, and merging components, such as buttons with icons in them. Combined with the WaveMaker runtime layers, these enhancements make it easy to assemble rich clients using only properties. WaveMaker's select editor (wm.SelectMenu) for example extends the Dojo Toolkit ComboBox (dijit.form.ComboBox) or the FilteringSelect (dijit.form.FilteringSelect) as needed. By default, a select menu has Dojo FilteringSelect as its editor, but it will use ComboBox instead if the user is on a mobile device or the developer has cleared the RestrictValues property tick box.

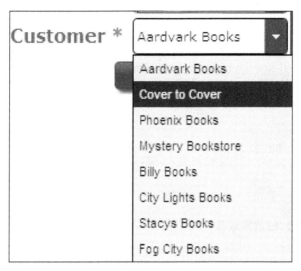

A required select menu editor

Let's consider the case of disabling a submit button when the user has not made a required list selection. In Dojo, this is done using JavaScript code, and for an experienced Dojo developer, this is not difficult. For those who may primarily consider Dojo a martial arts Studio however, it is likely another matter altogether. Using the WaveMaker framework provided widgets, no code is required to set up this inter-connection. This is simply a matter of visually linking or binding the button's `disabled` property to the lists' `emptySelection` property in the graphical binding dialog.

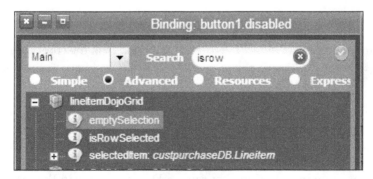

Now the button will be disabled if the user has not made a selection in the grid's list of items. Logically, we can think of this as setting the disabled property to the value of the grid's `emptySelection` property, where `emptySelection` is true unless and until a row has been selected.

Where WaveMaker most notably varies from the Dojo way of things is the layout engine. WaveMaker handles the layout of container widgets using its own engine. Containers are those widgets that contain other widgets, such as panels, tabs, and dialogs. This makes it easier for developers to arrange widgets in WaveMaker Studio. A result of this is that border, padding, and margin are set using properties on widgets, *not* by CSS.

Border, padding, and margin are widget properties in WaveMaker, and are not controlled by CSS.

Dojo made easy

Having the Dojo framework available to us makes web development easier both when using the WaveMaker framework and when doing custom work. Dojo's modular and object-oriented functions, such as `dojo.declare` and `dojo.inherited`, for example, simplify creating custom components, which we will discuss more in *Chapter 11, Mastering Client Customization.*

The key takeaway here is that Dojo itself is available to you as a developer if you wish to use it directly. Many developers never need to utilize this capability, but it is available to you if you ever do wish to take advantage of it. Running the CRM Simple sample again from either the console in the browser development tools or custom project page code, we could use Dojo's `byId()` function to get a `div`, for example, the main title label:

```
>dojo.byId("main_labelTitle").
```

In practice, the WaveMaker style of getting a DOM node via the component name, for example, `main.labelTitle.domNode`, is more practical and returns the same result.

If a function or ability in Dojo is useful, the WaveMaker framework usually provides a wrapper of some sort for you. Just as often, the WaveMaker version is friendlier or otherwise easier to use in some way. For example, `this.connect()`, WaveMaker's version of `dojo.connect()`, tracks connections for you. This avoids the need for you to remember to call `disconnect()` to remove the reference added by every call to `connect()`. For more information about using Dojo functions in WaveMaker, see the Dojo framework page in the WaveMaker documentation at:

```
http://dev.wavemaker.com/wiki/bin/wmdoc_6.5/Dojo+Framework.
```

Binding and events

Two solid examples of WaveMaker taking a powerful feature of Dojo and providing friendlier versions are topic notifications and event handling.

`Dojo.connect()` enables you to register a method to be called when something happens. In other words: "when X happens, please also do Y". Studio provides visual tooling for this in the events section of a component's properties. Buttons have an event drop-down menu for their click event. Asynchronous server call components, live variables, and service variables, have tooled events for reviewing data just before the call is made and for the successful, and not so successful, returns from the call. These menus are populated with listings of likely components and if appropriate, functions. Invoking other service calls, particularly when a server call depends on data from the results of some previous server call, and navigation calls to other layers and pages within the application are easy examples of how WaveMaker's visual tooling of `dojo.connect` simplifies web development.

WaveMaker's binding dialog is a graphical interface on the topic subscription system. Here we are "binding" a live variable that returns rows from the `lineitem` table to be filtered by the data value of the `orderid` editor in the form on the new order page:

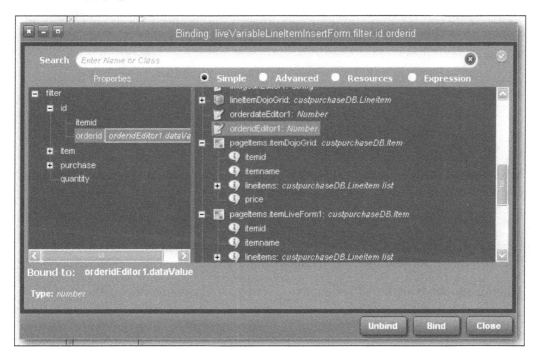

The result of this binding is that when the value of the `orderid` editor changes, the value in the filter parameter of this live variable will be updated. An event indicating that the value of this orderid editor has changed is published when the data value changes. This live variable's filter is being subscribed to that topic and can now update its value accordingly.

Loading the client

Web applications start from `index.html`, and a WaveMaker application is no different. If we examine `index.html` of a WaveMaker application, we see the total content is less than 100 lines. We have some meta tags in the head, mostly for Internet Explorer (MSIE) and iOS support. In the body, there are more entries to help out with older versions of MSIE, including script tags to use Chrome Frame if we so choose. If we cut all that away, `index.html` is rather simple. In the head, we load the CSS containing the projects theme and define a few lines of style classes for `wavemakerNode` and `_wm_loading`:

```
<script>var wmThemeUrl = "/wavemaker/lib/wm/base/widget/themes/wm_
default/theme.css";</script>
<style type="text/css">
  #wavemakerNode {
    height: 100%;
    overflow: hidden;
    position: relative;
  }
        #_wm_loading {
            text-align: center;
            margin: 25% 0px 25% 0px;
        }
</style>
```

Next we load the file `config.js`, which as its name suggests, is about configuration. The following line of code is used to load the file:

```
<script type="text/javascript" src="config.js"></script>
```

`Config.js` defines the various settings, variables, and helper functions needed to initialize the application, such as the locale setting.

Moving into the body tag of `index.html`, we find a `div` named `wavemakerNode`:

```
<div id="wavemakerNode">
```

The next `div` tag is the loader gif, which is given in the following code:

```
<div id="_wm_loading" style="z-index: 100;">
<table style='width:100%;height: 100%;'><tr><td align='center'><img
alt="Loading" src="/wavemaker/lib/boot/images/loader.gif"
/>  Loading...</td></tr></table>
</div>
```

This is the standard spinner shown while the application is loading. With the loader gif now spinning, we begin the real work with `runtimeLoader.js`, as given in the following line of code:

```
<script type="text/javascript" src="/wavemaker/lib/runtimeLoader.
js"></script>
```

When running a project from Studio, the client runtime is loaded from Studio via WaveMaker. `Config.js` and `index.html` are modified for deployment while the client runtime is copied into the applications webapproot.

`runtimeLoader`, as its name suggests, loads the WaveMaker runtime. With the runtime loaded, we can now load the top level `project.a.js` file, which defines our application using the `dojo.declare()` method. The following line of code loads the file:

```
<script type="text/javascript" src="project.a.js"></script>
```

Finally, with our application class defined, we set up an instance of our application in `wavemakerNode` and run it.

There are two modes for loading a WaveMaker application: debug and gzip mode. The debug mode is useful for debugging, as you would expect. The gzip mode is the default mode. The test mode of the **Run**, **Test**, or **Compile** button in Studio re-deploys the active project and opens it in debug mode.

This is the only difference between using Test and Run in Studio. The **Test** button adds `?debug` to the URL of the browser window; the **Run** button does not.

Any WaveMaker application can be loaded in debug mode by adding `debug` to the URL parameters. For example, to load the CRM Simple application from *Chapter 1, Getting Started with WaveMaker* in debug mode, use the URL `http://crm_simple. localhost:8094.com/?debug`; detecting debug in the URL sets the `djConfig. debugBoot` flag, which alters the path used in `runtimeLoader`.

```
djConfig.debugBoot = location.search.indexOf("debug") >=0;
```

Like a compiled program, debug mode preserves variable names and all the other details that optimization removes which we would want available to use when debugging. However, JavaScript is not compiled into byte code or machine specific instructions. On the other hand, in gzip mode, the browser loads a few optimized packages containing all the source code in merged files. This reduces the number of files needed to load our application, which significantly improves loading time. These optimized packages are also minified. Minification removes whitespace and replaces variable names with short names, further reducing the volume of code to be parsed by the browser, and therefore further improving performance. The result is a significant reduction in the number of requests needed and the number of bytes transferred to load an application. A stock application in gzip mode requires 22 to 24 requests to load some 300 KB to 400 KB of content, depending on the application. In debug mode, the same app transfers over 1.5 MB in more than 500 requests.

The `index.html` file, and when security is enabled, `login.html`, are yours to edit. If you are comfortable doing so, you can customize these files such as adding additional script tags. In practice, you shouldn't need to customize `index.html`, as you have full control of the application loaded into the `wavemakerNode`. Also, upgraded scripts in future versions of WaveMaker may need to programmatically update `index.html` and `login.html`. Changes to the `X-US-Compatible` meta tag are often required when support for newer versions of Internet Explorer becomes available, for example. These scripts can't possibly know about every customization you may make.

Customization of `index.html` may cause these scripts to fail, and may require you to manually update these files. If you do encounter such a situation, simply use the `index.html` file from a project newly created in the new version as a template.

Springing into the server side

The WaveMaker server is a Java application running in a Java Virtual Machine (JVM). Like the client, it builds upon proven frameworks and libraries. In the case of the server, the foundational block is the SpringSource framework, `http://www.springsource.org/SpringSource`, or the Spring framework. The Spring framework is the most popular enterprise Java development framework today, and for good reason.

The server of a WaveMaker application is a Spring application that includes the WaveMaker common, json, and runtime modules. More specifically, the WaveMaker server uses the Spring Web MVC framework to create a DispatcherServlet that delegates client requests to their handlers. WaveMaker uses only a handful of controllers, as we will see in the next section. The effective result is that it is the request URL that is used to direct a service call to the correct service. The method value of the request is the name of the client exposed function with the service to be called. In the case of overloaded functions, the signature of the params value is used to find the method matching by signature. We will look at example requests and responses shortly.

Behind this controller is not only the power of the Spring framework, but also a number of leading frameworks such as Hibernate and, JaxWS, and libraries such as log4j and Apache commons. Here too, these libraries are available to you both directly in any custom work you might do and indirectly as tooled features of Studio.

As we are working with a Spring server, we will be seeing Spring beans often as we examine the server-side configuration. One need not be familiar with Spring to reap its benefits when using custom Java in WaveMaker. Spring makes it easy to get access to other beans from our Java code. For example, if our project has imported a database as MyDB, we could get access to the service and any exposed functions in that service using getServiceBean().The following code illustrates the use of getServiceBean():

```
MyDB myDbSvc = (MyDB)RuntimeAccess.getInstance().
getServiceBean("mydb");
```

We start by getting an instance of the WaveMaker runtime. From the returned runtime instance, we can use the getServiceBean() method to get a service bean for our mydb database service. There are other ways we could have got access to the service from our Java code; this one is pretty straightforward. We'll dig into this in more detail in *Chapter 9, Custom Java Services*.

Starting from web.xml

Just as the client side starts with index.html, a Java servlet starts in WEB-INF with web.xml. A WaveMaker application web.xml is a rather straightforward Spring MVC web.xml. You'll notice many servlet-mappings, a few listeners, and filters. Unlike index.html, web.xml is managed directly by Studio. If you need to add elements to the web-app context, add them to user-web.xml. The content of user-web.xml is merged into web.xml when generating the deployment package. We will cover deployment in *Chapter 13, Deploying Applications*.

The most interesting entry is probably `contextConfigLocation` of
`/WEB-INF/project-springapp.xml`. `Project-springapp.xml` is a Spring
beans file. Immediately after the schema declaration is a series of resource imports.
These imports include the services and entities that we create in Studio as we import
databases and otherwise add services to our project. We'll be looking at a number
of these files in detail when we discuss services in the later chapters.

If you open `project-spring.xml` in `WEB-INF`, near the top of the file you'll see a
comment noting how `project-spring.xml` is yours to edit. For experienced Spring
users, here is the entry point to add any additional imports you may need. An
example of such can be found at `http://dev.wavemaker.com/wiki/bin/Spring`. In
that example, an additional XML file, `ServerFileProcessor.xml`, is
used to enable component scanning on a package and sets some properties
on those components. `Project-spring.xml` is then used to import
`ServerFileProcessor.xml` into the application context. Many users of WaveMaker
still think of Spring as the season between Winter and Summer. Such users do not
need to think about these XML files. However, for those who are experienced with
Java, the full power of the Spring framework is accessible to them.

Also in `project-springapp.xml` is a list of URL mappings. These mappings specific
request URLs that require handling by the file controller. Gzipped resources, for
example, require the header `Content-Encoding` to be set to gzip. This informs the
browser the content is gzip encoded and must be uncompressed before being parsed.

> There are a few names that use `ag` in the server. WaveMaker
> Software the company was formerly known as ActiveGrid, and
> had a previous web development tool by the same name. The use
> of `ag` and `com.activegrid` stems back to the project's roots, first
> put down when the company was still known as ActiveGrid.

Closing out `web.xml` is the Acegi filter mapping. Acegi is the security module used in
WaveMaker 6.5, discussed in *Chapter 12, Securing Applications*. Even when security is
not enabled in an application, the Acegi filter mapping is included in `web.xml`. When
security is not enabled in the project, an empty `project-security.xml` is used.

Client and server communication

Now that we've examined the client and server, we need to better understand the communication between the two. WaveMaker almost exclusively uses the HTTP methods GET and POST. In HTTP, GET is used, as you might suspect even without ever having heard of RFC 2626 (`https://tools.ietf.org/html/rfc2616`), to request, or get, a specific resource. Unless installed as a native application on a mobile device, a WaveMaker web application is loaded via a GET method. From `index.html` and `runtimeLoad.js` to the user defined pages and any images used on those images, the applications themselves are loaded into the browser using GET. All service calls, database reads and writes, or otherwise any invocations of a Java service functions, on the other hand, are POST. The URL of these POST functions is always the service named `.json`. For example, calls to a Java service named `userPrefSvc` would always be to the URL `/userPrefSvc.json`. Inside the POST method's request payload will be any required parameters including the method of the service to be invoked. The response will be the response returned from that call. PUT methods are not possible because we cannot nor do not want to know all possible WaveMaker server calls at "designtime", while the project files are open for writing in the Studio. This pattern avoids any URL length constraints, enabling lengthy datasets to be transferred while freeing up the URL to pass parameters such as page state.

Let's take a look at an example. If you want to follow along in your browser's console, this is the third request of three when we select "Fog City Books" in the CRM Simple application when running the application with the console open as we first did when exploring the sample application in *Chapter 1, Getting Started with WaveMaker*.

The following URL is the request URL:

`http://crm_simple.localhost:8094/services/runtimeService.json`

The following is request payload:

```
{"params":["custpurchaseDB","com.custpurchasedb.data.Lineitem",null,{"
properties":["id","item"],"filters":["id.orderid=9"],"matchMode":"star
t","ignoreCase":false},{"maxResults":500,"firstResult":0}],"method":"r
ead","id":251422}
```

The response is as follows:

```
{"dataSetSize":2,"result":[{"id":{"itemid":2,"orderid":9},"item":{"ite
mid":2,"itemname":"Kidnapped","price":12.99},"quantity":2},{"id":{"ite
mid":10,"orderid":9},"item":{"itemid":10,"itemname":"Gravitys Rainbow"
,"price":11.99},"quantity":1}]}
```

As we expect, the request URL is to a service (in this case named runtime service), with the `.json` extension. Runtime service is the built-in WaveMaker service for reading and writing with the Hibernate (`http://www.hibernate.org`), data models generated by importing a database. We'll learn more about the imported data models in *Chapter 7, Working with Databases*. Security service and WaveMaker service are the other built-in services used at runtime. The security service is used for security functions such as `getUserName()` and `logout()`. Note this does not include login, which is handled by Acegi. The WaveMaker service has functions such as `getServerTimeOffset()`, used to adjust for time zones, and `remoteRESTCall()`, used to proxy some web service calls. How the runtime service functions is easy to understand by observation.

Inside the request payload we have, as the URL suggested, a JavaScript Object Notation (JSON) structure. JSON (`http://www.json.org/`), is a lightweight data-interchange format regularly used in AJAX applications. Dissecting our example request from the top of the structure enclosed in the outer-most {}'s looks like the following:

```
{"params":[.......],"method":"read","id":251422}
```

We have three top level name-value pairs to our request object: `params`, `method`, and `id`. The `id` is `251422`; method is read and the `params` value is an array, as indicated by the [] brackets:

```
["custpurchaseDB","com.custpurchasedb.data.Lineitem",null,{},{ }]
```

In our case, we have an array of five values. The first is the database service name, `custpurchaseDB`. Next we have what appears to be the package and class name we will be reading from, not unlike `from` in a SQL query. After which, we have a null and two objects. JSON is friendly to human reading, and we could continue to unwrap the two objects in this request in a similar fashion. Let's examine the rest of this request in *Chapter 7, Working with Databases*, when we discuss database services and check out the response. At the top level, we have `dataSetSize`, the number of results, and the array of the results:

```
{"dataSetSize":2,"result":[]}
```

Inside our result array we have two objects:

```
[{"id":{"itemid":2,"orderid":9},"item":{"itemid":2,"itemname":"Kidnap
ped","price":12.99},"quantity":2},{"id":{"itemid":10,"orderid":9},"it
em":{"itemid":10,"itemname":"Gravitys Rainbow","price":11.99},"quanti
ty":1}]}
```

Our first item has the compound key of itemid 2 with orderid 9. This is the item `Kidnapped`, which is a book costing $11.99. The other object in our result array also has the orderid 9, as we expect when reading line items from the selected order. This one is also a book, the item `Gravity's Rainbow`.

Types

To be more precise about the `com.custpurchasdb.data.Lineitem` parameter in our read request, it is actually the type name of the read request. WaveMaker projects define types from primitive types such as Boolean and custom complex types such as `Lineitem`. In our runtime read example, `com.custpurchasedb.data.Lineitem` is both the package and class name of the imported Hibernate entity and the type name for the line item entity in the project.

Maintaining type information enables WaveMaker to ease a number of development issues. As the client knows the structure of the data it is getting from the server, it knows how to display that data with minimal developer configuration, if any. At design time, Studio uses type information in many areas to help us correctly configure our application. For example, when we set up a grid, type information enables Studio to present us with a list of possible column choices for the grid's dataset type. Likewise, when we add a form to the canvas for a database insert, it is type information that Studio uses to fill the form with appropriate editors.

Line item is a project-wide type as it is defined in the server side. In the process of compiling the project's Java services sources, WaveMaker defines system types for any type returned to the client in a client facing function. To be added to the type system, a class must:

- Be public
- Define public getters and setters
- Be returned by a client exposed function
- Have a service class that extends `JavaServiceSuperClass` or uses the `@ExposeToClient` annotation

 WaveMaker 6.5.1 has a bug that prevents types from being generated as expected. Be certain to use 6.5.2 or newer versions to avoid this defect.

It is possible to create new project types by adding a Java service class to the project that only defines types. Following is an example that creates a new simple type called `Record` to the project. Our definition of `Record` consists of an integer ID and a string. Note that there are two classes here. `MyCustomTypes` is the service class containing a method returning the type `Record`. As we will not be calling it, the function `getNewRecord()` need not do anything other than return a record. Creating a new default instance is an easy way to do this. The class `Record` is defined as an inner class. An inner class is a class defined within another class. In our case, `Record` is defined within `MyCustomTypes`:

```
// Java Service class MyCustomTypes
package com.myco.types;

import com.wavemaker.runtime.javaservice.JavaServiceSuperClass;
import com.wavemaker.runtime.service.annotations.ExposeToClient;

public class MyCustomTypes extends JavaServiceSuperClass {
  public Record getNewRecord(){
    return new Record();
    }
  // Inner class Record
  public class Record{
    private int id;
    private String name;

    public int getId(){
      return id;
    }
    public void setId(int id){
      this.id = id;
    }
    public String getName(){
      return this.name;
    }
    public void setName(String name){
      this.name = name;
}
}
}
```

To add the preceding code to our WaveMaker project, we would add a Java service to the project using the class name MyCustomTypes in the **Package and Class Name** editor of the **New Java Service** dialog. The preceding code extends JavaServiceSuperClass and uses the package com.myco.types.

A project can also have client-only types using the **type definition** option from the **advanced** section of the Studio **insert** menu. Type definitions are useful when we want to be able to pass structured data around within the client but we will not be sending or receiving that type to the server. For example, we may want to have application scoped wm.Variable storing a collection of current record selection information. This would enable us to keep track of a number of state items across all pages. Communication with the server is likely to be using only a few of those types at a time, so no such structure exists in the server side. Using wm.Variable enables us to bind each Record ID without using code.

The insert type definition menu brings up the **Type Definition Generator** dialog. The generator takes JSON input and is pre-populated with a sample type. The sample type defines a person object, albeit an unusual one, with a name, an array of numbers for age, a Boolean (hasFoot), and a related person object, friend. Replace the sample type with your own JSON structure. Be certain to change the type name to something meaningful. After generating the type, you'll immediately see the newly minted type in type selectors, such as the type field of wm.Variable.

> Studio is pretty good at recognizing type changes. If for some reason Studio does not recognize a type change, the easiest thing to do is to get Studio to re-read the owning object. If a wm.Variable fails to show a newly added field to a type in its properties, change the type of the variable from the modified type to some other type and then back again.

Studio is also an application

One of the more complex WaveMaker applications is the Studio. That's right, Studio is itself an application built out of WaveMaker widgets and using the runtime and server. Being the large, complex application we use to build applications, it can sometimes be difficult to understand where the runtime ends and Studio begins. With that said, Studio remains a treasure trove of examples and ideas to explore.

Let's open a finder, explorer, shell, or however you prefer to view the file system of a WaveMaker Studio installation. Let's look in the studio folder. If you've installed WaveMaker to c:\program files\WaveMaker\6.5.3.Release, the default on Windows, we're looking at c:\program files\WaveMaker\6.5.3.Release\studio. This is the webapproot of the Studio project:

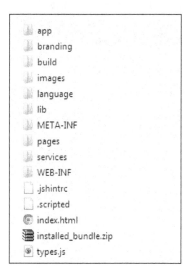

For files, we've discussed `index.html` in loading the client. The type definition for the project types is `types.js`. The `types.js` definition is how the client learns of the server's Java types.

Moving on to the directories alphabetically, we start with the `app` folder. The `app` folder can be considered a large utility folder these days. The `branding` folder, `http://dev.wavemaker.com/wiki/bin/wmdoc_6.5/Branding`, is a sample of the branding feature for when you want to easily re-brand applications for different customers. The `build` folder contains the optimized build files we discussed when loading our application in gzip mode. This `build` folder is for the Studio itself. The `images` folder is, as we would hope, where images are kept. The content of the doc in `jsdoc` is pretty old. Use `jsref` at the online wiki, `http://dev.wavemaker.com/wiki/bin/wmjsref_6.5/WebHome`, for a client API reference instead. `Language` contains the National Language Support (NLS) files to localize Studio into other languages. In 6.5.X, there is a Japanese (`ja`) and Spanish (`es`) directory in addition to the English (`en`) default thanks to the efforts of the WaveMaker community and a corporate partner. For more on internationalization applications with WaveMaker, navigate to `http://dev.wavemaker.com/wiki/bin/wmdoc_6.5/Localization#HL ocalizingtheClientLanguage`.

The `lib` folder is very interesting, so let's wrap up this top level before we dig into that one.

The `META-INF` folder contains artifacts from the WaveMaker Maven build process that probably should be removed for 6.5.2.

The `pages` folder contains the page definitions for Studio's pages. These pages can be opened in Studio. They also can be a treasure trove of tips and tricks if you see something when using Studio that you don't know how to do in your application. Be careful however, as some pages are old and use outdated classes or techniques. Other constructs are only used by Studio and aren't tooled. This means some pages use components that can only be created by code. The other major difference between a project's `pages` folder is that Studio `page` folders do not contain the same number of files. They do not have the optimized `pageName.a.js` file, for example.

The `services` folder contains the Service Method Definition (SMD) files for Studio's services. These are summaries of a projects exposed services, one file per service, used at runtime by the client. Each callable function, its input parameter, and its return types are defined.

Finally, WEB-INF we have discussed already when we examined web.xml. In Studio's case, replace project with studio in the file names. Also under WEB-INF, we have classes and lib. The classes folder contains Java class files and additional XML files. These files are on the classpath. WEB-INF\lib contains JAR files. Studio requires significantly more JAR files, which are automatically added to projects created by Studio.

Now let's get back to the lib folder. Astute readers of our walk through of index. html likely noticed the references to /wavemaker/lib in src tags for things such as runtimeloader. You might have also noticed that this folder was not present in the project and wondered how these tags could not fail. As a quick look at the URL of Studio running in a browser will demonstrate, /wavemaker is the Studio's context. This means the JavaScript runtime is only copied in as part of generating the deployment package. The lib folder is loaded directly from Studio's context when you test run an application from Studio using the **Run** or **Test** button. RuntimeLoader.js we encountered following index.html as it is the start of the loading of client modules. Manifest.js is an entry point into the loading process. Boot contains pre-initialization, such as the spinning loader image. Next we have another build folder. This one is the one used by applications and contains all possible build files. Not every JavaScript module is packaged up into an optimized build file. Some modules are so specific or rarely used that they are best loaded individually. Otherwise, if there's a build package available to applications, these them. Dojo lives in the dojo folder. I hope you don't find it surprising to find a dijit, dojo, and dojox folder in there. The folder github provides the library path github for JS Beautifier, http://jsbeautifier.org/. The images in the project images folder include a copy of Silk Icons, http://www.famfamfam.com/lab/icons/silk/, a great Creative Common licensed PNG icon set.

This brings us to wm. We definitely saved the most interesting folder for our last stop on this tour. For in lib/wm, we have manifest.js, the top level of module loading when using debug mode in the runtime loader. In wm/lib/base, is the top level of the WaveMaker module space used at runtime. This means in wm/lib/base we have the WaveMaker components and widgets folders. These two folders contain the most commonly used sets of classes by WaveMaker developers using any custom JavaScript in a project. This also means we will be back in these folders again too.

Summary

In this chapter, we reviewed the WaveMaker architecture. We started with some context of what we mean by "client" and "server" in the context of this book. We then proceeded to dig into the client and the server. We reviewed how both build upon leading frameworks, the Dojo Toolkit and the SpringSource Framework in particular. We examined the running of an application from the network point of view and how the client and server communicated throughout. We dissected a JSON request to the runtime service and encountered project types. We also learned about both project and client type definitions. We ended by revisiting the file system. This time, however, we walked through a Studio installation. Studio is also a WaveMaker application.

In the next chapter, we'll get comfortable with the Studio as a visual tool. We'll look at everything from the properties panels to the built-in source code editors.

3
Using Studio

It's time to check out the cockpit! In this chapter, we'll walk through the panels of the Studio Visual development environment. The topics we will cover include:

- Project management controls
- Service controls
- Source code editors
- The resource manager
- The Properties panel
- The binding dialog
- Revision control

As we work our way through the Studio IDE, we will see the application of many of the architectural concepts we discussed in the previous chapter. The example project WaveyWeb is used to demonstrate example code from this chapter.

Welcome to projects

When we first load Studio into our browser, we are greeted by the welcome dialog. The welcome dialog contains a number of links to key resources to help us get started, such as the developer community site and product documentation. At the bottom of the dialog is the version of WaveMaker Studio. On the **Projects** tab is a searchable list of possible projects found in the WaveMaker home projects folder. Changing the location of the WaveMaker home folder under **File | Preferences...** updates the listing in projects accordingly. However, it is via the **File** menu item that the bulk of the in-Studio project management takes place. In addition to setting the WaveMaker home folder, it is here we find **New Project...**, **Save**, **Close Project**, **Revert Project**, **Delete Current Project**, and **Copy Current Project...**, all operating on the current project. **Revert Project** is a handy version of bulk undo; it reverts the project to the last saved state. The **File** menu is also how we deploy our project. Deployment will be discussed in *Chapter 13, Deploying Applications*.

Note that we were specific to say "possible projects" and not "projects." As we've seen in our exploration of the file system, projects are organized by folders within the `projects` folder. It is not practical for Studio to verify every folder prior to listing. Any folder with at least one child folder is listed. This means it is possible to open a folder that is neither a project nor the root folder of a project.

As Studio opens a project, the first file it looks for is the `.wmproject.properties` file. The project properties file is how WaveMaker determines what version of Studio last edited the project. Project versions change whenever there is an upgrade task from the previous version and not every release increments the project version. Therefore, the version, in `.wmproject.properties` is not the same string as the product release, but instead is a numeric sequence incremented by each upgrade task. The project version for WaveMaker 6.5.3 is 0.54. The project version for other releases is listed on the release history page, `http://dev.wavemaker.com/wiki/bin/wmdoc/Releases`. If the version of the project we are attempting to open is lower, and therefore older than the version for the Studio we are running, Studio will attempt to automatically upgrade the project by performing the appropriate upgrade tasks needed to bring the project to the current level. If no project version was found, Studio alerts you to the issue by indicating `'Found project version "0"'`, and aborts opening the project. Projects with versions newer than the currently running Studio will not be opened either, as the project is likely to contain constructs that the older version of Studio cannot process.

A common cause of the no version property found condition for project folders is not having the project root folder in the `projects` folder. If you get this error for what should be a valid project, ensure the folder containing the `.wmproject.properties` file is in the immediate child folder of the `projects` folder of the WaveMaker home folder specified in preferences.

The easiest way to move individual projects across systems or users is to use **project export**. Generated from the file menu, when a project is open, a project export is a ZIP file of the non-replaceable files of the project, including any files or folders you may have added to the project such as resources or JAR files. Without the many class files, WaveMaker provided the JAR and JavaScript files, a project export is much smaller than zipping up the project. Project exports are often less than 1 megabyte in size, and can easily be e-mailed or shared via the community forums. When imported into Studio via the **File** menu, exports are expanded into the WaveMaker home projects folder with the rest of your projects. Imported projects will be compiled and have the runtime JAR files copied in upon test run deployment.

The WaveMaker home location preference is not the only Studio-wide setting in the **File** menu. **Modify Studio** contains two submenu items: **Upload Studio Patches** and **Import Partner Services**. Partner services are Studio extension packages. They are one way that organizations can customize Studio without having to maintain a custom fork of the Studio code base. Uploading Studio patches is an easy way to apply any recommended JavaScript patches to Studio and the runtime. It leverages `dojo.extend()` to redefine corrected functions with their fixes. The WaveMaker team posts key patches to the product wiki to be loaded automatically by the **Load Patches** button. Custom fixes can also be applied via this option. Unfortunately, this mechanism only works for JavaScript functions. Server side Java code can only be corrected via a more traditional patch of an update JAR file.

Hello WaveyWeb

We will now begin working with the WaveyWeb sample project. WaveyWeb demonstrates a number of techniques from localizing and adding custom events to loading custom JavaScript libraries for use from page code. WaveyWeb is part of the example project workspace we set up earlier, but can be found on GitHub by visiting `https://github.com/edwardcallahan/Easy-Web-Samples/tree/master/projects/WaveyWeb`.

Often, the first step when undertaking a project is among the hardest. Fortunately, WaveMaker makes getting started rather simple. Choosing **New Project** from the welcome dialog brings up the **New Project** dialog. Other than project name, we only have to make two decisions to get started, and neither choice is undoable. **Theme** refers to the CSS theme, and WaveMaker includes eight built-in themes out of the box. My favorite in WaveMaker 6.5 is **cool blue**. As you will see later, you can create your own custom themes using the theme designer. Like most cross-project artifacts, themes are saved to the common folder, the sibling to projects within the WaveMaker home folder. Storing such creatures in the WaveMaker home location separates them from the Studio installation. If the contents of common were stored inside the Studio installation instead, they could easily be deleted or otherwise lost during uninstallation.

The other decision we need to make is regarding the template. In WaveMaker 6.5, templates are single page constructs only. It is not until WaveMaker 6.6 that templates gain features such as the ability to include services. With that said, the six templates provided with WaveMaker 6.5 are quite useful and provide a quick start to both desktop and mobile targeted applications. For the desktop, Tabs Template is my runaway favorite, and it is what we'll be using for our WaveyWeb project.

There are a few key regions of the studio we will need to be able to reference. The following screenshot highlights them:

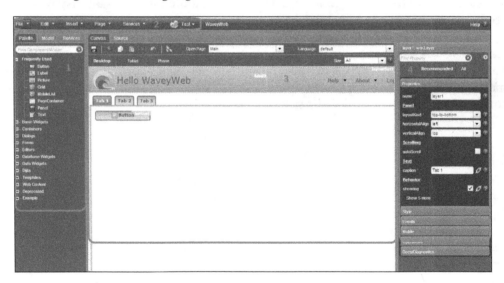

The key regions of the Studio are:

- The **Palette**, **Model**, and **Service** Trees(*1*)
- The top level menus(*2*)
- The **Canvas** and **Source** region(*3*)
- The **Properties** panel(*4*)

The **Palette**, **Model**, and **Service** tabs contain three tabs and four tree views. The **Palette** tab is the palette of visual widgets available to us for drag-and-drop designing of our application. The other tabs are views of the current project, organized by type. All three tabs are searchable using the search editor at the top of the panel.

Let's view our newly minted project via the **Model** tree. In the Model view, we see the visual client-side components of the current page in a tree format. From here, we can see the tabs template's beauty lies in its simplicity. It has a single top level panel, `panel3`, within the layout box. Within which we have a header panel, `panel1`, a body panel, `panel2`, and a footer panel, `panel6`. You can and should rename components in any project that is not throw-away or might otherwise be used for any length of time. For small, simple projects, you can get away with naming only core components. For larger, more complex projects, naming nearly all components consistently can provide a good return on effort. This is particularly helpful when searching for a specific component in the project. For an explanation of a commonly used naming convention, the Apps Hungarian Notation, visit `http://dev.wavemaker.com/wiki/bin/wmdoc_6.5/Component+Naming+Conventions`.

Within the main body panel, `panel2` in the template, we have a tab layer with three layers. This simple layout provides a functional and scalable layout that is suitable for building a variety of applications. For a large, multi-page application, the tab layers make great places to put page containers. We'll get back to that technique in the next chapter. For this trivial application, we'll put our widgets directly into the tab layers.

Add `wm.GenericDialog` to the project canvas by dragging and dropping the `GenericDialog` icon from the **Palette** tab to the **Canvas** region. Notice how it shows above the layout box, `layoutBox1`, in the model tree. This is because the dialog is not a child of the main layout. Dialogs, however, are constrained to the browser window at runtime.

Also in the top level menu we have the **Edit** menu. **Edit** contains what we'd expect it to contain: **Cut**, **Copy**, **Paste**, **Delete**, and **Undo**.

Undo is not absolute. **Undo** will not undo name changes, such as changing `variable1` to `varCurrentUser`. Instead, undo will undo the last addition or deletion. So, instead of reverting the variable name back to `variable1`, it might remove it outright if it was the last component added to the project.

Adding services

There is no single order in which you must build your project. However, as we learned in the previous chapter, types play an important role in projects, and project types come from the server. This means there is significant benefit to importing project services early in the creation of the application, as it enables us to use those service types to create type-specific forms and variables right away.

Try to minimize type iterations. While Studio will update existing typed components when you regenerate services with updated types, this is best avoided if possible. Studio is better at creating components of a type than updating component types. In the case of databases, this means finalizing your database schema as much as possible before importing it in order to avoid re-imports due to schema evolution. If you must make type updates, you might need to clear your browser cache or reload the project to get type updates to show.

Services are imported via the **Services** menu of the top level menus. The **Services** menu items all operate with server-side aspects. We'll discuss them in detail in later chapters. For the WaveyWeb project, we'll use the HRDB sample database. Selecting **Import Database** brings up the **New Data Model** dialog. The **Import Sample** button on the dialog automatically imports the sample HyperSQL Database (HSQLDB), (http://www.hsqldb.org/).

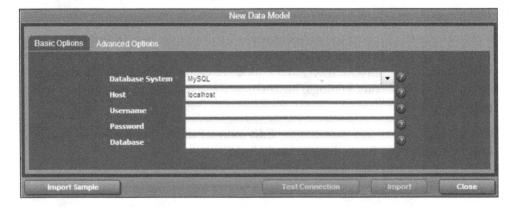

Human Resources Database (HRDB) is a sample database shipped with WaveMaker that defines a simple example Human Resources (HR) schema consisting of departments, employees, and vacations. There's also a user table that is good for examples using database security.

Now that we've added the HRDB service to our project, it shows up in the **Services** tree (the right tab in region one). The security service is automatically added to the project, but with security disabled by default. Selecting a service in the service tree expands that service item and brings us into the appropriate viewer for that service. For Java services, this is the Java source code editor. For a database service, this means we see a listing of all table entities and HQL queries in the services tree with the selected table entity shown in the data model editor. It is also by going into a service editor that we get the delete button to remove a service from our project.

In the lower-half of the **Services** tab is the **Components** tree. This is where we can find the non-visual client-side components of a project such as variables. Inserting a variable from the **Insert** menu immediately adds the variable to the components tree.

Services are server-side constructs, and all project services are siblings in the single tree. Components, however, can be owned by the page or the application. This is also called scope. Setting the owner of `wm.variable` to application enables the variable to be seen by all pages in the application and moves the variable to the **Project** section of the component tree. Application-owned variables are good choices for datasets that are used across multiple pages such as the logged in username and ID or the primary record being edited in the application such as a selected customer in a customer management application. Storing these values in application-scoped variables allows any page in the application to obtain values from the variable instead of needing to make a server call.

 Use application-scoped components judiciously. Unlike page-owned components, application-scoped data will be in memory for the life of the application as they cannot be garbage collected.

Inserting components

Many of the client-side, non-visual components are added via the **Insert** menu. Variables are named storage locations. More specifically, the insert variable menu item adds a `wm.variable` to the project. You can define and use JavaScript variables in JavaScript code as any JavaScript developer would expect. Unlike a JavaScript variable, `wm.variable` (`http://dev.wavemaker.com/wiki/bin/wmjsref_6.5/Variable`) is a variable type component class of which you can add instances of to a project. This means they can be used in the visual component tooling of Studio like other project components. JavaScript variables may be easier to manipulate in JavaScript, but `wm.variable` can often be exclusively managed via the visual tooling. JavaScript variables on the other hand can only be managed via code.

Subclasses of `wm.variable` include the service variable `wm.ServiceVariable` and its subclass, the live variable `wm.LiveVariable`. Service variables merge the ability to make server calls with the data storage capabilities of a variable. The resultant component can collect any inputs for a service call, make the call to the server-side function, and store its results. Live variables are server calls specifically for the read, write, update, and delete calls to WaveMaker database services. Live variables can only be used with database services that implement the `LiveDataService` interface. For the majority of all practical purposes, these are the services generated by the database import process.

Navigation calls are another commonly used component used for navigating between pages, layers, and dialogs in a project. A number of navigations can be performed without adding a navigation component to the project. As we have tab layers in our project, the showing of those layers are automatically available as tooled events. For example, if we add a button to `layer1`, its on-click event menu includes the navigation to `layer2` and `layer3`, a common task in layers without visible controls such as tabs. Let's set our `button1` on click event to `genericDialog1.show()`.

The other two call components are notification calls and PhoneGap calls. Notification calls are the componentized versions of alert, confirm, prompt, toast, and warn. Like `wm.variable`, we can use these notification components from the visual tooling instead of creating them in code. PhoneGap calls provide componentized access to some of the PhoneGap API, such as camera, contact database, geolocation, and microphone access. These only work when the application is deployed as a PhoneGap app, discussed in *Chapter 14, Mobile Deployment*.

The insert menu also includes a number of handy pre-configured client-side components for us to use. The **Prebuilt Variables** submenu is made up of exactly that, `wm.variable` that are pre-populated with days of the week, months of the year, the fifty states of the United States, and countries of the world. The data of any of these can be customized after being added to the project using the **Edit JSON** button of its properties.

Under **Graphics**, we have the image list component in three flavors. An image list is a component that lets us have a grid of icon images within a single image. Concatenating multiple images into a single file reduces the number of file requests needed to use any number of the images in the grid to a single request. Instead of downloading a new file every time we need an image, we specify the index of the sub-image within the single image file to be displayed. **Image list** is an un-configured instance. **Silk icons** use the silk icon files from `http://famfamfam.com/lab/icons/silk/` we saw in the Studio installation folder. The **Boolean Icons Imagelist**, `http://prax-08.deviantart.com/art/Boolean-1-1-166457851`, is also available to use and defaults to the Signage collection. The Boolean collection includes other collections that you can use simply by changing the URL property of the image list, say for example, you wanted to use electronics instead.

These provided icon lists make it really easy to liven up an application. For example, let's insert the Boolean image list and leave it as the default signage collection. Now take that button we added to show our generic dialog. Select **imageList1** from the image list drop-down property in the **Properties** panel. Finally, use the **editImageIndex** button to specify an image from the signage collection to display in the button.

This brings us to the **Advanced** submenu of **Insert**. Here we have an eclectic array of components. **LogoutVariable** and **LoginVariable** are for use with secured applications, which we will discuss in *Chapter 12, Securing Applications*. A timer is a componentized version of JavaScript `setTimeout()`, and is used to schedule something after a short delay or on an interval. See the client API reference for the timer for more details at, `http://dev.wavemaker.com/wiki/bin/wmjsref_6.5/Timer`.

We have discussed **TypeDefinition** in the previous chapter. You will recall that it is how we define client only types.

Rounding out the advanced insert menu we have **Composite Publisher** and **Template Publisher**. We'll discuss these further in *Chapter 11, Mastering Client Customization*.

The only top level menu items we have yet to discuss are **Page**, **Run**, and **Help**. The **Page** menu is where we manage project pages. We'll be discussing pages in later chapters. In addition to creating new pages and renaming and deleting existing pages, this menu allows us to specify the home page for the project as well as import pages from other projects. Note that when importing pages, only those components defined on the page are copied. Application-owned components, such as wm.variable we moved earlier, are defined in the application JS file, not the page's widgets file, and thus are not imported. This means that the import page menu item is functionally equivalent to copying a page folder into the current project's pages folder.

The **Run** menu item isn't a menu item like the others. If you click on it, it will run the project. In this case, run means deploy the project to the same embedded Tomcat server we are running the Studio application in and open a browser window on it. As we learned in the previous chapter, adding ?debug to the URL of any WaveMaker application uses the debug loading path. Instead of loading a limited number of gzip libraries, many smaller, uncompressed files are loaded individually. If we click on the downward arrow to the right of **Run**, we can choose the buttons action. The other options are **Test** and **Compile**. **Test** simply runs the application in debug mode with debug in the URL. Otherwise, it is, same as the **Run** menu item. This action is often referred to as "test run", which is reflective of the equivalence of the action. The test run deployed application is reachable to any browser that can reach the Tomcat server. Copying the URL, adding or removing debug, and launching the application in a non-default browser or a browser from another system on our network, is an easy way to begin testing you application in other browsers.

Compile, on the other hand, only compiles our project's services. This can be handy particularly when we are working with Java services that are being updated. If the project's server-side services do not compile, the application cannot be deployed or viewed in the browser.

 Compile undeploys the application. You'll also need to use **Run** or **Test** after compile to view the application in the browser.

Last but certainly not least is **Help**. The **Help** top level menu item opens a new tab on the product documentation page, http://dev.wavemaker.com/wiki/bin/wmdoc_6.5/. There's nothing special about this link, and you see the same documentation by pointing any browser at the product documentation URL.

The canvas

The canvas is the main work area and the largest screen region. You can adjust the width of the palette, model, and services tabs to the left and the properties to the right. When running Studio on a wide aspect screen, many find they have sufficient screen real-estate to widen those side panels. Conversely, when developing on a smaller resolution screen or designing for large screens, it may be necessary to adjust the width of the side panels to get a larger width for the canvas.

At the very top of the area, and just below our top level menu, we have the canvas tabs. When we first open our project, we have only **Canvas** and **Source** tabs. As we open services, additional service tabs are added to the tab row. Selecting our HRDB service from the service tree adds a **Database** tab as shown in the following screenshot:

Within the canvas tab, we have two rows of buttons and select menus that constitute the canvas toolbar. The first set of buttons mirror top level menu choices such as save, cut, copy, and paste. Many of these are also available as keyboard shortcuts, some of which are documented at `http://dev.wavemaker.com/wiki/bin/wmdoc_6.5/PageDesigner#HKeyboardShortcuts`.

The first option unique to the canvas controls is the toggle outline view just to the left of the **Open Page** dropdown. This toggles the dotted line outline and name label on widgets in the design area. While the outline view is helpful when getting started and easy to forget about, experienced users may find the information less useful and might prefer turning outline mode off. The page select is an easy way to open any page in the project.

The **Language** pull-down menu lets you specify which locale you are setting properties for. When language is left to **default**, properties such as label captions are defined in the page widgets file directly. The `widgets` file defined string is the caption used unless a locale-specific caption is set for the page. To set a local string, choose a locale code from the dropdown. Saving properties with a language selected saves those strings in a page language file in the `language` folder in the projects webapproot. These localized string properties are then shown instead of the default when browsers with the matching locale code load the page. Test running the application with a language selected also adds `dojo.locale=<code>` to the URL, where `<code>` is the selected locale code, so you can test the language files.

Under the canvas toolbar is the device view toolbar. The device view toolbar is the visual aspect of WaveMaker's mobile development tooling. Choosing a device view, either by the **Size** dropdown or choosing the **Desktop**, **Tablet**, or **Phone** view, has two outcomes: first, the canvas view is adjusted to match the target device; second, **Test** and **Run** append a `wmmobile` property to the URL. This `wmmobile` property adjusts the size of the launched browser window to emulate the chosen device screen size. The effects of the **Portrait** and **Landscape** toggles are similar, but for orientation.

If you want to also test touch events in a desktop browser, Chrome's Developer Tools settings screen allows you to enable touch events with **Emulate touch events** in the **Overrides** tab.

Working on the canvas

The canvas area itself is the visual representation of our project. Visual components are added by selecting a widget from the **Palette** and, dragging and dropping the widget onto the canvas.

Once placed on the canvas, widgets can be moved around using drag-and-drop and can also be edited using copy, cut, and paste. Widgets can also be rearranged directly in the model tree. For example, selecting the button we placed on layer1 enables us to drag-and-drop it into layer3. In both cases, Studio provides two indicators while the widget is droppable. First, a green or red bar indicates if the selected widget can be dropped there. Visual components can be deleted but they cannot be dropped off the canvas. Attempting to do so will show the red bar and the drop will be ignored. The orientation of the bar also indicates the orientation of the target panel.

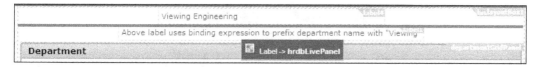

The other assistant is a pop-up box that indicates what is being put where. This confirms which widget is being moved and where it is being moved to. The target is expressed as into or after. These should be read as "placing widget X into container Y" or "placing widget X after widget Y (in Y's parent)."

 Sometimes you can't drop a new widget exactly where you want it on the canvas for one reason or another. In such cases, drop the widget anywhere on the canvas, usually close to where you want it, then move it to where you want it either via the model tree or placement within the canvas.

So far we've been using a left mouse button click-and-hold technique to manage widgets on the canvas. Widgets on the canvas also have a right-click pop-up menu. The best known use of the right-click menu is to **Edit Columns** of a Dojo grid. All of the choices in this menu are also available via the properties of the widget. However, the right-click menu can be a convenient shortcut to use. The **Wrap in Panel** operation, for example, can be most helpful when building out forms.

Source editors

The alternative use of the canvas area is for the source editors. Within the **Source** tab, there is a menu of choices. In general, each is an editor for a specific project file:

The Script tab

The most commonly used editor is the **Script** tab. **Script** is the page JavaScript source editor. This is the contents of the page JS file. For the main page, this is `pages/Main/Main.js`, as noted in the upper-right corner, just above the **Completions** panel.

The most common way to add page code is by using the `JavaScript` option in component events. Choosing JavaScript for an event automatically creates a function and places us in the source code script editor. For example, choosing JavaScript for the `onShow` event for `layer1` creates a stub `layer1` show event:

```
layer1Show: function(inSender) {
//Your on click event code here
  },
```

Alternatively, you can define the page function first and specify it for the on click event. In practice, it is usually easier to let Studio create the stub function.

 Studio does not automatically clean-up unused page functions. You need to manually delete any unused functions you no longer want.

Within **Script** is one of the most populous button bars of the source tabs. Starting from the left, we have save, which saves the entire project, and search, which searches within the source code currently being edited. Next we have import JS library, which imports the contents of a JavaScript source file from the resources folder by adding a combination of `eval` and `wm.load` to the bottom of the page source, just outside of the page declaration. This enables the contents of that imported library to be available to us in page code.

Next we have the blue circular arrows for the refresh button. If you choose to use an external editor to edit the page code while the page is open in Studio, use this button to refresh the code editor before saving the project to avoid losing your external changes. As we will see when we discuss Java Services, the Java equivalent of this button is invaluable when using a Java ID such as Eclipse.

The next two buttons deal with how our code looks. The reformat code button applies a code styling formatter to our code whereas the toggle line wrapping button toggles, well, line wrapping.

The lightning bolt auto complete is no longer needed now that the **Completions** panel is available. For many, one of the more intimidating aspects of the source code editor is facing a blank screen and trying to figure out what to type. To aid in that situation, Studio provides a completion engine that suggests possible completions. For example, enter `this.` in the page start function we added to our button and a few things happen:

```
start: function() {
    this.
},
```

First, a red X icon appears in the left margin as shown in the following screenshot:

This is the built-in syntax checker powered by Google's closure compiler, which can be found at `https://code.google.com/p/closure-compiler/`. The red X indicates that you probably have an error in your code. In this case, it says missing identifier, as `this.` is an incomplete statement. At the same time, the **Completions** panel updates with possible completions. In the context of page code, `this.` refers to the current page, and it is an easy way to access components on a page without hardcoding the page name into source. If we add a b for button, for example, `this.b`, our completion reduces to components starting with b. In this case, we now see only the `button1` we added to our layers earlier. Doubling-clicking on `button1` from the completions list completes our statement out to `this.button1` and refreshes the **Completions** panel to list a button's methods and members. We could then select `setCaption()`, the method for setting the caption of a component. The description panel below the **Completions** panel now describes the `setCaption()` function, complete with examples. Meanwhile, the `setCaption()` call is completed to match the signature with a placeholder value, `Click Me`, for the `inCaption` parameter of `setCaption()`.

```
this.button1.setCaption("Click Me");
```

Replace inCaption with whatever string the new caption should be. Don't forget to end your statement with a semicolon. It is not required, but is generally recommended, and it makes Doug Crockford happy too (http://javascript.crockford.com/code).

The next icon looks like a capital letter "A" and brings up the language dictionary editor. The script language dictionary is like the language dropdown in the canvas, but for localizing terms used in code. Continuing our button caption example, we could add a term to the dictionary for the button caption. The getDictionaryItem call, automatically inserted by the Add to Script button, replaces the term name with the localized term if a term was defined for the visitors' browsers locale. In the following example, the term has been called Main_continue_button_caption_term to indicate it is the caption of the continue button on the main page:

```
this.button1.setCaption(this.getDictionaryItem("SCRIPT_Main_continue_
button_caption_term"));
```

The rightmost button is yet another help button. This one is help for the editor. The editor embedded in WaveMaker 6.5 is Ace, http://ace.ajax.org. The editor help describes nine functions supported, such as *Ctrl* + *L* for go to line.

The other source panels

As we move to the right the next panel under **Source** is **CSS**. Here we can edit any CSS classes we have defined in the project. There's one tab for application-wide CSS and another for page-specific CSS. Again, the exact files being edited are noted in the upper-right corner.

As with page script, it is more common for users to populate this page using Studio. Creating a CSS class from the styles section of the **Properties** panel adds classes to the project CSS. We'll discuss CSS in detail in *Chapter 6, Styling the Application*. There's also a good styling section to the product documentation.
The styling wiki link the rightmost side of the **CSS** button bar gets you there: http://dev.wavemaker.com/wiki/bin/wmdoc_6.5/StylingWidgets.

The use of markup to add HTML to a project is deprecated. The **Markup** tab remains from when HTML was added to a project using the wm.Content widget and div IDs. Now, HTML can be added to the resources folder and presented using the wm.Html widget.

The **Widgets** tab is read-only. It shows you the current state of the page's widgets file, in which the JSON representation of our model tree is written. The widgets file is rewritten by Studio every time a project is saved. Expert users may use the widgets file to help diagnose a problem or even edit a project's content. Most users never need worry about this tab.

App Script and **App Widgets** are the application defined versions of **Script** and **Widgets** tabs. Components defined in the application scope are accessible to all pages in a project. Components defined with page ownership are only accessible to that page.

The **Themes** tab is where you'll find the theme designer. Here you can create themes that can be used to define the look and feel for multiple projects. Editing the Studio-provided themes is not recommended. If you want to start from an existing theme, make a copy first instead. Documentation for the theme designer can be found at http://dev.wavemaker.com/wiki/bin/wmdoc_6.5/ThemeDesigner.

The **Documentation** tab is the aggregation of any notes placed on components. The last layer of the properties of a component is **Docs/Diagnostics**. In which, developers can add notes to a component. This **Documentation** tab displays and prints those notes. Such a reference can be helpful to others in understanding your project. This can reduce the transition time for larger projects with many components, as even a good naming convention can take time to learn.

 Note that the **Documentation** tab doesn't have a refresh button. If you've been updating in Studio component notes, reload the project in Studio before printing to ensure everything is up to date.

Continuing from the left we have **Server Logs**. This tab displays the embedded Tomcat's output. The catalina.out file of the WaveMaker Tomcat can also be tailed as the file wm.log in the logs folder under WaveMaker home. The server's wm.log file is a great place to check for errors when things don't work server-side. Studio provides a view of the wm.log file for you. This can be very useful if you don't have access to the file system of the host running Studio's server.

The resource manager

This brings us to the **Resources** tab, also known as the resource manager (http://dev.wavemaker.com/wiki/bin/wmdoc_6.5/ResourceManager). The resource manager is Studio's built-in file manager.

The most common use case is to add image files to the project resource folder. The project's resource folder is under webapproot, so the files are available for loading at runtime. The resources folder in particular has been mapped into the project. You can use the binding dialog for resources. This absolves you of having to work out the correct path to the image when you want to set a picture widget's source property. We've already seen how JavaScript files can be imported into the page source just as easily.

The **Resources** tab can be used on mostly every part of the file system you might want to get at. You can upload JAR files to the project's classpath, for example. Adding JAR files to the project classpath allows you to use the classes of the JAR file from custom Java code. This access can be extremely useful. When running in the cloud such as the Cloud Foundry version of Studio, on the other hand, it may be the only direct file system access available.

The palette

There are two main ways to add visual components, better known as widgets, to a WaveMaker project's layout: call functions that create components from code or drag them off the palette and into the layout canvas in Studio. Most developers only use drag-and-drop.

The organization of the palette tree is rather good. It is also searchable if you can't find what you are looking for. Selecting a widget in the tree displays a question mark doc link and short description for that widget.

Importing a database adds each table entity of the schema to the database widget's section of the palette. These database objects are entry points to the `LivePanel` database form generator. The other way users commonly add new items to the palette is with custom widgets added to `common/packages/packages.js`. The **Example** button in the example group is an example of a custom widget added to the palette.

The Properties panel

This brings us to the **Properties** panel. All components have properties, and the **Properties** panel is where we view and edit those properties. The **Accordion** layer of **Properties** is the primary interface for defining component behavior. Properties shown depend on the selected component in the model, as not all properties are common to all components. Each layer in the accordion groups properties into common categories such as events and style.

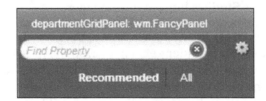

Properties can be viewed in **Recommended** or **All** mode. In **All** mode, all properties are shown straight off. In **Recommended** mode, the properties shown are reduced to the recommended set. The recommended properties are the most commonly used properties. These also tend to be less dangerous if you don't fully understand them. If there are additional properties beyond the recommended ones to be had, you can show them without leaving Recommended mode by clicking on the **Show more** link at the bottom of the set.

> Components can have additional properties that are not visually tooled but can be set via code. We can consider this to be **Expert** mode.

Like components, properties are searchable, and there is a single search editor across the views. Search will find those components not currently shown when in Recommended mode.

Also at the top of the **Properties** panel is the gear icon used to open a small settings pop-up box. In this box, we have a checkbox used to enable having multiple accordions open at once. The item in this box is a link to open the property publisher dialog. The publishing page properties enable us to have more modular and reusable pages. We will be discussing the use of publishing page properties in *Chapter 5, Navigating towards Reusability*.

The top layer is the **Properties** layer, and it contains the core properties of the selected component. Many properties have default values. These properties generally don't need to be considered until customization is desired. Studio auto-generates a name for the component upon creation and setting the name is often helpful, but is not required. Still, nearly all components have a few properties that you must set if the widget is to be effectively functional. These properties have the red asterisk used to mark required fields next to them.

On the far-right margin of each property there is a question mark help link. This opens the in-Studio help dialog for that property. The content shown in these dialogs is from the client-side API reference of the product documentation, or jsref for short. You can browse the JavaScript reference directly at:

http://dev.wavemaker.com/wiki/bin/wmjsref_6.5/WebHome

Not all properties are defined for every component. If there is no help defined for that property of that component, you can still view the general component documentation. An easy way to access the component reference is in the bottom most **Docs/Diagnostics** layer. Alternatively, use the **Open Wiki** link in the help dialog and remove the property name from the URL to access the component reference in your browser.

The **Data** layer is where we specify any inputs to variables and server calls. These include filters for searches and inputs to function calls. The fields are directly driven by the type of the variable or its operation. If the **Data** layer is not correct, check the **Type** and **Operation** specified in the **Properties** layer.

In the **Style** layer are three subtabs: **Basic**, **Styles**, and **Classes**. The **Basic** tab is used for setting border, padding, and margin. As we learned in the previous chapter, these are properties used by the WaveMaker layout engine and not CSS rules. The **Styles** and **Classes** tabs are used to create and apply component-specific CSS.

The **Mobile** layer is where we'll find mobile-specific properties for components. These properties control on what devices the widgets are shown and are generally only found on widgets due to their visual nature.

The **Events** layer is the visual interface to `dojo.connect()`. The **Events** tab is populated with the most commonly used events for that component. The drop-downs are populated with create options at the top and likely functions in the lower section. Choosing JavaScript creates a new empty event function and brings us into the page source script tab. It is important to understand that we are hardly limited to the tooled choices. A single JavaScript function can be used for multiple events from multiple components. Simply type in the name of an existing page function instead of selecting from the menu to reuse an existing function for an event. DOM events that are not visually tooled are not shown in the events tab, but can also be assigned handlers by calling `dojo.connect()` manually in the page's start function. The following line of code is an example of adding a mouse over event to a widget named `labelMouseOver`:

```
this.connect(this.labelMouseOver.domNode, "onmouseover", this,
"myMouseOverFunction");
```

When the user's mouse enters the DOM node for that label, the page function named `myMouseOverFunction()` is invoked.

A single event can trigger multiple functions. Next to the help link for each event is a plus sign icon. This is the "and then" button. Use it to add "and then" functions to events.

In the **Operations** layer are not properties, but buttons that perform useful functions on that component. Service calls can be invoked using the **updateNow** button, for example. Any operations accessible from the right-click menu for widgets, such as **Wrap in Panel**, are also here.

The last layer in the properties accordion is **Docs/Diagnostics**. We've already used the **Notes** tab to add custom notes for aggregation in the **documentation** tab under the **Source** tab. We've also seen how the **Docs** tab displays the JavaScript reference page for that component type. That leaves the **Description** tab, which is really the diagnostics part of this layer. This area generates a reference of event handlers as well as inbound and outbound bindings. A good use case for this tab is for checking if any other component is using the component under inspection. For example, prior to deleting a component, the diagnostics can confirm that the soon-to-be-deleted component is truly no longer being used.

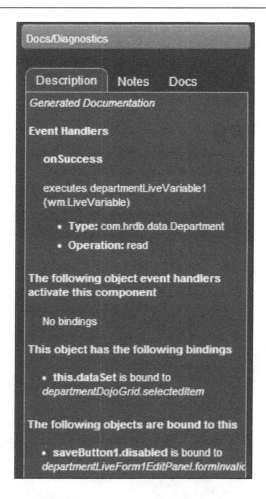

For a few components, the very last layer is **Deprecated**. This is where you will find deprecated features of components. You should only need this layer if you have an existing project utilizing deprecated features. In such situations, you should migrate the functionality to non-deprecated methods.

The page and project properties

At the beginning of our discussion of the **Properties** panel, we said that all components have properties. Most users find it intuitive to select a widget or component to view its properties. What is sometimes less obvious is that the pages and the project itself in the components tree also have properties. As you might expect, page and project properties apply to all components owned by the page and project respectively.

Project properties include specifying a currency locale code used for displaying currencies unless specifically overridden for a widget and how older versions of MSIE should be handled. It is here in the project properties that we specify the project's theme.

Binding dialog

The last area of Studio we need to cover is the binding dialog. This is the graphical tooling for subscripting to topic notifications. The primary topic of interest here being the "has changed" event. Consider the binding in the following screenshot:

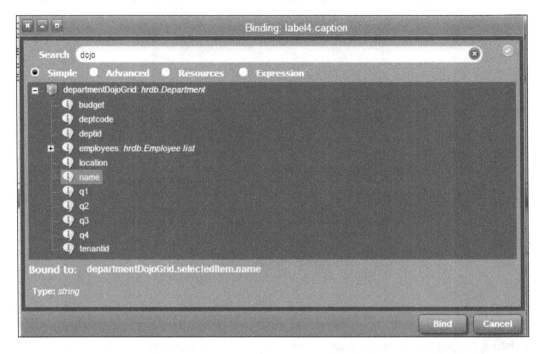

Here we have bound the caption of a label named `label4` to the name of the department selected in the department grid. This binding causes the label to be notified when the selected department changes. The grid publishes a "has changed" notification when the selected item changes. Upon receiving that notification, the label can then get the new value and update its caption accordingly.

There are four view modes to the binding dialog: **Simple**, **Advanced**, **Resources**, and **Expression**. A search editor is available to quickly find source components. Type information is also used to provide a green, yellow, or red indicator icon in the top-right corner. Matched types are indicated by the green checkbox, whereas the yellow warning and red X icons indicate decreased confidence and outright distrust of the selection accordingly.

The title of the dialog is the name of the target component. In the footer of the dialog, the source component is indicated by the **Bound to:** label and the target type is provided as an aid. The source is the component providing the notification and value, as that is the source of the information. The target is the component receiving the information or the target of the binding.

In Simple view mode, a single tree of likely sources is presented. In Advanced mode, all components are listed in either the visual or non-visual tree. The Advanced mode trees quickly become large. Searching is extremely helpful in finding the correct component quickly, especially if you know the component's name or you have utilized a naming convention that allows you to quickly filter the tree down by type or class. Another way to quickly get to the component you seek is by selecting it in the model tree or on the canvas. That's right, with the binding dialog open you can drive the search editor by selecting in the canvas or model tree. Advanced mode also enables you to bind to components on other pages with the page selector in the top-left corner.

The resources view enables us to bind to file resources uploaded to the project's `resources` folder. The classic use case here is setting the image source of a picture widget to an image file.

Last but certainly not least is the **Expression** view. Binding expressions as they are called, are JavaScript expressions that are executed in a context where this refers to the window instead of the page. This means we can use logical operators and conditionals in our bindings without needing to code full functions. The lower part of the **Expression** view allows us to add component references to our expression via selection. Selecting the selected department name of our department grid from the tree adds `${departmentDojoGrid.selectedItem.name}` to the expression, for example. The department name string could be concatenated with other component properties or static values as desired. For example, we can change the binding of the `label4` label's caption to:

```
"Viewing " + ${departmentDojoGrid.selectedItem.name}
```

This adds the static string `Viewing` with a space in front of the selected department name.

Binding expressions are an advanced feature and are nicely documented in the product documentation at `http://dev.wavemaker.com/wiki/bin/wmdoc_6.5/Binding+Expressions+Display+Expressions`.

Using revision control software

WaveMaker does provide revision control for projects. It is strongly suggested to utilize a revision control system, such as Git (`https://en.wikipedia.org/wiki/Git_(software)`) and GitHub (`https://github.com/`), for any valuable project. Version control enables developers to track and control changes to the project. Storing projects in such systems enables a team of developers to collectively work on a single project. Solo developers also benefit from using version control, most notably by being able to revert to a previous state should something catastrophic occur.

The example projects used here are examples of a project workspace using GitHub (`https://github.com/edwardcallahan/Easy-Web-Samples`). For more information and examples of using revision control, visit `http://dev.wavemaker.com/wiki/bin/Software+Configuration+Management`.

Summary

In this chapter, we toured the visual IDE of Studio. We've touched upon every working area of the Studio tooling, from the top level menu down to the small properties settings. We have examined how to create a new project, add components, add custom JavaScript perform bindings, and set component properties. We have also looked at the benefits of using revision control software such as Git.

This chapter builds upon the architectural concepts introduced in previous chapters. You should now find yourself becoming more comfortable connecting the mouse clicks in the Studio tooling with the concepts happening underneath it all.

In the next chapter, we will apply our understanding and discuss designing applications.

4
Designing a Well-Performing Application

At this point, you should be comfortable with both the use of Studio as well as the structure of the applications produced by Studio. Let us now consider the structure of our own applications. By failing to prepare, you are preparing to fail is Benjamin Franklin's version of the well-known sentiment that planning pays off. WaveMaker makes it easy to build a web application; however, building a good application still requires some planning.

In this chapter, we will address design considerations for a successful application. First, we will consider screen sizing to ensure that the application fits correctly on our users' devices. We'll also continue working with pages to improve application loading times. Finally, we'll improve the overall application performance by looking at how we can optimize our use of data and server calls.

By considering these aspects before building the application, the resultant application will be easier to use, maintain, and better performing.

Begin with the end in mind

Planning the application begins with determining what the application will and will not be when it is done. What must the application be able to do to be successful, and how does that definition of success compare to average requirements? Questions to consider while answering this include the following:

- Will the application be used on a multitude of devices of varying screen sizes and input types, or will users primarily be using a single class of devices?

- What type of network connectivity will users' devices have?

- Which browsers will they be using?

- Will the application be installed on a mobile device as a PhoneGap application?

- Will some users be installing an application while others are using the hosted version?

Answers to these types of questions quickly start to drive some design considerations.

Let's consider a few examples. If the application needs to be used by modern devices with slow network connections, but possessing plenty of local resources, minimizing network usage is going to be critical to a good user experience. This is common with field service workers. We can equip the field staff with good devices, but we are likely to be dependent upon a cellular provider for connectivity that could be limited to 3G service in a service area. Here, we can look to cache as many of our resources as possible to minimize network utilization. We may have some larger sets of data that are beneficial to keep around in the client-side and we may use client-side querying to create local views on that dataset.

If, however, the application is to be used continuously on older desktops with adequate network connectivity but with little memory to spare, our focus changes. This was the situation for a mid-sized electronics retailer's return merchandise authorization (RMA) system. They needed to modernize their RMA application, but they were constrained in their ability to upgrade the hardware installed at each location. In this case, we need to keep the memory footprint consistently small. We are likely to favor fetching data in small distinct chunks instead of filtering views on locally cached datasets. As we have a strong network, we can afford to make more service calls that return smaller datasets in order to avoid overrunning available system memory.

Finally, if the application is to be used by a variety of devices with a variety of browsers and screen sizes, suitability to all these devices becomes a driving factor. Do we develop several versions of the application, one for each target device class, or do we have a single set of pages that provide a lowest common denominator approach?

These examples only scratch the surface of the considerations that may drive other considerations. WaveMaker applications have been deployed in an amazing range of configurations. Sometimes, a single requirement can dictate many aspects of the project. It is also important that the application performs well; users hate to wait.

With the application's driving design considerations determined, we can begin to design our application. Combined with some understanding of performance factors, we can be confident of successful results.

Leveraging layouts

Before we can properly take up screen sizing, we need to understand how visual components are laid out in a WaveMaker application. The layoutBox, of type wm.Layout, is the page's widget container. It is the parent of all the visual components on the page. The layout box is the container into which the widgets of the page go. As such, its properties affect every widget on its page:

First, we have **width** and **height**. These both default to using percentage-based sizing at 100%, which means that the app will be of the full width and height of the browser. Percentage layout allows us to specify the size of a widget in terms of the percentage of the space available in that dimension. Let's say both components in a panel are set to 100% width in a left-to-right panel. Each widget would get one half of the available width. That is, each widget would get 100% of the 200% allocated. If one widget was set to 100% and the other 200%, the first would get 1/3 of the available space, 100/300, while the second receives the remaining 2/3 of the available space.

The alternative option is to specify size in pixels. Choose **px** in the dropdown or simply enter a number ending in px, such as 80px, in the editor. This allows us to specify the exact pixel dimensions of the container. Using pixel-based sizing gives the developer direct control over the size of the widget. Images will always be the same size no matter what the user's screen size is. If the specified size does not fit in the available space, and scrolling is enabled, scrollbars or touch scrolling will be present. Pixel and percentage sizing can be mixed in a single container with good results. For example, a picture may always be 200px while the components sharing the panel share the remainder of the available space.

Next, we have **layoutKind**. In the top-to-bottom layout, which is the default for **layoutBox** box, widgets are stacked from top to bottom as they are added to the container. The other value of **layoutKind** is **left-to-right**, in which components are stacked within a shared container from the left to the right. With a **top-to-bottom layoutBox**, if we want to have two widgets next to each horizontally, we'll need to add a container with the **left-to-right** layout kind within the **top-to-bottom** container. The **Top-to-bottom layoutKind** is a good default to most application's **layoutBox**. As the page grows, it gets taller. Users are accustomed to scrolling down to get to additional content. At the same time, layouts requiring users to scroll both horizontally and vertically are more cumbersome, requiring the user to spend more effort in positioning the window.

> Changing panel properties can sometimes be disruptive to the layout of a panel when changed. One option is to use the **wrap in panel** operation in Studio's right-click menu when a desired addition to a panel requires a change in the kind of layout. Instead of changing the value of **layoutKind** of the existing panel, create a new panel with the desired layout kind and move existing widgets into the new panel.

Horizontal and vertical alignment dictates how widgets align within the panel. The top setting for **verticalAlign** works well for most cases. However, for a versatile layout, the center **horizontalAlign** container works well with tablets and desktops. The CRM Simple example project demonstrates this. The minimum size properties **minWidth** and **minHeight** are useful in such situations to ensure things stay large enough to be usable.

Finally, **autoScroll** will automatically add scrollbars to the panel when needed.

Screen-sizing strategies

If all users are using an application from the same device, the task is simple: provide an application that works great on that device. However, this is not common with web applications. Business applications might only concern themselves with desktop users, but even here it is likely that there is some range in screen resolutions and browsers being used. This is hardly new to web development, and the task is well understood. A single layout can be used without too much trouble.

Increasingly however, we need to also consider tablet and phone users. In the case of CRM Simple, we used a single page for all screens. The layout is simple and condensed enough to remain usable on a 7-inch tablet. If the screen gets much smaller than that, it becomes unusable. At the same time, while it may look overly simplistic, it's still usable on a desktop. Although phone screen sizes continue to drift upwards, they're still small enough to require significant simplification of the interface. You simply cannot present as much information at once on a phone. A well-designed mobile application does less, but does it well. This leaves us with a few options to consider when targeting multiple devices:

- Multiple versions of the application
- One page for all devices
- A page per device
- Some combination of the above

Multiple versions of an application or all in one?

Creating a new project for each device is an obvious solution, but it does incur the cost of having multiple versions to maintain. On the other hand, building a separate version for PhoneGap enables it to be optimized for mobile. For example, the installed version could be designed for offline operation, utilizing local storage, indexedDB, and so on. This can be a logical addition to a successful web application with a growing phone user base. New applications needing mobile support but with no immediate desktop support needs are also good candidates for PhoneGap-optimized application.

One screen for all devices

A single set of pages for all devices can work well as long as you do not try to support both phones and desktops from the single page. A page can be designed for the smallest target device screen size and allowed to scale up in size, but only to an extent. For example, on a phone, a task menu where the user picks from a short task list is a common model. However, as a full-screen window on a high resolution desktop, a six-button home page would be odd, impractical, and ugly. This means that we are most likely to be able to use some set of pages for both larger tablets and desktops and laptops. It is also likely that some phone pages are usable on tablets.

A screen for each screen size

As we saw earlier, by selecting the project in the **Services** tab, Studio allows us to specify a different page for phones, tablets, and desktops in the **Projects Properties** under **Mobile**. This feature allows us to have a single application with pages optimized for each device class.

This is a good strategy; using the same services for all client views means there is only one server to maintain. The potential trap when using this approach is the logic being repeated on each page. To minimize page code duplication, create a shared JavaScript file under **Resources**. These can be easily imported using the **Import** button in the **Source** tab. By putting as much logic as possible in the shared resource script file, you can reduce the amount of page code duplicated in each page. The shared JavaScript functions would be a good place to put management information of any global objects our application is using, as a simple example.

The very bottom of the main script page of WaveyWeb has an import of `waveytools.js`:

```
eval(wm.load("resources/javascript/waveytools.js"));
```

`Waveytools.js` defines a namespace called `waveytools`. Using namespaces is a good thing; it keeps its functions out of the global namespace and avoids potential collisions with other functions. This is why all functions in WaveMaker start with a prefix such as `app`, `main`, `wm`, and `this`.

In the `waveytools` namespace, we've defined a `logMessage` function. An example of calling this function is shown in the `layer1 onShow` event function:

```
layer1Show: function(inSender) {
    //this is using the log function defined in waveytools.js
    waveytools.logMessage("Now showing layer 1");
},
```

The hybrid approach

Often the most practical approach is a combination of these approaches. If the application is large, maybe the tasks should be divided into multiple applications. In the version for bigger screens, you can have more complete applications with one page for all screens. Meanwhile, for the smaller screens, use a smaller, task-focused, specialized application.

If a single page in the desktop version of an application performs some complex task, most probably it will be necessary to divide that task into multiple pages for the tablet version. A single page of the desktop may require multiple pages in the tablet version to accomplish the same task.

Now that we have planned our layouts, let's consider how we'll keep things moving along smoothly.

Going faster

Most often, any definition of a successful application includes being "fast enough". What is and is not "fast enough?" Well, it depends. What we can easily say is that a slow application is no fun to use. Users will complain or stop using the application outright if performance is too poor. Building a well-performing application does not "just happen"; it requires planning. Let's look at some of the key design factors of performance.

Using page containers effectively

As we have seen, the widgets file of a page defines all of the components of a page in the JSON format. The higher the number of widgets and components on a page, the more JSON code needs to be parsed before the page can be rendered. Therefore, the higher the number of components on a page, the longer it takes to load. Reducing page load time is one of the most significant performance knobs available to developers.

Page containers have a **deferLoad** property, as shown in the following screenshot:

When enabled, which is the default state, the page container does not automatically load any page. Instead, it remains empty until the page is needed or explicitly loaded. Deferring the loading of widgets after application initialization is a powerful technique for reducing application load times.

Let's look at the WaveyWeb application from the last chapter. In **layer2** of **tabLayers1**, just below **labelMouseOver**, we have our first page container named **pageContainer1**. The page name property is set to `PageRichText`. Run the application.

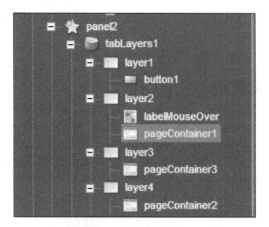

After the application has loaded, open the **Network** tab of the Chrome **Developer Tools** and clear the previous requests using the **Clear** button. The **Clear** button is the circle with the angled line through it, as shown in the following screenshot:

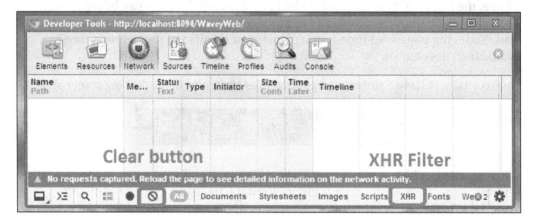

Optionally, use the **XHR** filter button to filter out only XHR requests if you like. This makes service calls easier to see. Now click on the tab labeled **Connect**. Notice how `PageRichText.a.js` is fetched upon the showing of the tab layer containing the page container:

Name Path	Method	Status Text	Type	Initiator	Size Content	Time Latency
PageRichText.a.js?dojo.prev /WaveyWeb/pages/PageRichTe:	GET	200 OK	text/jav...	dojo_build.js:567 Script	674B 428B	37ms 33ms
wm_editors.js /wavemaker/lib/build/Gzipped	GET	200 OK	text/plain	dojo_build.js:567 Script	45.47KB 183.18KB	62ms 54ms
wm_richTextEditor.js /wavemaker/lib/build/Gzipped	GET	200 OK	text/plain	dojo_build.js:567 Script	51.79KB 203.19KB	51ms 42ms
wm_richTextEditor_en-us.js /wavemaker/lib/build/nls	GET	200 OK	text/jav...	dojo_build.js:567 Script	2.95KB 7.57KB	48ms 43ms

If you reload the application with the **Network** tab open, you'll see that
`PageRichText` is not loaded with the application. We could force the page container
to load a page before being shown, for example, by calling `loadPage()`. This is easy
to demonstrate in the **Developer Tools** console by calling `main.pageContainer1`.
`loadPage("PageRichText")` before the page loads, for example, by opening the
layer containing the page container:

Developer Tools - http://localhost:8094/WaveyWeb/#

Elements   Resources   Network   Sources   Timeline   Profiles   Audits   Console

```
> main.pageContainer1.loadPage("PageRichText")|
```

This instructs the page container to load `PageRichText`. Now, when we
show **layer2**, `PageRichText` is already loaded and there is no fetch. Notice
that once `PageRichText` is loaded, like `main`, it gets loaded in the memory and
not re-fetched. Clicking through all three layers does not result in further loading
of `PageRichText`. The browser already has `PageRichText` (and `main`) loaded and
does not need to re-fetch these pages.

Using page containers with `deferLoad` is a good way to reduce the amount of work that the browser needs to do before the application is ready for the user. Using cut and paste, entire panels of widgets can be moved across pages easily. However, WaveMaker 6.5 Studio does not support multiple widget selection. You can select an entire panel, but not multiple individual widgets. You can move many widgets by copying a panel, but non-visual components and code must be processed individually. Furthermore, source code must be manually moved. The lesson here is that while you can break up a page into multiple pages afterwards, it is convenient to use multiple pages from the beginning.

Pages have no performance impact until they are loaded. Once loaded, however, they consume browser memory. Therefore, we need to consider how many pages the application shows at the same time.

How many page containers?

An effective application could utilize a single-page container. Consider a `main` page with headers, footers, menus, and so on, and a single-page container for the body. Such a layout could have two pages loaded at any time; `main`, and another page in the page container. Each navigation event changes the page loaded in the page container. This is an efficient design that keeps the memory footprint down. When a page is replaced by a new page, all references are removed enabling the replaced page's components to be garbage collected.

Another common pattern is to have a layer of page containers, such as we have done in the WaveyWeb application. This enables the application to have multiple pages loaded at the same time at the price of increased memory consumption. It also enables commonly used pages to remain loaded, generally improving the overall user experience.

Such a layout enables direct communication between pages, reducing the need for global variables. Components with application as their owner are available globally across all pages of the application and are called **global variables** as a result. These application-owned components are not unloaded until the application is destroyed. This means they are always in memory and always available. This can be a convenient means to share data across pages, but at the cost of consuming more memory.

When directly sharing data across pages, it is important to verify that the page your code calls into exists. Check the value returned from the other page before using it, or otherwise prevent the user from getting into the situation outright. For example, the following `if` block checks that the variable `data` has a value before using it:

```
if(data && data.length > 0 ){
}
```

Once again, which is best depends on the applications' goals. For an application that is being run on older hardware with little memory and less-than-ideal browsers, every bit of memory usage is costly. Older versions of Internet Explorer are infamous for their performance degradation as memory utilization increases. For an application targeting such platforms, the single-page container with many small pages is a good choice. At the same time, having too many pages loaded simultaneously can be overbearing to all but the most powerful systems. For many, a balanced approach will be the best. Using a few pages loaded simultaneously often reduces the complexity needed to manage the state. This will generally consist of one or two common pages being always loaded with one or two page containers for worker pages to perform specific tasks.

Don't forget that it is possible to have page containers within page containers. Within a page loaded in a page container, such as on the `main` page, we can repeat the pattern of a single-page container or a layer of page containers. Be careful not to overload the browser by nesting too many pages when using this pattern.

Reducing module loading

Deferring the loading of content via page containers improves load times by reducing the number of components that need to be created and rendered before the application is ready for the user. However, even the simplest application requires time to load and parse the WaveMaker runtime and component classes. The libraries containing component classes must be loaded before the page can create instances of those components.

As we know, in the debug mode, each module file is loaded independently as needed. By contrast, in the gzip mode, these modules are combined into minified compressed files. These modules are divided into groups. These groupings have been carefully selected to provide good loading for most situations. With a little bit of knowledge and planning, we can use these groupings to gain additional loading advantages.

Let's add a rich-text editor to `PageRichText` of our WaveyWeb application and repeat our network observation. Rich-text editors are heavyweight components. When we go to the **Connect** layer, causing `PageRichText` to load, we see two additional network requests: a 51.8 KB gzip build file and a 3.0 KB NLS file. Because the page contains a rich-text editor, `wm_richTextEditor.js` is loaded immediately after `PageRichText.a.js`. In parsing the components of `PageRichText`, the page loader finds that the page needs the `wm.RichText` class. Most applications use editors, but only some applications use heavy rich-text editors. As such, the rich-text editor is in its own build file, thus saving applications that don't use the rich-text editor from ever having to load and parse that 51.8 KB file. The NLS file contains localizations for the labels such as cut, copy, and paste, and is specific to the user's locale. Therefore, the NLS files are not included in the component package.

There are 24 gzipped files in the `lib\build\Gzipped` folder. The names will give you a good idea about the modules they contain. The `Wm_editors.js.gz` file contains all editors except the basic text editor and the rich-text editor. It also contains the Dojo grid. A direct list of component classes and their module can also be seen by entering `wm.componentList` on the console. This returns an array of classes and the build modules they require. By being conscious of these loadings and organizing your pages accordingly, you can reduce or defer the amount of downloading needed to use the application.

It is possible to create your own custom build files. This can be tricky and is beyond the scope of this book. For users wishing to create their own minified, compressed files, the product documentation can be found at `http://dev.wavemaker.com/wiki/bin/wmdoc_6.5/Performance#HTheJavascriptBuildSystem`.

Optimizing the use of data and service calls

Server calls are expensive. Optimizing the number of calls and the frequency of those calls often provides good performance returns. Not only does a service call require client resources, it also calls the server. Excessive refreshing of datasets can cripple the usability of an application. Let's explore how the application will use services and how we can optimize that usage.

Developers who haven't been watching the **Network** tab in **Developer Tools** can be astonished by the sheer volume of server calls their application is making. Requiring many service calls to initialize the application can significantly increase the duration it takes the application to be ready for the user. Optimizing the use of service calls is one of the other significant performance knobs developers have at their disposal.

As the application starts to come together, make a point to inventory the JSON network calls. Can you account for each and every one? Yes, I said every one. Do you understand why it was needed? How large is the dataset that is being returned? Was the call really needed at that time? Let's look at some common issues.

Beware of autoUpdate

The **autoUpdate** option is easy to use, but can often be the biggest performance drag on applications that use it. Let's see why.

Service variables can be invoked in the following different ways:

- Having its `update` function called from code.
- Selecting the service call from an event dropdown. This is the code-free equivalent of calling `update()`.
- Lazy loading of related data model entities by grids.
- Using the **startUpdate** option. This fires the service call when the page loads for the first time.
- Using the **autoUpdate** option. This fires the service call whenever any of its inputs change.

The **autoUpdate** option is too easy to use. You check the box and you get the data. If any bound input to the service call changes, such as an input to a query, the service call fires. Call `setValue()` from the code on an input and it also fires. **AutoUpdate** really means update (fire, or trigger the call) whenever any inputs change. It's very simple and easy.

However, don't use it. Trigger every service variable from the events and code instead. Often the use of autoUpdate results in the service variable firing too often. This is a performance drag on client, server, and the network. Don't use autoUpdate in anything but trivial applications and avoid having to untangle a mess later.

A chain of service variables is a common pattern in AJAX applications. The `onSuccess` event of one service call invokes another service call that is dependent upon data from the first. For example, selecting a value in one select menu can often filter the options presented in another select menu. Likewise, selecting a row in a grid often triggers other service calls filtered for the selected item. With autoUpdate, these chains can get long and messy. Pretty soon, you would have lost control of your network utilization. The application is making dozens of service calls whenever values change, and it is difficult to know what is what anymore. Sometimes, service variables fire multiple times for no known reason.

Instead, invoke each service variable directly. Use the onchange events of components to invoke service calls instead of using the autoUpdate feature. Let binding update the input parameters to the service variable, but invoke the service variable yourself.

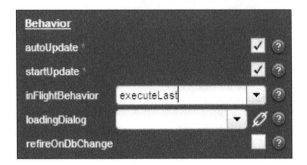

AutoUpdate can also result in the user seeing incorrect data. By default, when a service variable is triggered, such as by a bound value change event, and the service variable is still "in flight" from the last time it was triggered, the second call is ignored. This means that the data returned to the user was never updated to the most current inputs. In WaveMaker 6.5, service calls now have an **inFlightBehavior** property that will queue the last request for execution and another that queues all in-flight calls. The **executeLast** option is good for read operations. The **executeAll** option should be used judiciously. If the user is likely to be doing volume operations often, consider adding a bulk operation Java service instead. Consider the application with a common usage pattern of marking multiple items as resolved. Instead of selecting X items to be marked as resolved and calling an update X times, send an array of items to be resolved to a single server-side function. In that function, iterate over the items and mark them as resolved. We'll discuss creating such Java services in *Chapter 9, Custom Java Services*.

Controlling the result set size

Service variables have a property that specifies the maximum number of rows returned by the call. It is called maxResults and defaults to 500. The other maximum results property, DesignMaxResults, applies only to design time, or when data is being loaded into the application while working in Studio.

The `maxResults` property prevents thousands upon thousands of rows from being returned and overwhelming the browser. Consider a read operation on a table containing hundreds of thousands of entries. Even an accidental unfiltered read on such a table could leave the most modern browser struggling to manage such a dataset. Combined with the `firstRow` property, large datasets can be paginated into the client. By advancing the `firstrow` property to the next row to be returned and triggering the service call, data can be brought into the browser in chunks. The `DataNavigator` component is a widget available on the palette to easily paginate data from live variables. Pagination with service variable data is possible, but requires exposing parameters to control pagination in the service methods.

While reducing the size of result sets is generally good for performance, sometimes a slightly larger result set is better overall. Let's say an application uses a table listing the 193 member nations of the United Nations. Using a service variable with a `maxResults` value of anything less than 193 means that all results are not returned in the single read call. This may be desirable if the results are segmented somehow, but if the goal is to have a single list from which users can choose a member nation, populating the list in a single call is more efficient.

Client-side querying of variable results

Another tool in optimizing service usage is the client-side query mechanism in `wm.Variable`. The `Variable.query()` function can be performed on a `wm.Variable` that contains a list of data and supports greater than, less than, not, and wildcard searches. The query returns a new `wm.Variable` containing the results that match the specified query.

Client-side variable querying enables developers to avoid making calls to the server to filter moderate-sized datasets. This is particularly well suited for datasets that are not subject to change while the application is in use. Our United Nations member nations use case is a good example, as new members being added to the U.N. are extremely unlikely while the user has the dataset loaded.

More information about variable querying can be found at `http://dev.wavemaker. com/wiki/bin/wmjsref_6.5/Variable_query`.

Live views and related data

It is important to understand that live views return all columns of a related table, regardless of whether those columns are used or not. This can increase the size of the dataset returned significantly. We'll discuss live views further in *Chapter 7, Working with Databases*. For application planning, it is important to remember that all columns of the related table are always returned. A related table containing a blob, for example, is better retrieved using an HQL query in which we have specific control over the columns returned.

Lazy loading

Lazy loading is an alternative to live views and retrieve related data. When using database data with relations, WaveMaker will just-in-time fetch related data if needed. For example, if our employee live variable does not include the department information in its view, any request for department information will require a synchronous lazy load. Yuck! This enables the call to return a result as expected; however, the entire application stops until the call returns as a result.

In WaveMaker 6.5, `dojoGrid` does not lazy load. Adding a custom column such as `${deparment.departmentname}` to the employee grid will provide only an empty column. The **Lazy Loading** tab of WaveyWeb loads `PageLazy`. There is a button on `PageLazy` that takes the selected item index and requests the department of the selected item from the live variable that populated the grid. This is a shortcut to give an example of lazy loading, and is not something we would normally do because we are working across two datasets. If the user sorts the grid, the selected item index will no longer match the index of that employee in the live variable. The following is the code for the **Get Department** button:

```
this.employeeLiveVariable1.getItem(this.employeeDojoGrid.
getSelectedIndex()).getValue("department");
```

We have combined two calls. The first call, `this.employeeDojoGrid.getSelectedIndex()`, returns the integer index of the grid selected item. The second call, `this.employeeLiveVariable1.getItem(n).getValue("department")`, gets the *n*th item from the employee live variable and then fetches the value of its department. In our case, *n* is the selected item index. As the employee live variable does not include the department in its live view, each call to a different *n* results in a lazy load. Watch for yourself in the **Network** tab. Each click of **Get Department** for a new selected item results in a `runtimeService` JSON call, filtered by a full employee. Lazy loading uses the full item as a filter, even when just a Primary Key would have been sufficient. This causes more data than needed to be sent in the request.

Lazy loading reduces the initial loading of the dataset at the cost of incurring synchronous reads when related data is required. WaveMaker does this for us, and most of the time, it is a good thing; however, for some models, fetching the related data as part of the initial read may be the more efficient pattern. More information on lazy loading can be found at `http://dev.wavemaker.com/wiki/bin/wmdoc_6.5/LazyLoading`.

Related editors

Another source of service calls is related editors. Related editors have an `autoDataSet` property. By default, this is enabled, and means that each related editor has its own live variable and dataset. Clearing the `autoDataSet` property shows the `dataSet` property, enabling us to specify the related editor's dataset. The auto dataset feature is convenient, but when we have lookup editors on large datasets that can be filtered down, it is often more efficient to provide our own dataset. Providing our own dataset also lets us control when the dataset is refreshed. Again, in our United Nations example, we don't need to refresh the member nation list during the application's use.

Summary

In this chapter, we have learned about key considerations when planning our application. The aspects we discussed are primarily those of the layout of the application and the performance of the application. By starting with a layout well suited to the user's device and keeping our application nimble, we are much more likely to have a successful application. Using page containers to segment the application and controlling the use of service calls are key performance factors. Spend some time in the beginning planning the application layout. Experiment with a few test applications on target devices if you can. Restructuring an application midway through its creation is best avoided as much as possible.

In the next chapter, we will continue our study of client-side application structure. Now that we have seen how important pages are to building scalable applications, we will learn how to use pages more effectively.

5
Navigating towards Reusability

In the last chapter, we learned about the importance of using pages to reduce both application load times and memory usage. We also started thinking about our application's layout and its use of the available screen real estate. These logically lead us to the topic of navigating around within the application. Now that we've segmented our application into pages of similar concerns, how do we move about these pages to form a smooth flowing application? In this chapter, we will discuss application navigation and the navigation components available to us. We'll start with the navigation call, layers, and page containers. We'll continue to review all the components available to us, from simple notifications such as alerts, confirms, toast, to simple dialogs and page dialogs. The tooled component versions of these are straightforward to understand and use. We'll also show how you can use these components from JavaScript for a highly customized user experience.

After that, we'll look at some advanced aspects of pages that we can use to improve page reusability. First, we will look at published page properties, which will allow the page and its page container to interact. The back button and page history can be troublesome with an AJAX application. We'll look at the tooling provided by WaveMaker that we can use to smoothen out those rough spots. Finally, we'll look at URL management. We'll see how URL management is a complex issue and we'll examine the use case of creating URLs that contain grid selection.

The example project for this chapter is `CustpurchaseNavigation`, available at `https://github.com/edwardcallahan/Easy-Web-Samples/tree/master/projects/CustpurchaseNavigation`.

Navigation, layers, and page containers

WaveMaker provides navigation calls for navigating around within an application. Navigation calls are client-side components of the type `wm.NavigationCall`. They may feel like service calls, but they do not call the server. Not every application navigation requires the use of a navigation call. Tab layers, in which the user selects the visual tab of the layer they want, are the most notable example. Navigation calls are configured by their properties to specify both the type of navigation and the specific instances involved. Navigation calls can be used for a variety of things, from showing a toast message to replacing the home page outright. To load a page into a page container, for example, select `gotoPageContainerPage` for the operation of the navigation call and set the `pageName` and `pageContainer` properties.

Shown in the previous screenshot is **navigationCallMobileSite** from the `CustpurchaseNavigation` example project. The application provides a link to its mobile version in the menu bar in the top-right corner. This menu item invokes the **navigationCallMobileSite** navigation call using the **onMobile_VersionClick** event shown in the following screenshot:

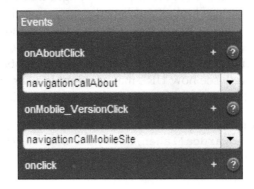

A **gotoPage** operation replaces the entire main page with the page specified, **PageMobile** in this case. This can be used to bring the user to a different version of the application, such as between mobile and desktop as we have done or between simple and advanced mode.

In the same menu, an about item uses the **gotoDialogPage** operation to display the **PageAbout** page in a dialog box.

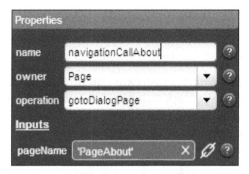

This utilizes the default application dialog as a page container. It is an application-owned component that can be accessed via code as app.pageDialog. It is very important to note that there is only one instance of this dialog in an application.

When using multiple pages with a single page container, navigation calls are an easy way to change the page shown in the page container. An example of how easy this is to use is provided on the tab titled **Page Container** in the example application. A select menu containing a list of destination pages is presented in the following screenshot:

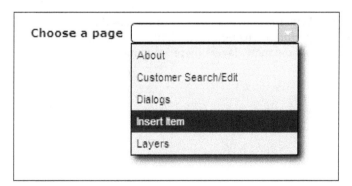

The select menu's onChange event triggers the gotoPageContainerPage navigation call, which gets its pageName property from binding the select menu's selected item, selectMenuPageChooser.selectedItem.dataValue.

Pages can also be loaded into page containers without a navigation call by using `setPageName()`. If you are using page code to determine the next page to navigate to, `setPageName()` is often easier to use. For example, to load the page `PageAbout` into the page container `pageContainerPageContainer`, we would use:

```
this.pageContainerPageContainer.setPageName("PageAbout");
```

Layer navigations can also be specified from the script. For example, we could set our tab layers, `tabLayers1`, to the layer named `layersDialogs` using the following code line:

```
this.tabLayers1.setLayer("layersDialogs");
```

A more efficient use of layer navigation calls can often be utilized using the `nextLayer` and `previousLayer` operations. This saves us from the need to create a new navigation call for each and every layer, particularly in wizard-like constructs. The example application demonstrates this on its `PageLayers` page, shown on the **Layers** tab:

 With the above, all navigation across the layers is performed using two navigation components, regardless of how many layers there are to move across.

Simple notifications

Good applications must inform the user of a number of events and conditions. Unexpected errors and failures, successful task completion, and drawing attention to unmet requirements are all use cases for such notifications. WaveMaker provides a range of components to assist with these needs. In this section, we will look at the simple notifications provided by choosing **NotificationCall** from the **Insert** menu:

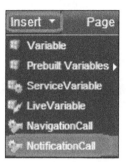

Alert!

The most basic of navigations are the simple notifications. The most basic of these is **alert**. They are the simple dialogs with a message and an **OK** button to dismiss the dialog. It remains nearly impossible not to encounter alerts on the Web. In raw JavaScript, you use `alert("Some Message");` and an alert is shown. What more could there be to know about alerts?

The JavaScript `alert()` uses the browser to display the message. We know that browsers are inconsistent creatures, and their handling of alerts is no different. Some browsers even freeze all execution during the alert. Also, browser alerts look like browser windows and lack any application styling. In short, they don't match the look and feel of your application.

In the `CustpurchaseNavigation` example project, we will show you how to alert a message in four variations. One button is using the standard JavaScript alert; the others are using the WaveMaker app alert notification. Also in the **Alert** panel is a text editor, `textAlertMsg`. This editor is the source of the alert message:

The right-most button is called `buttonAlertSimple` with the caption **Alert by JS Alert**. This button uses JavaScript in its on-click event to call the standard JavaScript alert: `alert(this.textAlertMsg.getDataValue());`. We obtain the editor's value by calling `getDataValue()` on the editor and pass it in as our value to the old alert.

Moving to the left we have a button that calls `app.alert(this.textAlertMsg.getDataValue());` directly in its on-click event script. Again, we obtain the text editor's data value via script. This time, however, we use the `app.alert()` call to show the message. Now, instead of the "the page says" box, we get our message in a more appealing dialog:

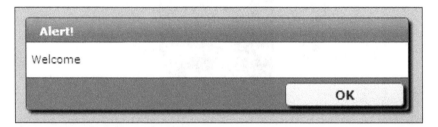

Continuing to the left, we introduce **notificationCallAlert**, a notification call component added to the project and visible in the service's components tree. The text property of **notificationCallAlert** is bound to the data value of the `textAlertMsg` editor. The `buttonAlertNotifiction` function calls the `notificationCallAlert` component directly from its on-click event. This is the code-free way to show an alert:

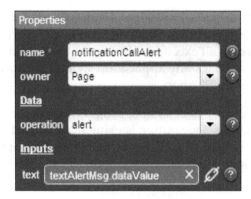

The left-most button uses script to customize the alert message before showing it. The `buttonAlertUpdateClick` function, the on-click event function for the button labeled **Alert by Update**, is shown in the following screenshot:

```
buttonAlertUpdateClick: function(inSender) {
    var msg = "Important notice: " + this.textAlertMsg.getDataValue();
    this.notificationCallAlert.setValue("input.data", {text: msg});
    this.notificationCallAlert.update();
},
```

First we get the data value from the alert message text editor, as we did before in `buttonAlertScriptClick()`. However, this time we append the editor value with `Important notice:` and save the result in a JavaScript variable named `msg`. Next, we set the value of the notification's text message. This overrides the text value from the binding. Finally, we use `update()` to invoke the notification call from the script. This is very similar to how we might set the input and trigger a service call.

Toast

Toast is the modern, gentler version of alert. Alerts are modal; they prevent the user from proceeding until they acknowledge the alert. A toast message pops up, like toast from a toaster, to deliver information without forcing the user to stop what they were doing.

The message is shown for some time and fades away. While the lower-right corner is the default position for the message, toast can be shown from any corner or center point of the application window including the center of the window.

In the **Toast** panel of our example application, previously shown, we display a toast using a notification call, using script, and again using more advanced script. **Toast by Notification**, like its alert equivalent, directly invokes the notification component, `notifictionCallToast`. Toast can be shown using either a notification call or a navigation call component. This example uses the notification call variety.

Toast by Script uses JavaScript to invoke `app.toastSuccess()` directly. Like alert, this provides us with an easy-to-use but consistent looking toast dialog:

```
buttonToastScriptClick: function(inSender) {
    app.toastSuccess("Well done!");
},
```

Finally, **Toast by Script - Advanced** uses JavaScript for its click event to display a toast message in an advanced, fully manual fashion:

```
buttonToastScriptAdvancedClick: function(inSender) {
    if(app.toastDialog === undefined){
        app.createToastDialog();
    }
    app.toastDialog.showToast("Oops, something went wrong processing: "
+ this.textToastMsg.getDataValue(), 3000, "Error", "bottom center");
},
```

Unlike the `notificationCallAlert` property, we do not use `update()` and `setValue()`. There is a single `toastDialog` variable in the application. So, the first thing we must do is ensure it has been initialized. This is done by calling `app.createToastDialog()` if the `app.ToastDialog` value is undefined. With that done, the toast is shown with the parameters specified.

Again, this is an advanced way of using toast. Most users will not need to use this method. However, it is a good example of how we can have complete control of the toast dialog at runtime without creating a toast notification of every possible combination at design time. Reusing the single notification not only saves us development effort, it also reduces the number of components the application needs to initialize at runtime.

The input properties of a tooled-notification call component in Studio can be used as a guide for parameter values. If we look at the values in the drop-down for `dialogPosition` in the **Inputs** properties of `notificationCallToast`, we can see the list of possible values for `dialogPosition` to use in our script.

Confirmations

Next up we have a confirmation. Confirmations are message boxes with an **OK** and **Cancel** button:

They are used to present the user with an immediate choice. The previously shown confirmation was created by using wm.NotificationCall with the operation property set to confirm. This time, however, we likely want to know the results of the dialog. Did the user choose **OK** or **Cancel**? The onCancel and onOk events are used to take the appropriate action. In our example project, we use JavaScript to set the caption of the results label according to the user's selection. The onCancel and onOk events could just as easily cancel or complete the submission of a form, or whatever we may need to do.

Here we have a great use case for the **And then** event feature as shown on the confirmation button **onclick** event in the following screenshot:

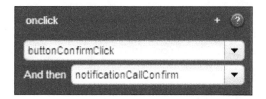

First, the confirmation button click uses JavaScript to clear the results label:

```
buttonConfirmClick: function(inSender) {
    this.labelConfirmResult.setCaption("");
},
```

And then invokes the confirmation dialog notification component, **notificationCallConfirm**. Clearing the caption ensures the label caption is always reflective of the user's choice.

Warn and prompt dialogs

The other notification operation options are warnOnce and prompt.

Warn once is simply an alert dialog with a "Don't warn again" tick box on it. It has a built-in saveInCookie property that is used to store the user's preference if they check the tick box in the dialog. You must specify both a cookie name and text message to use a warn once notification call. While any string can be used for the cookie name, as always, using a self-describing name is recommended.

Prompts are confirmations with a built-in text editor:

The editor's value is passed to the onOk event function as the inResult parameter:

```
notificationCallPromptOk: function(inSender, inResult) {
  this.labelPromptResult.setCaption(inResult);
},
```

This sort of functionality is also easily delivered using designable dialogs should the prompt operation of wm.Notification not meet your needs.

Dialogs

WaveMaker provisions four dialogs in the dialogs section of the palette. They provide a range of customization and functions, from canned dialogs to fully customizable pages.

Generic dialog

The first is the generic dialog. A generic dialog is a lightly customizable dialog that can be modal or non-modal according to its `modal` property. Dialogs are displayed in front of the application window. In other words, the dialog is on top of the application in Z order. Modal means that the user can no longer interact with the application window while the dialog is shown, as done with alerts. In addition to allowing the user to operate around them, non-modal dialog can be docked or minimized so the user can refer back to them at a later time, such as referencing other fields to populate an input form in the dialog.

 Modal dialogs need a means of dismissal. If you don't provide the user with a close button or otherwise dismiss the modal dialog, they will be stuck.

In addition to the `modal` property, generic dialogs have a number of properties we can use to customize the dialog. For example, we can set their size, caption, message, and display position. The `positionNear` property allows us to position the dialog near another component. In the **Children** section of its properties, we can enable up to four buttons on the dialog. Each button's caption and event can be controlled like any other button.

Loading dialog

The loading dialog is used to cover a section of the application while a service call is actively calling the server. It informs the user that something is happening while preventing the user from attempting to interact with that part of the application. As such, it is the least customizable of the provisioned dialogs. You only need to specify the widget or panel to be covered and the `service` variable to be tracked.

A Java service called `SleepSvc` has been added to the `CustpurchaseNavigation` example project. This service contains a `takeNap()` function that sleeps for a specified period of time. The button labeled **Loading Dialog** invokes the service variable, `serviceVarTakeNap`, and covers the button's parent panel while the service call is in flight.

While the server call is outstanding, or "in flight", the panel is covered with a *gray scrim* with a spinner image and the words **Loading…**, all of which are customizable from properties.

The designable and page dialogs

The most customizable dialogs are **designable dialogs** and **page dialogs**. Page dialogs are dialogs in which we load a page. They are effectively page containers in a dialog. Designable dialogs have a container widget, their version of the layout box. In this container widget, we can place widgets just as we do with a page's layout box. One of the components we can put into a designable dialog is a page container.

The **Designable Dialog** button in the example application demonstrates a designable dialog. In the dialog, we have a label, a text editor, and a close button:

Here we are only limited by the size of a dialog, which we also control in its properties. Notice that all these dialogs are part of the page. They show up in the visual components of the page in the model tree. This means that components of the designable dialog are no different than any other page component. They can access the page using `this` and they must be parsed when the page is loaded. In our example, project page code accesses the favorite color editor, `textFavColor`, in the designable dialog using `this.textFavColor.getDataValue()`, because the editor is just another page component.

A page dialog, or a designable dialog using a page container, gains the benefits of deferring page loading with the functionality of a dialog. However, this also means we need to pass values across those page boundaries, which we will address shortly. The **Page Dialog** button in our example project displays a page containing an insert form in a dialog. This is one way we can begin reusing pages within an application. Instead of creating a new item insert form for the possibly multiple places in an application, a user might want to insert a new item, we can show the single page in dialogs as needed.

Published page properties

Pages should be designed as independent entities. Within a page, any assumption about application state is risky. Even for an assumption that is always true now further revision of the application may render that assumption invalid. A simple renaming of a variable could break any child page accessing that variable directly. Depending on a specific application state, in page code also limits the page's reusability. This means that accessing parent page components from page code should be strictly avoided.

You can code in the logic of a page to verify the parent page state. However, this introduces unnecessary complexity into our page code. Also, any changes to the parent page now require updating all child pages utilizing that state. Yuck!

To address situations where the page and its parent page need to interact, we can publish page properties. Publishing page properties exposes component properties and events to the page container containing the page. This enables the two to be loosely coupled, as it is now the page container that can provide specific inputs into the page.

Let's look at the example of the **Insert Customer** button on the **Dialogs** tab of the example project. The page named `PageItemInsert` publishes the `onInsertSuccess` property of the `itemDBForm` widget, shown in the following screenshot. This event is called whenever a new item is inserted into the item table:

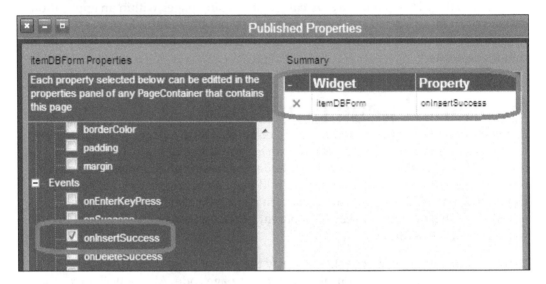

The green up arrow next to **onInsertSuccess** in the **itemDBForm** events panel informs us that the event has been published:

Back on the page named **Page Dialogs**, the page container `pageContainerDesignableDialog` now sees the published **onItemDBFormInsertSuccess** event in its events list, as shown in the following screenshot:

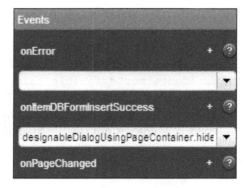

This enables the page container to augment the page logic with its own logic. In our example, the page container simply closes the dialog after a successful insert.

 Only page containers see published properties. Page dialogs do not currently see the published properties of the contained page. That is why the example uses a designable dialog with a page container to access published page properties.

Accessing components of a page container page

We use published properties to pass parameters into a page. Getting results out of the page container, however, is easier. Since we are already using the **onItemDBFormInsertSuccess** event, we can use the **And then** feature of the event to add a JavaScript event handler in addition to the call to hide:

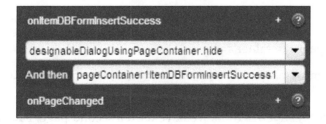

Now we can access the form's data output from our event handler function. In our example, we get the name of the newly inserted item and store it in a JavaScript variable:

```
var newItemName = inSender. pageItemInsert.itemDBForm.getDataOutput().
getValue("itemname");
```

The page has been hidden, but the page still exists, so we can continue to access its components. Note how we must use the page container from `inSender` to access the `itemDBForm` widget and its `dataOutput`. This is because the page is a child of the page container, and using `inSender` enables our script to be ignorant of its page container. `inSender` is the `pageContainerDesignableDialog` container itself. Within page functions, this is a reference to the current page. Therefore, from the `pageDialogs` page, we could access the designable dialog's page container as shown in the following code line when `inSender` is not readily available:

```
this.pageContainerDesignableDialog.pageItemInsert.itemDBForm.
getDataOutput().getValue("itemname");
```

Things get even more interesting with nested page containers. From our example project's main page, we could access the same data output via the two page containers:

```
this.pageContainerDialogs.pageDialogs.pageContainerDesignableDialog.
pageItemInsert.itemDBForm.getDataOutput().getValue("itemname");
```

Note how this makes two assumptions about the state of the application; first that the `pageContainerDialogs` container contains the `pageDialogs` page, and then that `pageContainerDesignableDialog` contains `pageInsertItem`.

We can avoid needing to know the name of the page loaded in the page container by using code instead of the page name:

```
this.pageContainerDialogs.page.pageContainerDesignableDialog.page.
itemDBForm.getDataOutput().getValue("itemname");
```

However, this will still fail to get us to the form if either page assumption is invalid as there will not be an `itemDBForm` widget as expected. If you must use such a reference, be certain to check the result.

The page in the page container will continue to exist until a new page is loaded into the page container. If we want to clean up right away, we can use `setPageName("")` to clear out the page container's page:

```
this.pageContainerDialogs.pageDialogs.pageContainerDesignableDialog.
setPageName("");
```

From this one page, `PageDialogs`, we have used a second page, `PageItemInsert`, twice; once from the **Page Dialog** button and again from the **Insert Customer** button. By using published page properties, we altered how the user interacts with the single page without altering the page's logic.

Pages can publish any event or property of its components to create reusable pages. For more examples of publishing page properties, refer to the documentation available at `http://dev.wavemaker.com/wiki/bin/wmdoc_6.5/Creating+Reusab le+Components+with+PageContainers`.

History and back button

One particularly problematic aspect of AJAX applications is that they break the browser's back button and history features. Since the browser only sees a single page in the traditional HTML sense, the browser is not aware of the intra-application navigations. This means an accidental click of the back button sends the user out of the application, often exclaiming something to the effect of "oh no" at the same time.

WaveMaker 6.5 introduces state management to help with this situation. History management, along with URL management, are in the **History/URL** section of the project's properties:

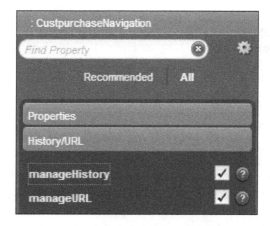

Enabling the history management property throughout the tree of components enables the browser history to work within the application. For example, if you move across the tabs of the example application and then use the back button, it will reselect the previous tabs instead of navigating the user away from the application.

In the tab labeled **URL** of the example program, the page `PageCustomerSearchEdit` demonstrates manually adding to the application history for those components that do not automatically handle state. First, in the grid selection change event, we get and store the ID of the selected customer:

```
customerDojoGridSelectionChange: function(inSender) {
    var custid = inSender.selectedItem.getValue("data.custid");
    var company =
        this.customerDojoGrid.selectedItem.getValue("data.company");
    app.addHistory({id: this.getRuntimeId(),
                    options:{custid: custid},
                    title:company});
},
```

The `custid` value is then stored in the application history using the runtime ID of the page as its key with the `addHistory()` function. The previous code enables the browser's back button to go back to the previously selected item in the grid.

For more information and examples of history management, refer to the documentation available at the following link:

`http://dev.wavemaker.com/wiki/bin/wmdoc_6.5/Back+Buttons+and+State`

The history and URL management features are new features to WaveMaker 6.5. They are temperamental features in this release. If things are not working, carefully check the history and URL management properties for all components involved. Users using these features should look for additional hardening of these features in future releases.

URL management

The other classic AJAX application issue is the use of the URL. It can be desirable to be able to send a colleague a URL that brings them to the desired page and record, or to easily bookmark our place within the application. Sending a colleague a URL to the application and providing navigation instructions, traversing to the customer page, finding the customer XYZ, and so on, is far less desirable.

This example code requires WaveMaker 6.5.3 to work.

URL management is often a tricky business, and thus is disabled by default. Reproducing the entire state of the application could easily include:

- Loading pages
- Navigating tabs
- Setting filters on service calls
- Updating those service calls
- Acting upon the results of those service calls

To use URL management, it must be enabled for the application, the page container containing the page, and any components with the property in-between. In the **URL** tab of the example program, a `PageCustomerSearchEdit` page is loaded. The page container for this page, the project's main tab layers, and the project all must have URL management enabled in order for URL management to work.

Once enabled, we implement the `generateStateUrl` method:

```
generateStateUrl: function(inLocationState) {
  var custid =
    this.customerDojoGrid.selectedItem.getValue("data.custid");
  inLocationState[this.getRuntimeId()] = {"custid": custid};
}
```

As with history, we use the page's runtime ID as the key for the key/value pair in the `inLocationState` array.

Now that the URL contains the selected customer ID, we need to implement the use of this ID in the page's start function. Since the `live` variable populating the grid may not have returned results at the time of the execution of the `start()` function, we declare a page-level variable just inside of our page declaration to store the `custid` value:

```
dojo.declare("PageCustomerSearchEdit", wm.Page, {
    selectedCustomerID: -1,
    ...
```

Then, in the start function, if `inLocationState` exists and contains a customer ID, we store the ID in our variable:

```
start: function(inBackState, inLocationState) {
if (inLocationState !== undefined) {
    var selCustID inLocationState[this.getRuntimeId()] .custid;
  if (selCustID !== undefined) {
      this.selectedCustomerID = selCustID;
  }
}
},
```

Note that the `inBackState` and `inLocationState` parameters were added as arguments to the `start()` method manually. The page start function did not contain these arguments originally.

 In JavaScript, it is not required for the method signature to match as in Java.

Finally, in the `live` variable success event, we check for the status of `this.selectedCustomerID`, our page variable:

```
customerLiveVariable1Success: function(inSender, inDeprecated) {
    if(this.selectedCustomerID !== -1){
        var query = {custid:this.selectedCustomerID};
        this.customerDojoGrid.selectByQuery(query);
        this.selectedCustomerID = -1;
    }
},
```

If it's been set, and is not -1, we use it to form a grid query for `selectByQuery()`.

 Using the selected customer grid selection index would be easier than using a query to find the customer by its ID. However, the order of the results will change. If the grid is sorted alphabetically, inserting new records starting with a will change the index order of all customers starting with b and beyond.

The result is that the URL is populated to contain the full information needed to restore the state. If we select the customer with ID 4, for example, we can send our colleague the following URL:

```
http://localhost:8094/CustpurchaseNavigation/#{"main.
tabLayers1":4,"main.pageContainerURL.pageCustomerSearchEdit":
{"custid":4}}
```

This will bring them to the tab layer containing our customer search page, and pass the customer ID 4 for our grid to select upon loading.

For more information about URL management, see the URL management section of the history management page in the documentation, available at the following link:

```
http://dev.wavemaker.com/wiki/bin/wmdoc_6.5/Back+Buttons+and+State#Hm
anageURLProperty
```

Summary

In this chapter, we discussed navigating in and around a WaveMaker application. We looked at navigation in general and used navigation calls for everything from loading pages into page containers to changing layers. We explored the diverse range of notifications that the WaveMaker framework provides, from alerts and toasts to confirmations and warns.

We began leveraging navigation to reuse pages with dialogs. Page container dialogs and designable dialogs allowed us to reuse pages within dialogs. Publishing page properties enabled the page to remain independent of its parent while allowing the page container to influence how the page looks and behaves. We also saw how it is easy to obtain data values from a page now that we know how to navigate within page containers.

Finally, we looked at new advanced features for managing browser history and URL state. These new features are both tricky and require the latest WaveMaker Studio updates to work properly. Once working, however, they enable us to provide a rich user experience, such as being able to message a colleague a URL to record within an application.

In the next chapter, we'll look into CSS and styling of applications.

6
Styling the Application

With the layout of the application now understood, we will naturally want to style the application to control how the application looks and feels. WaveMaker, being a standard browser application, uses cascading stylesheets (CSS) to define presentation semantics.

In this chapter, we'll discuss using CSS to style WaveMaker applications. How you style a WaveMaker application depends on your objective. We will also discuss the styling tools and techniques available to the WaveMaker developer. We will use the style property panel to style individual widgets, groups of widgets, and create and apply CSS classes. We will also look at the theme generator tool included in Studio.

Since CSS can be a tricky creature to work with, we will need to learn how to sleuth our way around the CSS of page elements. For this, we will use the developer tool's inspect feature to diagnose what style was applied. Finally, we'll take a sneak peek at the widget theme's designer tool being worked on for the next release of WaveMaker.

This chapter does not cover much about CSS itself. Readers seeking to learn more about CSS itself will find no lack of resources on the topic, such as the MDN `https://developer.mozilla.org/en-US/docs/Web/CSS`. Instead, we will be focusing on how to style WaveMaker applications. While no small part of styling applications is using CSS with WaveMaker, our focus is not CSS itself, but styling the application. The example project for this chapter is `StylingApps`, available at the following link:

`https://github.com/edwardcallahan/Easy-Web-Samples/tree/master/projects/StylingApps`

CSS in WaveMaker

CSS is the acronym and common name for cascading style sheets. The CSS language specification is maintained by the World Wide Web Consortium, or W3C, the same standards organization for HTML and XML. In a nutshell, CSS is used to separate the content of a web page from the presentation aspects of the page.

All modern browsers support CSS; however, here too, there is a variation across browsers. Internet Explorer has never provided particularly good CSS standards support, for example. Versions prior to MSIE 10 were notorious for their lack of CSS support, and there remains numerous variations listed on MSDN available at `http://msdn.microsoft.com/en-us/library/ff405926`. As a result, it is important to test your CSS across all targeted browsers along with the rest of the application. This is particularly true when doing things like rounded corners or gradients.

From the Dojo Toolkit perspective, WaveMaker uses the Tundra Dijit theme. If you see Tundra in the class names, that's where it comes from. Most of the Dojo names we will see in the style classes are self-documenting. For example, it is not hard to map `.dojoxGridRow.dojoxGridRowSelected` to the Dojo grid widget from dojox when we see it somewhere in the developer tools.

Having Dojo available can be handy for styling as well. Take an example where we want to draw attention to a particular tab at runtime; maybe to highlight that there is something on that tab that requires the users' attention. We can use `dojo.style` to apply the change we seek. With `dojo.style`, we can simply use the div `id` we see from the CSS inspector. Right-click on the element of interest; here, we are interested in the selected tab, and select **Inspect element**:

Chrome's CSS inspector will highlight the element in the document in the DOM:

```
<button id="main_tabLayers1_decorator_button2" type="button" style class="wmtablayers-tab">Customized
Panels</button>
<button id="main_tabLayers1_decorator_button3" type="button" style="background-color: rgb(100, 225, 227);"
class="wmtablayers-tab wmtablayers-selected">Custom</button>
</div>
```

Now pass the div id and the desired `style` class body to `dojo.style()` to change the style:

```
dojo.style("main_tabLayers1_decorator_button3",{"background-color":"#
FF8700"});
```

In CSS, specificity determines which CSS rule is applied by the browser to an element. **Specificity** is one of the more difficult parts of CSS to understand, and is the most common reason why an intended rule isn't being applied. It is calculated based on rules of selectors. A simplistic mental model is that the most specific rule gets applied, and in the case of equal specificity, the newest rule is applied.

Text boxes, select menus, and the grid get their base styling from the Dojo Tundra theme. We have been using the WaveMaker provided theme named `wm_coolblue` in our example projects. Themes are built on top of the Dojo styling. Consider the lines 817 - 819 of `theme.css` available at `https://github.com/SpringSource/wavemaker/blob/master/wavemaker/wavemaker-studio/src/main/webapp/lib/wm/base/widget/themes/wm_coolblue/theme.css` for `wm_coolblue`, shown in the following code line:

```
.wm_coolblue div.dojoxGrid, .wm_coolblue .wmlist {
font-size: 8pt;
}
```

The `font-size` rule is specified for both `dojoxGrid` and `wm.list`, enabling the two components to be used better interchangeably while making the rule more specific than Dojo's rules.

Every project has a theme. If a project does not have a specified theme, it uses the theme named `wm_notheme`. On top of the project theme, we may define application CSS rules and/or page specific CSS rules using the source tabs as shown:

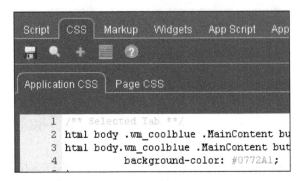

The net result of all of this is that there are often a number of stylesheets in the stack for any given element. This means you often need to use very specific rules and sometimes several of them in order to style your application just right. For example, to change the selected tab color for all tabs in a project using the cool blue theme, we would put this into the **Application CSS** tab:

```
html body .wm_coolblue .MainContent button.wmtablayers-tab.
wmtablayers-selected,
html body.wm_coolblue .MainContent button.wmtablayers-tab.wmtablayers-
selected{
        background-color: #0772A1;
}
```

Some elements in WaveMaker just cannot be styled using CSS. Recall that `border`, `margin`, and `padding` of a widget are properties used by the WaveMaker's layout engine. All nodes in WaveMaker are positioned using absolute positioning. As such, height, width, left, and top cannot be set by CSS. Every other aspect of a widget that you would expect to be able to set with CSS can be set using CSS.

 The framework does not manage the layout of every element on the screen. For example, `margin` and `padding` for grid cells are not managed by WaveMaker. This means you could use CSS on them.

Those exceptions aside, how you go about styling a WaveMaker application depends on what you want to do. Start with a theme, choose an existing theme or create your own. If you want to customize an existing theme, make a copy of it first. Within that theme, if you want to customize a single instance of a widget, the tooled styling is perfect. If you want to create a class of widgets, Studio makes it easy to create a class from a widget. If you have an existing look and feel you want to apply to a project, you can create a theme for it or import the CSS.

Tooled styling

The **Style** tab of the **Properties** panel contains the bulk of Studio's tooled styling. Under **Basic** are the `border`, `padding`, and `margin` properties. Under **Styles** is a tooled CSS editor:

The styles we specify here are added directly to the widget's definition in the page-specific `widget.js` file. For the previous panel, when we look in the page's `widgets.js`, we can see the specified styles in the `styles` parameter:

```
CustomizedPanel: ["wm.Panel", {"height":"125px","horizontalAlign":"lef
t","styles":{"backgroundGradient":{"direction":"horizontal","startColo
r":"#3737b9","endColor":"#011d65","colorStop":80},"color":"#f00000","t
extAlign":"center"},"verticalAlign":"top","width":"100%"}, {}, …
```

Within the widget definition for `CustomizedPanel`, we now have a `styles` object.

Defining classes

Tooled styling is fine for single-instance editing. If we want to make a class of these panels so we can have multiple instances of a widget styled the same way in the application, we will use the **Create CSS Class** button. This creates a class out of styles that we can apply to other widgets. Creating a CSS class from the preceding panel includes all the style directives, including a multi-browser gradient in a single class:

```
html.WMApp body .CustomRedTextHorizGradientPanel {
background: -webkit-gradient(linear, left center, right center,
from(#3737b9), color-stop(80%,#011d65), to(#011d65));
background: -moz-linear-gradient(left, #3737b9 0%,#011d65 80%,#011d65
100%);
background: -o-linear-gradient(left, #3737b9 0%,#011d65 80%,#011d65
100%);
background: -ms-linear-gradient(left, #3737b9 0%,#011d65 80%,#011d65
100%);
filter: progid:DXImageTransform.Microsoft.gradient(
startColorstr='#3737b9', endColorstr='#011d65',GradientType=1);
color: #ff0000;
text-align: center;
}
```

Now, our panel, and any other widget we apply this class to using the **Add Class** button under the **Classes** tab, will include the `style` class name in its widget definition in the page `widget.js`:

```
ClassPanel: ["wm.Panel", {"_classes":{"domNode":["CustomRedTextHorizGr
adientPanel"]},"height":"125px","horizontalAlign":"left","verticalAlig
n":"top","width":"100%"}, {}, {
```

Here, instead of the styles being specified in the panel definition, only the class name is needed. As the widget definition is specifically passed the class name, the selector is little more than the class name.

This panel definition includes the styles directly in the previous highlighted JSON. The `StylingApps` example application has a tab labeled **Customized Panels**. It contains two panels styled exactly the same way but using the two different techniques. The top panel defines the styles directly in the **Styles** properties. The lower one uses the `CustomRedTextHorizGradientPanel` class we defined from the **Styles** panel. The application and management of the class can be found in the **Classes** subtab of **Styles**:

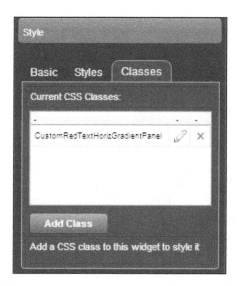

Avoiding !important

The CSS property `!important` gives a declaration more weight than it would otherwise have. Most of the time, but not always, `!important` will cause the declaration to take precedence over any other rule. As a general rule, its use should be reserved to situations where no other solution exists.

When creating CSS rules for use in WaveMaker, `!important` can often help get the declaration applied. Before using `!important` in the declaration permanently, there are a few things you can try to make your selector more specific.

Since every widget is within the document's BODY tag, it has the body as a parent. This means we can add body to the rule. The same applies to html. Every widget node is inside of the document HTML tag, so we can add html to our rule. We can also add in the theme name and page name to help our rule be even more specific. Consider this class in the main.css file from from StylingApps example:

```
html body .wm_coolblue .MainContent button.wmtablayers-tab.
wmtablayers-tab:hover,
html body.wm_coolblue .MainContent button.wmtablayers-tab.wmtablayers-
tab:hover{
        background-color: #63AFD0;
}
```

Note that when we use the theme name in the rule, we need to use two rules. One rule is for the body space theme and the other is for the body dot theme, as shown in the preceding example.

The selected tab layer and other commonly requested rules can be found in the documentation at the following link:

```
http://dev.wavemaker.com/wiki/bin/wmdoc_6.5/Stylin
gWidgets#HCommonCSSrulesyou27llwant
```

Most of them use the theme name. Don't forget to change the theme name in the rule if you are not using wm_default.

In StylingApps, we started the application using a tab layout template with the wm_coolblue theme. Let's say that we want to customize the tabs to convey more meaning to the user. Great! We find in a community forum post that .wm_coolblue button.wmtablayers-tab.wmtablayers-selected is how you style selected tabs. Unfortunately, even after adding both html and body, our rule still requires !important to get applied, as shown in the following code snippet:

```
html body .wm_coolblue button.wmtablayers-tab.wmtablayers-selected,
html body.wm_coolblue button.wmtablayers-tab.wmtablayers-selected{
        background-color: #0058FC !important;
}
```

We don't want to use !important if we can avoid it. Remove the !important property and use the inspect element feature of the developer tools again. With the element selected, open the **Matched CSS Rules** layer in the right half of the developer tools:

```
Matched CSS Rules
.dj_ie6 .wm_coolblue .MainContent .wmtablayers-tab.wmtablayers-        theme.css:1667
selected, .wm_coolblue .MainContent .wmtablayers-tab.wmtablayers-selected,
.wm_coolblue .MainContent .wmtablayers-tab.wmtablayers-selected:hover, .wm_coolblue
.MainContent .wmtablayers-tab.wmtablayers-selected:focus {
    color:   #ffffff;
    background-color:  #007cc2;
    background-image: url(images/repeatx/brightThickEdge0.png);
    background-position: ▶ top left;
    background-repeat: ▶ repeat-x;
}

html body .wm_coolblue button.wmtablayers-tab.wmtablayers-selected, html   localhost:1
body.wm_coolblue button.wmtablayers-tab.wmtablayers-selected {
    background-color:  #0058FC;
}

.wm_coolblue .MainContent button.wmtablayers-tab {                       theme.css:1648
☑ font-family: Verdana;
☑ color:  #333333;
☑ font-weight: bold;
```

We see our declaration loading from localhost almost at the top of the stack, but it is crossed out to indicate that it has been overruled. The style from **theme.css:1667** is being applied instead. Furthermore, notice how both our class and the applied class have a rule in bold. It is showing us that our rule HTML body `.wm_coolblue` `button.wmtablayers-tab.wmtablyers.selected` is less specific than `.wmcool_` `blue .MainContent .wmtablyaers-tab.wmtablayers-selected`. This informs us that adding `.MainContent` to our rule will make our rule more specific. Sure enough, once we add `.MainContent` to our rule, we no longer need `!important`. Here's the full class:

```
html body .wm_coolblue .MainContent button.wmtablayers-tab.
wmtablayers-selected,
html body.wm_coolblue .MainContent button.wmtablayers-tab.wmtablayers-
selected{
        background-color: #0058FC;
}
```

Using `!important` in a declaration is an easy way to get the style you want applied. However, inspecting the element and viewing its **Matched CSS Rules** can make it easy to get the desired style applied without having to use `!important`.

Testing rules with dojo.query()

Sometimes, our class rule doesn't show up at all in the **Matched CSS Rules** layer. Our rule may be plain old wrong. Maybe we forgot to change the theme name. Maybe we made a typo. Fortunately, dojo.query() gives us an easy way to test our rule. Simply pass the selector part of the rule to dojo.query() as a string on the console. For our selected tab example, we would use:

```
dojo.query("html body.wm_coolblue .MainContent button.wmtablayers-tab.
wmtablayers-selected");
```

dojo.query() will return any matching elements. We can hover over the returned elements and they will be highlighted in the application. If no elements are returned by dojo.query(), our rule is likely wrong, as there were no matched elements in the current document.

Themes

Themes define the overall look and feel of a project while providing the ability to easily reuse that style with other projects. Themes can set everything from rounding and fonts to background colors and button styles.

The project's theme is a property of the project. The property dictates which theme a project is loading. When the project is selected in the **Services** tree, the theme can be changed just like any other select menu tooled property. The themes themselves are managed under the **Source | Themes** tab. This theme designer can be used to create a new theme or to make a copy of an existing theme for customization. The theme designer is documented at the following link:

```
http://dev.wavemaker.com/wiki/bin/wmdoc_6.5/ThemeDesigner
```

As we've seen, most of the CSS classes you add to your project are likely to have the theme in the name. This means you are likely to find yourself doing a find and replace to change the theme in your rules if you added some CSS rules to your project and then need to change the theme name. For this reason, you'll want to make the theme name one of the first styling decisions of a project.

Subthemes

Like most web projects, WaveMaker themes provide subthemes. Subthemes are variations of the main theme for contrasting different parts of the application. This enables us to easily differentiate the header from the main content from emphasized content while remaining within the same palette and style of the theme.

The subtheme is a property in the **Style** tab of container widgets such as panels and layers. It is labeled **themeStyleType**:

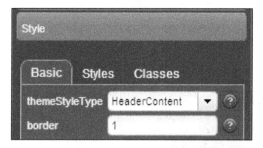

The **Sub Themes** tab of the StylingApps example application demonstrates the use of subthemes within the wm_coolblue theme:

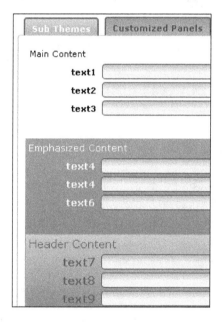

The three panels are identical and save their subtheme settings. The WaveMaker project templates utilize subthemes as well. In the subthemes example, you will notice that the **Header Content** panel shares the background color and gradient of the **Header** panel from the tabs template.

Managing themes

The main options for working with themes are:

- Copy and edit an existing theme
- Create a new theme from scratch
- Import a theme

If you like an existing theme but want to adjust it more to your liking, the easiest thing to do is to make a copy of the theme and modify it accordingly. The theme designer is very useful for this case. This approach enables you to quickly get a fully styled look with some customization of your choice.

On the other hand, creating a new theme gives you the most control over how an app looks, and is a small project in itself. Determine the color palette of complementary colors to be used and the general feel you want. Find a theme with font and rounding settings similar to what you want. Copy this theme to use as your starting point. For further information about creating your own theme, visit the following link:

```
http://dev.wavemaker.com/wiki/bin/wmdoc_6.5/
ThemeDesigner#HCreatingafulltheme
```

Importing and exporting themes

In WaveMaker 6.5, exporting and importing projects does not include the theme in the import or export. The tooled import and export of themes is introduced with WaveMaker 6.6. For WaveMaker 6.5 and earlier, you must manually copy the theme to and from the `themes` folder in the common folder of the WaveMaker home folder.

If you are using exports for a project using a custom theme, place a copy of the theme in the root of the project. This will automatically include the theme in exports without having the theme be part of the deployment package. Developers importing the project will still have to copy the theme into their common folder, but they'll always get a copy of the theme with the project. If you forget to update the copy, it will be out of date. That is still better than no theme!

Importing CSS

If you have existing CSS files, you can import them into your project. The recommended process is to upload the files using the resource manager. Like the **Script** editor, the **CSS** editor in Studio includes an import button using a green plus sign icon.

Importing a CSS file this way adds the appropriate @import statement to the current **CSS** editor. This @import statement can be moved as needed.

Borrowing parts

Another technique worth noting is the *borrowing* of fully styled widgets from other applications and templates. Consider the case of a search editor. While we could create our own, we may have noticed that **Fancy Template** from the **Templates** menu contains a search editor that would fit our needs just fine. Here's a way to extract that editor from the template:

- Immediately upon page creation, add **Fancy Template**
- Move the desired component out of the template and into the layout box
    - In this example, we need panel5 to include the magnifying glass image
- Delete the FancyTemplate widget from the **Model** tree
- Delete any components added by the template
    - In this example, the monthsVar, varTemplateLogout, and varTemplateUsername components can be deleted

Similarly, widgets can be copy and pasted out of a page that was imported into the project for the sole purpose of providing parts into a project.

Other styling tools

Styling applications is a complex topic with many aspects. In this chapter, we've already been using the Chrome developer tools inspector feature to examine our CSS. This and the similar developer tools for other browsers are a near necessity when styling applications.

Most of the time in Chrome, we can right-click on our page and choose **Inspect element** as we have been doing; however, sometimes you cannot. The **Custom** tab of the StylingApps example includes a page with an editable grid. We cannot right-click on the editable grid as row selection is managed by Dojo, and the normal techniques will not work. To inspect these elements, we need a different approach.

Open the developer tools and enable inspection mode by clicking on the magnifying glass icon in the bottom row. Inspection mode is enabled when the icon is blue.

Now that inspection mode is on, the selected element of the page is shown in the developer tool's **Elements** panel for inspection.

If you are new to CSS, you are likely to find yourself wanting a few additional CSS tools. A color picker or two is a handy tool to have available. A color picker allows you to determine the color code of anything on the screen, usually by clicking on or selecting the region of interest. The other kind of color picker lets you choose a color from a map and determine its code. This kind of color picker is included in the color property editor of the **Style** properties tab. Another useful tool is a color scheme designer. A scheme designer lets you plan a color palette of complementary colors.

New in WM 6.6

While the WaveMaker 6.5 theme generator is useful for generating new themes, many developers can find it frustrating when their primary need is to define themes for widgets.

For this, WaveMaker 6.6 introduces the theme designer, which takes a different approach to the problem. If you wish to create a new theme but the theme generator is not the right tool for you, try the 6.6 theme designer. It can be found next to the theme designer under **Source | Themes**.

The previous screenshot is from a development version of WaveMaker 6.6 and is subject to change.

Note that the current theme designer has been renamed as theme generator.

Summary

In this chapter, we looked at styling WaveMaker applications. We learned how CSS is applied in WaveMaker applications. We looked at the tools WaveMaker provides for styling applications. The three main areas in Studio for styling are the **Style** properties tab, and the **Themes** and **CSS** tabs under **Source**. In the **Style** properties tab, we styled widgets and created classes from those styles. In the **CSS** source tab, we created custom classes to style widgets. We also looked at the 6.5 theme designer tool.

While creating our custom CSS class, we learned how useful the developer tools inspect feature can be. In our example, we used it to avoid needing to use !important in our declaration. We also took a quick sneak peek at the new theme designer tool for WaveMaker 6.6.

In the next few chapters, we'll start moving server side. We'll begin that journey with database services, which combine client-side form logic with server-side hibernate services.

7
Working with Databases

We have seen how WaveMaker makes it easy to build JavaScript applications. The primary function of these applications is almost always to find, display, edit, update, create, and/or delete data of some form or another. A commonly used data source is relational databases.

Databases work particularly well with WaveMaker. The structure of the data is well defined. This enables WaveMaker to generate types directly from the database schema. The operations allowed by a relational database are limited to what is referred to as **CRUD** (Create, Read, Update, and Delete). Combined with the type information, Studio can then generate fully-functional database forms that users can customize.

In this chapter we will look at how databases are used in WaveMaker applications. We'll start with the generated hibernate data model. The most common way to use the data model is with the live panels generated by dragging a database type from the palette. We'll dissect these generated panels and examine how they work. We'll also introduce the use of the **Hibernate Query Language** (**HQL**) when we need more advanced querying and look at how we can integrate those results with live data components. As capable as HQL is, sometimes you just want good old-fashioned SQL. We'll finish this chapter with a quick look at the `createSQLQuery()` function.

This chapter shows examples from the sample project named Databases, available in the Easy-Web-Samples repository on GitHub at `https://github.com/edwardcallahan/Easy-Web-Samples/tree/master/projects/Databases`. We will continue to use the same `custpurchase` MySQL database used in other sample projects.

Generating the data model

Data in modern relational databases has almost always been "normalized" into rows and tables with relationships. In order to convert between the relational data formats of relational databases and the objects of Java, WaveMaker, like many Java applications, uses an **object-relational mapping (ORM)** layer. In particular, WaveMaker uses the open source ORM library named Hibernate. To generate the domain model at design time, WaveMaker uses an additional Hibernate component known as **Hibernate Tools**.

Importing an existing database

The easiest and accordingly most common way to use databases with WaveMaker is to provide a **Java Database Connectivity (JDBC)** connection for an existing database to Studio. Studio utilizes the connection to attempt to generate an ORM data model using Hibernate Tools. This model is then used to create a database service in the project.

From the **Services** menu, choose **Import Database**:

Studio provides specific import options for the following database systems:

- IBM's DB2
- HyperSQL HSQLDB
- MySQL
- Oracle
- Postgres SQL
- Microsoft's SQL Server

The import dialog is customized for each database type:

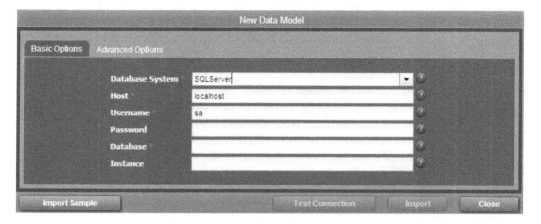

Choosing **SQLServer**, for example, causes an editor for the SQL Server instance name to be displayed, as shown in the preceding screenshot. Some choices may also utilize mappers with system-specific mappings. The WaveMaker documentation for importing databases giving a full walk through of the process can be found at `http://dev.wavemaker.com/wiki/bin/wmdoc_6.5/Database#HImportingDataModels`.

Any database for which a Type 3 JDBC driver and a Hibernate 3 dialect are available should be importable using the **Other** option from the **Database System** dropdown in the import dialog. See the untooled database instructions at `http://dev.wavemaker.com/wiki/bin/Dev/UntooledDatabase` for more information about importing such databases. Examples in the documentation include FireBird, CouchDB, and MS Access.

> The importing of NoSQL or big data data stores is not tooled in WaveMaker 6.5. However, thanks to the Spring Framework, it is still possible to use these newer data storage engines in your projects. See the community-provided example for using MongoDB with WaveMaker at `http://dev.wavemaker.com/forums/?q=node/7619` and `http://dev.wavemaker.com/forums/?q=node/7507`.

For larger schemas, the table and schema filters in the **Advanced Options** can be used to reduce the number of tables included in the import. Use regular expressions such as cust* for all tables starting with cust or ^system* to exclude all tables starting with system. More details on all of the advanced options can be found at http://dev.wavemaker.com/wiki/bin/wmdoc_6.5/Database#HAdvancedOptions.

> Do not forget to consider any JDBC parameters you may want to append to the value of **Connection URL** in **Advanced Options** after it is assembled from the other field values. Not all situations need parameters, and syntax varies by database system. That said, some parameters are very helpful. For example, adding ?useUn icode=true&characterEncoding=UTF-8 to the JDBC URL is effectively required with MySQL when storing UTF-8-encoded characters in a database. This is common when working with extended character sets and languages with unique characters.

Importing the sample database

The Databases sample project includes a MySQL database export file in the src folder named custpurchase.sql. It is also available from GitHub at https://github.com/edwardcallahan/Easy-Web-Samples/blob/master/projects/Databases/src/custpurchase.sql.

The export can be used to create your own copy of the database. If you are unfamiliar with this process, visit any one of the many blogs and articles on the topic, such as http://www.itworld.com/it-management/359857/3-ways-import-and-export-mysql-database.

Once created, you can import the schema using **Import Database** as previously described:

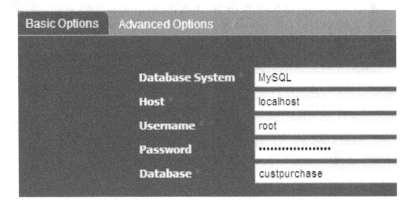

Creating a new schema

If you don't have an existing database schema to import, you can create a new data model from within Studio by using the **Design Database** item from the **Services** menu. The process is described in the documentation at http://dev.wavemaker. com/wiki/bin/wmdoc_6.5/Database#HCreatingNewDataModels.

That said, it is important to understand that the data model editor in WaveMaker is generic to relational databases in general. This means that it does not provide tooling for database-specific features and types. Studio's data model editor is not going to be the best tool for editing schemas for any specific database as a result. Furthermore, the data model editor in WaveMaker 6.5.X is outdated and needs updating to be easier to use.

Instead of creating a new schema in the WaveMaker data model editor, many find it easier to use their favorite database tool such as **SQLyog** (https://code.google.com/p/sqlyog/downloads/list) or the tools provided by the database vendor instead. After the schema is defined to your satisfaction, import the database as if it were an existing database. Studio's built-in data model editor is useful for making project-only changes to the model, but for more significant tasks such as creating a new domain model, database-specific tools are often preferred.

Exporting a schema

After defining a new schema in the data model editor, it must be exported to a database in order to be used as a data store. The export process is documented at http://dev.wavemaker.com/wiki/bin/wmdoc_6.5/ Database#HExportingaDataModel.

The **Data Definition Language** (DDL) generated by the export process uses the drop table statement. This means that any records in the table will be lost. Be certain not to export to existing tables if you wish to retain existing data.

Keeping the use of `drop table` in mind, exporting a schema from Studio can be quite useful in the following situations:

- Migration of a schema from one database system to another
- Creation of a database when a project export does not include a SQL dump file

In these cases, the database-neutral design of the data model editor becomes an advantage, and the schema defined in the project domain model can be easily exported to a new database.

Making project-only schema changes

Sometimes, it can be advantageous to modify the project local schema and not export those changes back to the database system. The most common example of this is adding relationships for a database that does not have formal relations in its schema.

Older databases may use numeric columns for relations without actually defining relationships. This causes the Hibernate mapping to see a numeric value instead of a related object. It is often not possible to modify the existing database to add Foreign Key constraints. While such a schema can be used in WaveMaker, the object-relational mapping can be easier to use with a defined relationship. For example, database forms can only use related editors for relationships defined in the schema.

Product documentation for creating relationships in the data model editor can be found at `http://dev.wavemaker.com/wiki/bin/wmdoc_6.5/Database#HCreatin gandWorkingwithRelationshipsandForeignKeys`. Note that the changes must be saved, but in this case, should not be exported back to the database server.

Examining the service

So what happened beneath the covers when we generated our data model? Once again, examining the filesystem artifacts will show us the full story. In short, we find that database services are specialized Java services.

Let's look at the `CustpurchaseDB` service generated by importing the `custpurchase` database, such as the one in the `Databases` example project.

 An SQL export of the `custpurchase` database is included in the project's `src` directory, in case you would like to import the database into your own MySQL server.

Like all services, the `custpurchaseDB` service source resides within the `services` folder of the project. In this GitHub project browser, this folder is found at `https://github.com/edwardcallahan/Easy-Web-Samples/tree/master/projects/Databases/services/custpurchaseDB`. Note that this is not the same as the `services` folder under `webapproot`. The `webapproot/services` folder only contains the SMD service method definition files used by the client at runtime. Service sources are not part of `webapproot`.

Within the `services/custpurchaseDB/src` folder is the `custpurchaseDB.properties` file. This file contains all of the properties specified when importing the service, from the Hibernate dialect to the JDBC driver class name. Although the password is not in clear text, it is still recommended to use caution with passwords for any publically-reachable service. Also in this folder is the `custpurchaseDB.spring.xml` file. This is the SpringSource beans definition file for our database service. It is to be noted that in defining the data source, the properties are loaded from the values defined in the properties file. For example, consider the following:

```
<property name="url" value="${custpurchaseDB.connectionUrl}"/>
```

In the preceding line of code, `custpurchaseDB.connectionUrl` is defined at line 5 of `custpurchaseDB.properties`. This means that there is exactly one place in the project where the connection URL is defined, keeping the maintenance of the URL simple.

The other item in the `src` folder is the folder named `com`, present at the top of our database service package (`com.custpurchasedb`). There are two files named `CustpurchaseDB.java` and `CustpurchaseDBConstants.java`, and one folder named `data` in the `/src/com/custpurchasedb` folder.

`CustpurchaseDBConstants.java` is, as its name implies, for constants—values that do not change. In this case, the class provides the mapping for query names to static string values. This enables the service to refer to queries without using their exact names.

`CustpurchaseDB.java` is more interesting among the two as it defines the service's operations. Here we find the `read`, `update`, `delete`, `begin`, `rollback`, and `commit` functions needed for database operations as well as any Java-defined queries of the service. These operations all utilize the `DataServiceManager` class provided by WaveMaker through the `dsMgr` reference. `CustpurchaseDB` also implements both the `DataServiceManagerAccess` and `LiveDataService` interfaces, enabling it to be used by the client-side live data form-building tools and components. It is here that we see an intersection point of the Java service generated from the schema, the WaveMaker live data runtime services, and the client-side live family of components. The example Java-defined query is `getCpuserById`, defined in lines 28 to 35 of `CustpurchaseDB.java`. This query was generated as part of the import and is an example of how queries can also be defined in Java, although in practice, few utilize this feature.

Heading further down the directory structure we have the `data` folder. Here reside the data entity type definitions. There is a Java class for each entity; for example, the Java class `Customer` is the entity type for the customer table, and it provides setters and getters for each member field of the customer type. For each entity type, there is a matching Hibernate mapping XML file. In the example of `Customer.java`, its entity mapping is `Customer.hbm.xml`. The Hibernate mapping file contains information needed by Hibernate to load and store the persisted objects. For example, the table-to-class name mapping is found on line 3 of `Customer.hbm.xml`, as shown in the following line of code:

```
<class name="com.custpurchasedb.data.Customer" table="customer"…
```

These data class entities and their corresponding mapping files were generated by Studio using Hibernate Tools during the import process.

Among all the class and mapping file pairs, we also have a single file for queries. When we define HQL queries in Studio's query editor, they are stored in `app-queries.ql.xml`. We'll return to this file and the `output` folder momentarily.

Customizing database services

Studio generates a fully-functional but straightforward Hibernate persistent mapping. Users with more extensive database knowledge are likely to want to modify the database service. While not required, such customization is certainly possible. One common modification is to replace the driver manager data source of Spring with C3P0's (`http://www.mchange.com/projects/c3p0/`) pooled data source instead. Instructions for enabling C3P0 connection pooling can be found in the WaveMaker wiki at `http://dev.wavemaker.com/wiki/bin/Dev/Databases#H DatabaseConnectionPooling`.

While such modifications are possible, it is important to note that any customizations will be lost upon database re-import.

Re-import

Importing a database creates the entity types used in the project. As with other type defining actions in WaveMaker, the sooner in the development process we define our types, the better. Database services are no different. Furthermore, the creation of custom queries or use of database operations from Java services further integrates the service types with the project code. Therefore, it is best practice to complete and refine the database schema before performing the database import to avoid re-importing due to modifications to the schema.

When schema changes are required, the re-import feature found in the **Database Connection Settings** dialog replaces the database service with a new, freshly generated data model:

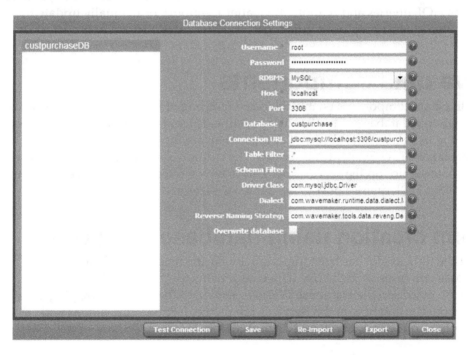

This means that, at the very least, all customizations will be lost upon re-import. Unfortunately, there is no tooled mechanism to update just the modified parts of the data model. In conjunction with the downstream impact of type changes, re-import can be a tricky proposition. Some strategies for dealing with re-import can be found at http://dev.wavemaker.com/wiki/bin/Dev/TNT02.

An alternative to re-import is to manually edit the service. This can be accomplished by applying matching changes within the data model editor as noted in the preceding TNT article or by manually editing the files of the service. If you are unclear of the edits required but are not successfully able to use re-import, one strategy is to import the new database schema into a test project. The data model from the throwaway test project can be used as a guide for changes needed for the real project's data model.

 Problems with re-import in WaveMaker 6.5.2 have been corrected with WaveMaker 6.5.3. This is another reason for using the latest version of WaveMaker.

The success rate of re-import depends directly upon the type of changes being made and the number of dependencies that the project has built around the data model to be regenerated. Be certain to backup any project before making any significant change such as re-import. If re-import is not successful, either remove dependencies such as HQL queries and reapply them after re-import, or manually update the data model using a test project for guidance.

Live data components

The live data components enable the rapid building of highly-customizable forms for relational databases. This family of client-side components includes the live form, the live panel, and the live variable. They are the easiest to use with the WaveMaker-provided **runtime service**. The runtime service calls into the generated Hibernate service on the server-side. This is why we see live forms post to runtime service but HQL queries post to the database service.

Form creation using database objects

After the data model has been imported, by far the most common use of those database entities is with the live data components used and created by the database objects in the **Database Widgets** section of the palette. Dragging a table from the database in the **Services** tab project tree onto the canvas will also bring up the **Pick LivePanel Layout** dialog.

However you get there, the dialog provides a good selection of useful layouts. All but two of the layouts use the wm.LiveForm component, generally referred to as **live form**.

Editable Grid creates a live variable to populate a grid with the live editing property enabled. The **Live Variable** option is the other option that does not utilize live forms. It creates only a live variable and is surprisingly handy as an option.

If you need something different from a full list, edit, insert, and delete form, such as an insert-only or update-only form, there's another option in the **Beta Widgets** subsection of the **Forms** palette that is worth being aware of:

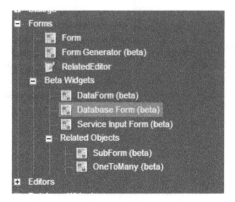

The **Database Form (beta)** is a beta widget that uses live data and provides its own configuration dialog:

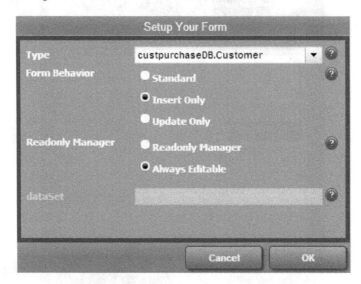

The **Setup Your Form** dialog will quickly set up an insert- or edit-only form by choosing a value for **Form Behavior** while providing some quick setup for read-only management as well. The wm.DBForm database form has its own live variable. Optionally, you can specify a dataset if you will be updating existing entries selected from other lists. The JavaScript client reference, also known as jsref, has a good synopsis on the features of DBForm at http://dev.wavemaker.com/wiki/bin/wmjsref_6.5/DBForm.

The other beta forms widgets are not database specific, but can be used with database types as desired. Database services are simple specialized Java services after all.

Dissecting the live panel

While these dialogs may seem magical, they are really only conveniences. We can easily recreate their results, albeit in several more mouse clicks.

To easily understand what gets generated, import the custpurchase database into a new, empty project. Next, drag a **Purchase (custpurchaseDB)** database widget from the palette onto the canvas:

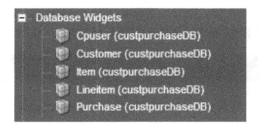

When prompted, select the **Grid on Top** layout for a **Purchase** database object. What do we have?

In the services tree, we have a new live variable named `purchaseLiveVariable1` of type `custpurchaseDB.Purchase`. Both `autoUpdate` and `startUpdate` are enabled, but that's about it for the live variable's configuration.

In the model tree, we have several new components:

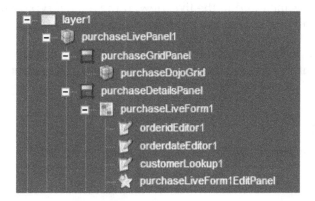

The parent of all the new visual components is a live panel, **custpurchaseLivePanel1**, with two panels in it: a **purchaseGridPanel** on top of a **purchaseDetailsPanel**. The **purchaseGridPanel** contains only the **purchaseDojoGrid**, a grid using the newly-minted live variable for its dataset. Below that, in the **Details** panel, we have **purchaseLiveForm1**, which is a live form and its associated **Edit** panel. The live form uses the grid selected item, **purchaseDojoGrid.selectedItem**, as a value for **dataset**, as shown in the following screenshot:

The **onSuccess** event of the live form refreshes the grids dataset by invoking the purchase live variable, **purchaseLiveVariable1,** as shown in the following screenshot:

That's all there is to it. The other layouts are similar, but with the form in a dialog or the grid next to it instead of on top of the form.

Related data

When the schema has the formal "to one" or "to many" relationships, live data makes working with the relationships rather simple. As Studio knows the domain model, it knows about the relationships. However, live variables will not handle related data unless the relation is included in the live view. If the related type is not included in the live view, we are not able to use the related object in our forms.

We first noted this in *Chapter 4, Designing a Well-performing Application*, where related data can unknowingly increase the size of the result set. Let's see how we control this related data.

Live views

In the properties of **purchaseLiveVariable1** is a button labeled **Edit View**:

This brings up the **LiveView Editor** with the live variable's type, in our example **Purchase**, as the base:

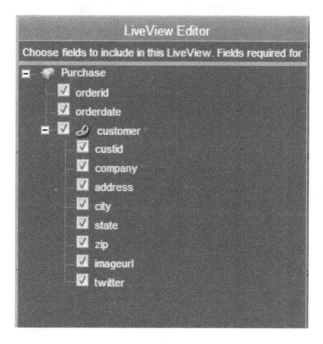

Studio has already included the customer relation in the view. This means that every purchase record we fetch will include its full related customer record. Even if we clear the checkbox for a field, say **imageurl**, the full customer object, including the **imageurl** field, will be returned on read and sent on update. The clearing of a field checkbox only removes the field from automatic editor generation. When cleared, the field is still retrieved with the full related object; however, the field is not included in forms and grids unless manually added.

> Don't be afraid to turn live views of data upside down. When working with related data, sometimes the object you want to work with is not the right object to build the view upon. Some cases are better addressed by using the to-many side of the relation as the base object and displaying the to-one relation instead. The to-one relation can be displayed via a related editor or form, which is easier than trying to work the to-many side of the relation, which requires a grid or list.

With the customer object included in the view, we can use a **RelatedEditor** in our forms. Studio has already added **customerLookup1** to our **purchaseLiveForm1** with its **formField** property set to **customer**, as shown in the following screenshot:

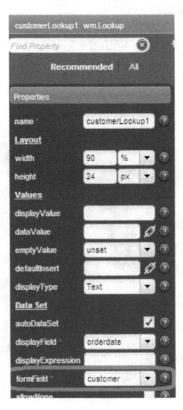

This lookup editor can be customized just like any other widget. A common configuration step for lookup editors is to set the value of **displayField** to a field or expression that enables the user to easily identify the related record.

Query by example

The form tools provide us with quick and easy list and edit components, but if we want to search for a record to edit, we'll most likely want a search of some sort.

In *Chapter 6, Styling the Application*, we styled an editor into a single-value search input. We could bind such an editor's data value as the input value of any one of the filter fields of the live variable. In which case, the service variable's **matchMode** would dictate how that filter value was used to find matches.

What if we need the ability to search against other fields or multiple fields? For multiple field input, the **DataForm** widget will quickly generate an editor for every field of a type. However, when working with live variables for reading, it is important to remember that they are always **Query By Example** (**QBE**). QBE means, as its name implies, querying by passing an example of what you want. Providing multiple filter values contribute to defining the example to be matched. The match mode setting determines only how the example is applied.

This means QBE always performs AND queries. Let's say we bind an editor with the value "San Francisco" as the filter input for city to a customer live variable. Upon firing, the live variable will return all customers with the value of city "San Francisco". If in addition to a city filter we also bind the value "M" for company name, still using the start match mode, the service call would then return companies with names starting with "M" and in the city of San Francisco. In our example custpurchase database, the live variable only returns "Mystery Bookstore."

QBE is an inherent AND query because every additional input adds additional fields to the example to be matched. We cannot do OR or range queries, such as greater than or less than, with live variables. In order to perform such queries, we need to either use an HQL query or access the database via Java services.

> The client-side querying method query() on wm.Variables does perform some of these range operations, but it does so in the browser and does not utilize the database engine in any way. It should not be used against very large datasets as a result.

HQL

Hibernate's SQL-like query language is called **Hibernate Query Language** (HQL). HQL is a full object-oriented query language that can perform joins, aggregate functions such as count, expressions such as "or" and "not", as well as utilize group and order by clauses. HQL queries are the tooled means to perform the advanced queries we could not perform using live variables. The HQL query editor can be accessed by using the **Query** option from the **Services** menu:

If your project uses multiple database services, be certain to select the correct database from the **Data Model** dropdown:

The WaveMaker documentation at wiki includes comprehensive documentation for HQL, including examples, links to Hibernate documentation, and an online tutorial called *HQL_Guru*. Visit the HQL tutorial at http://dev.wavemaker.com/wiki/bin/wmdoc_6.5/HqlTutorial.

To invoke HQL queries, we add a service variable to the project and specify the database service and query operation just like a Java service. HQL queries are saved to the `app-queries.ql.xml` file. Let's now return to our exploration of the `custpurchaseDB` service of `CustpurchaseNavigations`.

In `webapproot/services/custpurchaseDB/src/com/custpurchasedb/data/app-queries.ql.xml`, the sole query defined is `CustomersByState`.

```
<query name="CustomersByState" >
   <query-param name="state" type="java.lang.String"/>
   SELECT cust.company as company, cust.city as city FROM Customer
cust where cust.state = :state
</query>
```

Within the query definition, we see the same HQL syntax we entered into the query editor as well as the input type, a string. What `app-queries.ql.xml` does not tell us is the return type. If we attempt to bind a widget such as a grid to the queries service variable, we'll see that the service variable returns a list of **CustomersByStateRtnType**.

What is this type and where did it come from? If we look at the service definition file for the service, `webapproot/services/custpurchaseDB/designtime/servicedef.xml`, we see the operation with the fully-qualified class name of the return type, as shown in the following code snippet:

```
<operation operationType="other" name="customersByState"> <parameter
name="state" typeRef="java.lang.String" isList="false"/><return
typeRef="com.custpurchasedb.data.output.CustomersByStateRtnType"
isList="true"/></operation>
```

The fully qualified name of the return type is `com.custpurchasedb.data.output.CustomersByStateRtnType`. Within the database service `com.custpurchase.data` namespace is a namespace named `output`. It is here, in `output`, that we find our custom return types. If we go into `webapproot/services/custpurchaseDB/src/com/custpurchasedb/data/output`, we find the file named `CustomersByStateRtnType.java`, which defines a Java type based on the `select` statement from our HQL query. Our example query returns the city name and the company name, which are both strings. In the process of creating that query, Studio creates a corresponding custom return type specific to the query. The type contains only the two string fields we selected from the customers table and not the full customer object.

If you don't provide alias names for returned fields, Studio will assign a less meaningful C0 or C1-like name to the member variables. For example, if we had used SELECT cust.city FROM city instead of SELECT cust.city as city FROM, Studio would have been forced to name the city member variable of CustomersByStateRtnType C0.

Now this raises an interesting question. If live variables can only perform QBE, how can we perform advanced queries but still utilize the live data form components?

Mixing HQL and live data

In our example HQL query, we selected specific fields from the customer object: company and city. Had we instead returned the full customer object using FROM Customer cust where cust.state = :state, our return type would have been the same entity type used by live data, com.custpurchasedb.data.Customer. When we return the table entity type, we are able to seamlessly use the results in a live form. A common use case for this is to populate a list or grid with the results from an HQL query returning table entity types. The live form can then be bound to the grid-selected item, just like the form created by using the database object from the palette. This enables us to have more advanced queries and use live data form components on the results.

This presents us with a trade-off. If we use SELECT to reduce the number of columns returned by a query, we return a custom return type that cannot be used with the live data form components. If instead we return the full object using only the FROM syntax, we return all of the table's columns, increasing the size of the returned payload, but enabling us to directly bind a live form to a returned record.

What if we want to restrict the number of fields returned from an HQL query but still want to edit the results in a live form? In these cases, we can defer the network overhead and return only the full record just before it is to be edited. Specifically, we populate the grid or list with our HQL query results, being certain to include the Primary Key or other unique constraint in the select statement. Instead of binding a live form directly to the grid-selected item, use the grid-selected item as the filter input to a live variable of that type. Also, use the grid selection event to fire the live variable. The live form can then be bound to the live variable's return. As the live variable filter input included a unique identifier, it returns only one instance. By using the live variable as an intermediary, the grid-selected item is converted from a custom return type to a standard entity type, thus enabling it to be edited by the live form. While this method incurs the additional network call between selection and editing, it allows us to reduce the size of the query return. When returning many records from tables with many large columns, the additional live variable server call can be a small price to pay.

Calling SQL and stored procedures from Java

Sometimes we just want to use SQL statements. Maybe we have an existing query that is just too complicated to convert to HQL, or there is an existing stored procedure we want to utilize. Fortunately, Hibernate allows us to use native SQL as well. Hibernate documentation on the topic can be found on the Hibernate documentation site at `http://docs.jboss.org/hibernate/core/3.3/reference/en/html/querysql.html`.

To utilize this Hibernate feature in WaveMaker, we call `createSQLQuery()` from a Java service. Multiple examples of this are available in the WaveMaker documentation wiki at `http://dev.wavemaker.com/wiki/bin/wmdoc_6.5/JavaServices#HUsingcreateSQLQuery5C5C`.

The `createSQLQuery()` call technique can also be used for stored procedures. Stored procedures can also be mapped to a service such as HQL queries manually. Examples of this technique can be found at `http://dev.wavemaker.com/wiki/bin/Dev/Stored+Procedures`.

Summary

Importing a database into a WaveMaker project generates a Hibernate ORM model and adds a database service utilizing that model to our project. The client-side live data components such as live form and live panel make it very easy to use this domain model in the project to create forms. However, the live variable query model is strictly AND-based and therefore not useful for all queries. WaveMaker Studio tools HQL queries for such situations. By being aware of our HQL query return types, we can integrate the more advanced HQL queries we need with the convenience of the live data client form tooling. For situations where HQL is still not enough, we can utilize the database service from custom Java code to gain even further control.

Next, we will further explore Java services and ways in which we can integrate project services with Java.

8

Utilizing Web Services

Web services enable software systems to exchange data more easily. Whether using the SOAP protocol or REST style, web services are, quite frankly, everywhere. As such, they can be a valuable source of data for any web application.

Studio's Web Services tools generate services from basically a URL; either an example URL or the URL to the WSDL. Not all web services can be imported successfully. For those that do import, there's no faster or easier way to use web services in a project. In this chapter, we will examine the four types of web services supported for WaveMaker applications. Specifically, we'll look at how to utilize the following:

- Web Feed Services
- SOAP services by importing a WSDL
- REST services that return XML
- REST services that return JSON

Installing wsdl4j-bin.jar

Choose **Web Service** from the **Services** menu to begin adding a web service to a project:

When using an installed version of WaveMaker Studio, the first time you do this, you'll be prompted to install the web services description language for the Java JAR file, wsdl4j.jar, into the installation, as shown in the following screenshot:

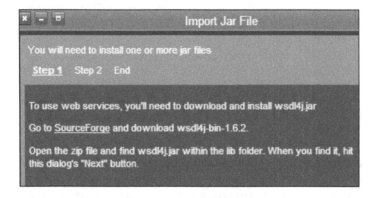

You'll need to complete this task before being able to use the web services tooling. The wsdl4j library is distributed under Common Public License 1.0 from SourceForge (http://sourceforge.net). Like the dependency bundle we installed when first setting up Studio in *Chapter 1*, *Getting Started with WaveMaker*, the wsdl4j license effectively prohibits the library from being distributed as part of the Apache-licensed installation package. The **Import Jar File** dialog will assist you in completing the task.

Should you encounter problems installing the library using the dialog, you can manually install the library. First, you'll need the ability to add files to the Studio installation folder. If the WaveMaker Studio server does not have sufficient permissions to copy the JAR file to the installation folder, the import will fail. Starting Studio with increased privileges, such as starting WaveMaker as root on Linux and OS X or using the **Run as administrator** feature in Windows, should address most permission problems:

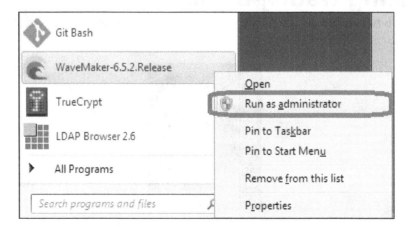

If everything else fails, you can manually copy the JAR file into the `studio/WEB-INF/lib` folder of the installation and restart the WaveMaker Studio Java server.

Feed services

Rich Site Summary (RSS) and **Atom services** are not true web services. Instead, they are a family of web feed formats that allow sites to publish content updates in a standard format. Regardless of their proper classification, consumption of feed services is enabled in the **Web Services** panel.

Selecting **Feed** from the web service type selector simply prompts us to import the pre-built WaveMaker feed service into the project:

There is no further configuration to be performed in the **Web Services** tab after importing the feed service. The feed service is now part of the project services tree with two functions: `getFeed` and `getFeedWithHttpConfig`. Service variables are then used to consume a feed using the `FeedService` service and one of the two functions. Simply set the properties of a service variable, in this case the URL, and then invoke the service variable in the same way as you would do for any other service variable.

A service variable on the `getFeed` method takes only the URL of the feed. The `getFeedWithHttpConfig` method can take a username and password for HTTP basic authentication as well as a connection timeout parameter. The username and password are encoded and added to the request as basic authorization. Yes, you can use the connection timeout with or without setting a username and password.

Binding the feed

The results of the service variable are used like any other service variable results. We can get the result from JavaScript, or more commonly, we can bind the results to a component, as shown in the next screenshot. However, the structure of the feed return value is not a list, and therefore will not show up in a grid's quick dataset dropdown.

Instead, the returned `FeedService.Feed` object is a single object that includes an entry list. That is, the list is a member of the singleton return object. Most often, you will want to bind to the **entries** element of the return:

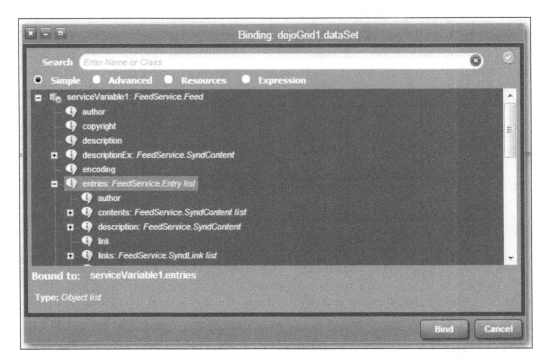

The preceding screenshot shows the **entries** list of **FeedService.Entry** objects that contains the title and the URL values.

SOAP

The verbosity of the XML used by the SOAP protocol enables WaveMaker to leverage tools such as JAX-WS's `wsimport` tool and JAXB's `xjc` to generate full Java clients from *some* WSDL files. This generated client, as you likely suspected, is but a service in the project, and we'll use service variables to invoke the operation.

Unfortunately, the tooling for building Java services from WSDL files is stale in WaveMaker 6.5.X. Some WSDLs will import nicely. Service generation may work, but others won't work at all. The generator will fail due to some error, but others still will generate a service that will not compile. Sometimes, the broken service can be quickly fixed up, for example, by providing a missing import. Sometimes there are more serious projects, such as missing classes, and fixing the generated service requires more skill and effort. WaveMaker has never supported RPC/encoded-style WSDLs. At the other end, WSDLs are using features new to protocol, since the tooled versions of JAX-WS and JAXB are likely to fail as well.

If service generation is not successful

Depending on the source of the error, you may be able to modify the WSDL to enable it to import correctly. Relative paths can be problematic, for example, and getting the service imported can be as simple as fixing an import path within the WSDL. The location of the XSD schema location import may just not be reachable from your network. Another condition is importing a copy of a WSDL from the filesystem can cause the import tooling to expect the imports on the filesystem as well. Sometimes, you can easily change the import location. Other times, it is easier to place a copy of the imported file in the location where the tooling is looking for the file. However, you choose to solve it; with a careful read of the error message, sometimes a failed import can be resolved by a quick tweak of a file.

If the service generates but fails to compile, you also *might* be able to correct the service. Missing `import` statements are an easy fix. Other issues, such as missing type classes, can be more difficult to patch.

REST

REST web services, in contrast to SOAP services, do not define types in the inter-application contract. Participants need to know what format the data is, but the structure of the data payload varies by resource and representation. In general, web services returning data in XML are best used with the **Build-A-Service** option, shown in the following screenshot. On the other hand, JSON-returning services are best used with the **XHR/JSON** web service import choice. There is also a significant difference in how the two types of services are implemented. The XML **Build-A-Service** is implemented as a Java service. While we still use service variables to invoke it, the **XHR/JSON** is a client-side-only service that adds definitions to the browser client without adding a server-side Java service to the project.

REST services returning XML

When you import a web service of the type **Rest (Build-A-Service)**, WaveMaker builds a WSDL file, which it then uses to generate the Java service. The easiest way to populate the inputs and outputs of the service is by using the **Populate From Sample Call** feature:

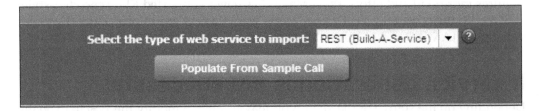

Enter the working URL of the service you want to import:

If you need to pass headers, use POST instead of GET or provide HTTP basic authentication values for the call to succeed. You can do so using the **More Settings** panel. The goal of the **Populate From Sample Call** button is to specify a URL that will return a successful response. The inputs and response from the sample call are then used to model the input and response types of the service method:

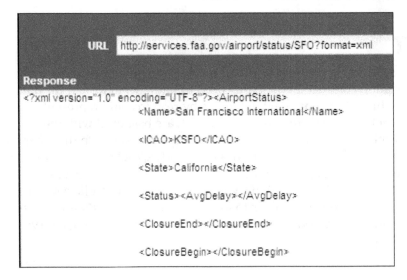

Of particular interest is the response. The XML response value is used to generate a new type. If you cannot perform a successful sample call for any reason, any copy of the XML response from the service can be pasted into the **XML Schema** section of the **Service Output** panel. The **XML Schema** button under **Sample XML Response** will cause Studio to generate a type from the XML.

If providing a sample response is just not possible, the **Raw String** checkbox can be used. The **Raw String** option can also be used when the service returns something other than XML. Whatever the case, using the raw string response type means that unless the response is a simple single string, you may need to parse the results.

Finally, you may need to rework the **Service URL** before importing the service. Take the example of the FAA's airport status service shown in the preceding screenshot (`http://services.faa.gov/airport/status/SFO?format=xml`). Studio assumes all name/value pairs after the question mark to be variables, and all values prior to the question mark to be static. This means that Studio will suggest that the value of **Service URL** should be `http://services.faa.gov/airport/status/SFO?format={format}`, where `{format}` is an input parameter named `format`. We instead want the service URL to be `http://services.faa.gov/airport/status/{airportCode}?format=xml`, where the format is fixed and the airport code is the variable. Instead of a variable named `format` in the query string, we want a variable named `airportCode` in the path so that we can get the status of the various airports managed by the FAA. We need to remove `format` as an input parameter, add `airportCode` instead, and adjust the **Service URL** accordingly before importing the service.

With the service imported, we only need to create a service variable on the service's operation and pass the airport code string for the airport we want the FAA status for, and then we invoke the service variable as appropriate.

After the service is imported, opening the service in Studio shows us the generated WSDL Studio. We are no longer able to edit the input and output parameters and types. We can, however, adjust the value of **Endpoint Address**:

Service Name	faa
HTTP Basic Auth Username	
HTTP Basic Auth Password	
Connection Timeout (milliseconds)	
Request Timeout (milliseconds)	
Endpoint Address	http://services.faa.gov/airport/status/xairportCodex

Changing the endpoint address may be required prior to deploying the project. During development, we might use a test server, for example, particularly if the service accepts POST or PUT methods that update resources. In such cases, we are likely to want to change the service URL for deployment to connect to the production server instead of the test server we used during development. As there are no means to update the endpoint in the deployment dialog, such changes need to be made and saved here prior to deployment.

REST services returning JSON

JSON continues to grow in popularity, and many RESTful web services now are capable of returning JSON. Other services may prefer or even only return JSON. WaveMaker 6.5.X introduces the **XHR/JSON** services for utilizing services that return JSON. The **XHR/JSON** import panel has four sections (**Service Settings**, **Fixed Headers**, **Inputs**, and **Return Type**), as shown in the following screenshot:

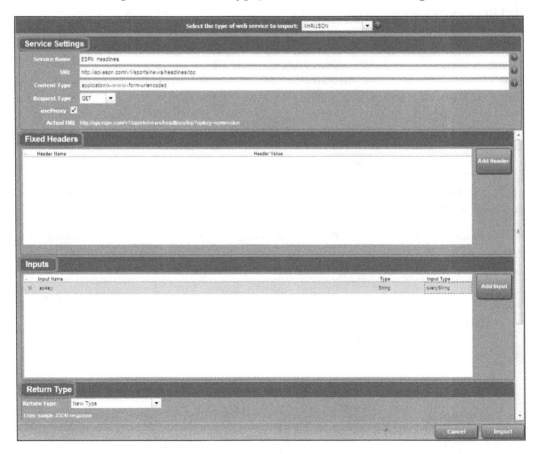

In **Service Settings**, we specify the base service settings: **Service Name**, **URL**, **Content Type**, and **Request Type**. Also note the **useProxy** checkbox, which we'll address shortly.

Fixed Headers are for header parameters with static or fixed values. This can be useful for API keys or other header-passed values that will always be the same. Header values set here will not be shown as inputs on the service variable.

> Be certain that you don't make a private password or API key public by accidentally checking it into a shared repository such as GitHub. See the considerations for using public and shared repositories before checking a password in as part of a project at http://dev.wavemaker.com/wiki/bin/ation+Management#HConsiderations whenusingsharedorpublicrepositories.

Inputs is used for **queryString**, **header**, or **path** values specified with the **Input Type** dropdown, as shown in the following screenshot:

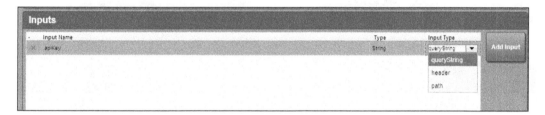

Unlike **Fixed Headers**, the inputs specified here will show up as input parameters of the service variable, and thus can vary from call to call. **Query String** values are passed as name = value pairs after the question mark of the URL as part of the query string. With **path** inputs, the values are inserted into the URL path as name/value, where name is the input name and value is the value given for the parameter. The **header** input passes the value in the header of the request as a name = value pair like **Fixed Headers**, but the input is shown in as a service variable input and the value can vary per call.

Some service inputs don't fit well into this model and may require some jiggery-pokery to get the URL just right. For example, a path variable that lacks a name can be entered using part of the path for the input name. If the desired path includes /news/{API KEY}, where {API KEY} is the key value, we could enter the input with the input name news, thus tricking Studio into building the desired URL. If we enter news in the URL and use apiKey as the input name, we would instead get /news/apiKey/{API KEY} in our path.

WaveMaker 6.6.0 reworks this panel and addresses a number of the complications encountered with the 6.5.X version. Note that the 6.5.X XHR service definitions are not compatible with 6.6.0 as a result, meaning XHR services must be redefined between 6.5.X and 6.6.0.

Return Type is just that—the type of the return from the service call. If an existing type is returned, select it from the **Return Type** dropdown to avoid creating duplicates. If not, paste a sample JSON response into the text area labeled **Enter Sample JSON response**. Similar to the XHL web service return type, the response can be obtained from anywhere, such as another tab in your browser:

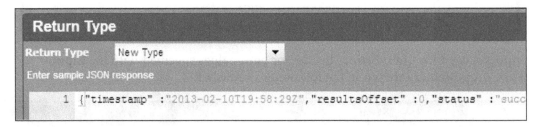

The XHR proxy

The XHR service is the only one of the four that is not a Java service. The **useProxy** option determines if the WaveMaker server is to be used as a proxy for XHR calls. This will generally be required whenever we are using the WaveMaker Java server in a web application deployment due to the same origin policy. PhoneGap applications, however, are loaded from the local device, and are not subject to the same origin policy (`http://www.w3.org/Security/wiki/Same_Origin_Policy`). This means that you can turn off the proxy settings in the PhoneGap deployment dialog.

Using the proxy routes, all requests through the server's WaveMaker service requests using the path `wavemakerservice.json`. This means the browser sees all requests as going to the same server that the application was loaded from and are thus of the same origin.

Using the proxy, however, brings some constraints of its own. Most notably is that `accept-encoding` gets set to `text/plain` even if you specify a header value otherwise.

Summary

WaveMaker tools contain four web service import options: **Feed** for RSS and Atom services, **SOAP** for importing SOAP WSDLs, **REST (Build-A-Service)** for XML returning services, and **XHR/JSON** for JSON returning services. Importing a web service through the tooling adds a service to the project that can be invoked using a service variable.

While these options can be used for many of the web services available, some web services simply cannot be made to work with one of these tooled options. If a Java client for the service can be obtained by another means, the web service can be accessed via a custom Java service.

In the next chapter, we will learn about custom Java services, the workhorse of server-side functionality in WaveMaker. Mostly, for any situation in which the tooled services do not meet our needs for any reason, a Java service can be used. If it can be done in Java, it can often be done in a custom Java service.

9
Custom Java Services

So far, we have seen how WaveMaker provides a framework in which we can easily build applications. We've also seen how the Studio can generate server-side services from as little as a JDBC connection to a relational database schema or web service URL. In this chapter, we'll cover the root of all server-side functionality, custom Java services. If it can be done in Java, it can probably be done in WaveMaker using custom Java services.

It is impossible to address all the possible ways you could use custom Java services in a project. Instead, in this chapter, we will equip you with the building blocks needed to build your own solutions in Java. The following are the areas we will address:

- The classpath
- Using external editors
- RuntimeAccess
- Accessing other service beans
- Servlet stuff
- Logging

The example project for this chapter is named `JavaServices`. It demonstrates using the `custpurchase` MySQL example database from a custom Java service.

Java or web service

Before adding a custom Java service to a project, ensure that a Java service is the best way to provide the desired functionality. A straight Java service may not be the best solution if you expect to reuse the functionality in other projects.

One option is to package the core functionality up into a JAR file. This makes it easier to reuse the functionality provisioned by a set of classes. Subsequent projects will still need to use a Java service; however, they don't need to recompile another copy of the Java sources. Instead, the JAR file is added to the classpath and the Java service class uses the classes of the JAR just like any other JAR file import. This can be a good option if your organization produces JAR files as artifacts from other projects. Simply take the output targets from those builds and bring them into the WaveMaker projects. The downside to this approach is that any updates to the classes in the JAR file must be propagated to each project using the JAR.

Therefore, if the functionality will be reused by multiple projects, a well-designed web service is almost always the better choice. When published as a web service, REST or SOAP, there is a single service to maintain. When bugs are fixed or improvements are made, there is only one place to test and apply the update so long as the external API does not change. Using a web service also provides more flexibility in your deployment architecture. The web service can be deployed on a host other than the host running the WaveMaker application server JVM. This keeps the load off of the application deployment host while distributing the workload amongst resources.

Custom Java services are powerful tools. As the Linux sudo tool often reminds us, with great power comes great responsibility. Before building out the ultimate backend, take a moment and ask if the functionality is better provisioned as a web service.

Adding a custom service

Adding a custom Java service to a project is a simple matter of choosing **Java Service** from the **Services** menu. The **New Java Service** dialog asks for only a **Service Name** and a **Package and Class Name**:

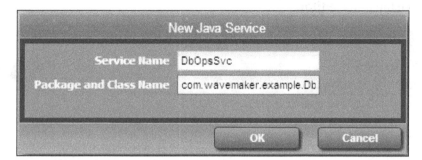

The **Service Name** is the name we'll see in the project services tree, service drop-down, and so on. The **Package and Class Name** is just the package and class name together. Take the desired package name and the desired class name together to form the fully qualified name of the Java class to be created.

In the previous example, the service name is DbOpsSvc, as in "database operations service". The fully qualified class name entered into the **Package and Class Name** editor is com.wavemaker.example.DbOpsSvc. This creates a class named DbOpsSvc in the com.wavemaker.example package. The class name and the service name do not need to match. However, using the same name for both, or at least a similar name, makes it easier to remember which class is associated with which service.

Adding a Java service to the project adds a single Java source class to the project. This class is packaged as a Spring bean defined in the service's spring XML file, for example, DbOpsSvc.spring.xml. The service bean definition is imported into the project in project-services.xml. If we have not violated a Java naming constraint and all goes well, we'll be taken to the Java service editor with that newly minted class source file in the editor:

```
Canvas    Source    Java    WebServices

1  package com.wavemaker.example;
2
3  import com.wavemaker.runtime.javaservice.JavaServiceSuperClass;
4  import com.wavemaker.runtime.service.annotations.ExposeToClient;
5
6  @ExposeToClient
7  public class DbOpsSvc extends JavaServiceSuperClass {
8      /* Pass in one of FATAL, ERROR, WARN,  INFO and DEBUG to modify your
9       * recommend changing this to FATAL or ERROR before deploying.  For
10      */
11     public DbOpsSvc() {
12         super(INFO);
13     }
```

We'll discuss how to use an IDE such as Eclipse shortly.

 When working with the code editors within Studio, sometimes large areas or the whole editor gets selected. An easy way to clear the selection is to use the up arrow or down arrow.

Dissecting the template class

The initial version of the class is generated from a template. It's pretty simple, but it is important to understand it too:

```
package com.wavemaker.example;
```

The package name comes directly from the package name we specified in the creation dialog.

In *Chapter 2*, *Digging into the Architecture*, we learned that a service class must extend `JavaServiceSuperClass` or use the `@ExposeToClient` annotation in order to be able to expose methods to the client. The template does both, and there are two imports: one for the super class and the other for the annotation:

```
import com.wavemaker.runtime.javaservice.JavaServiceSuperClass;
import com.wavemaker.runtime.service.annotations.ExposeToClient;
```

In between two comments, the first noting the class as client-facing and the second using the log command, is the class declaration:

```
@ExposeToClient

public class DbOpsSvc extends JavaServiceSuperClass {
```

In the preceding code, we can see the use of the annotation and the extension of the base class. There is also a constructor that calls the base class constructor and a sample operation called `sampleJavaOperation()`.

Extending the `JavaServiceSuperClass` class provides the log methods and the initialization of the service logger; it is not necessary, however, as using the client annotation is sufficient, and we can extend our own class if needed. However, if we choose to extend a class other than `JavaServiceSuperClass`, we must use the `@ExposeToClient` annotation on the class or on individual methods for them to be included in the service definitions. This is most commonly required when your model requires you to extend a specific class, and thus the service class is not able to extend the service super class.

The classpath

One of the things you will need in the initial stage of creating custom Java services is the ability to add things to the classpath. The classpath is the set of locations in which Java looks for classes and packages. If it is not on the classpath, we cannot use it in Java. Therefore, we need to add any additional classes we wish to use in our Java service to the classpath before we can use them. Where files should go to get on the classpath is driven by what they are and their desired reach.

JAR and class files

JAR files (`.jar`) and compiled class files (`.class`) specific to a project are added to that project's root `lib` folder. For a project named `Project1`, this would be the `/projects/Project1/lib` folder within the WaveMaker home folder. JAR files placed in the `lib` folder are copied into `/WEB-INF/lib` as part of preparing the project for deployment, including the local deployment when using the **Run** button. You do not want to put files directly into `/WEB-INF/lib`. Use of the `lib` folder keeps the storage of your JAR files separate from the Studio provided JAR files. This also enables you to keep all of the `/WEB-INF/lib` folder out of any file repositories such as SVN or GitHub. Use your repository's ignore statement on the `/WEB-INF/lib` folder. Your local working copy of the folder will be repopulated by Studio upon deployment.

If, however, the JAR file is needed in every new project, such as a custom JDBC driver, place the JAR file in the `/commons/lib` folder instead. The `commons` folder is the sibling of `projects` that stores user cross-project files such as custom themes that we first saw in *Chapter 2, Digging into the Architecture*. The contents of `/commons/lib` are copied into the project's `/lib` at the time of project creation. This absolves the developer of having to do this for every new project. The copying out of `commons` only occurs at project creation, and is the same as any other JAR file in the `lib` folder thereafter.

Java source files

Adding a Java service to a project creates a single new client-exposed class. This class is the browser's interface to the service. Only the exposed public methods of this class are callable by the client. However, we are not constrained to using a single class in the implementation of our service. We can add as many source files we need into the project's `/src` folder. Java classes in the `/src` folder are compiled and copied into `/WEB-INF` whenever the project is deployed or compiled.

In fact, if the Java service is to be of any significance, you certainly want to use multiple classes. Here too, it is prudent to keep hand-added and generated files distinct on the filesystem. In this case, however, we can have overlapping package names while keeping the files separate. Because we can have a hand-coded package in `/src`, we can share base package names amongst classes while keeping the files segmented on the filesystem.

Let's take a look at the "spin up" application that can be found in the WaveMaker source code applications folder `https://github.com/SpringSource/wavemaker/tree/6.5.X/wavemaker-desktop/applications/projects/WM_Spinup_App2`. This is the source for an application that was used to deploy WaveMaker Studio to Version 1 Cloud Foundry accounts. It is an interesting example because it does a bit of it all. The project contains two services: `SpinUpService` and `userlogDB`. In addition to these services, the project adds a handful of JAR files to the `lib` folder and uses classes in those JAR files from manually added classes. One JAR, `cloudfoundry-client-lib`, is the Java client for Cloud Foundry web services. Those custom classes are used by the main project service, `SpinUpService`. The other service, `userlopDB`, is a single table database used to log application usage. It is only used from the main project service, `SpinUpService`.

The `SpinUpService` class is given in the following link: `https://github.com/SpringSource/wavemaker/blob/6.5.X/wavemaker-desktop/applications/projects/WM_Spinup_App2/services/SpinUpService/src/com/wavemaker/spinup/wmclient/SpinUpService.java`. The service defines only two client-facing operations, `login` and `launchStudio`, and is in the package `com.wavemaker.spinup.wmclient`. The manually added Java source files are under `/src` in the package `com.wavemaker.spinup.web` (`https://github.com/SpringSource/wavemaker/tree/6.5.X/wavemaker-desktop/applications/projects/WM_Spinup_App2/src/com/wavemaker/spinup/web`). The classes all share the `com.wavemaker.spinup` package name. Within the `wmclient` space is the client-facing service, and within the web space is the supporting classes used by `wmclient`.

Using an external editor

For any significant hand-coding, or just a better experience at editing the service class, you can use the editor of your choice instead of Studio's built-in editor. The editor in Studio is a fine editor, but if you prefer to use a Java IDE such as SpringSource Tool Suite (STS), Eclipse, or NetBeans, you can do so by importing the WaveMaker project into a Java IDE.

NetBeans

To import a WaveMaker project into NetBeans, choose **File** followed by **New Project** from the NetBeans menu. In the **New Project** dialog, choose the **Java Web** category with the **Web Application with Existing Sources** project type.

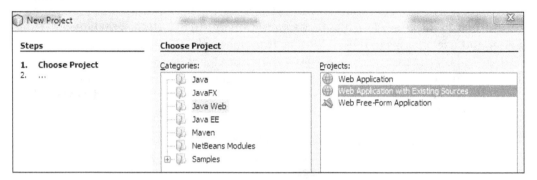

Then, specify the project root for the **Location** field as shown in the following screenshot:

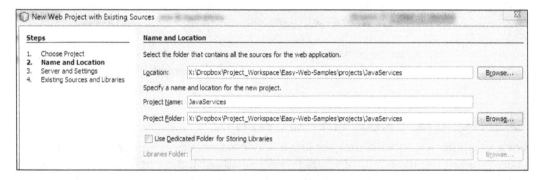

You'll also need to specify the project's `webapproot` folder for the **Web Pages Folder** field before you can complete the wizard.

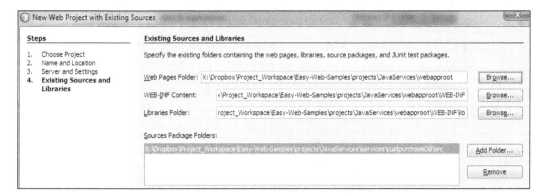

 NetBeans will warn you that the project already contains class files. You can ignore the class file warning without deleting the class files as suggested by NetBeans.

Eclipse/STS

To import a WaveMaker project into Eclipse or STS, select **File | New | Java Project** from the STS menu. In the **New Java Project** dialog, clear the **Use default Location** checkbox and specify the project folder in the **Location** editor. The Eclipse project name should exactly match the WaveMaker project name.

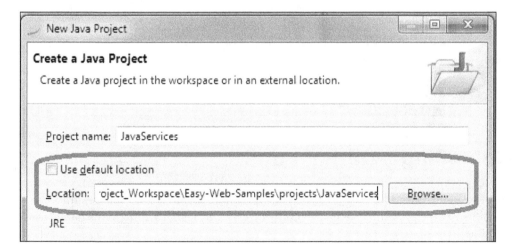

WaveMaker 6.5.X requires JDK 6. Use only a Java 6 JRE for the project.

The project is now available in STS, and we can edit it like any other Java project.

Compiling external edits

You can compile and test your classes from the IDE if you like; however, in order to have Studio be aware of the changes and compile your changes into the project's WEB-INF, Studio needs to compile any changes from the external editor into the project.

You could close and re-open the project in Studio, but that takes too long. Instead, the refresh button in the Java editor can be used.

The refresh button causes Studio to reload the open Java service file and recompile the project. If you have not edited any of the service source files that are open in the editor within Studio, then you can alternatively use the save or test/run button instead. The save button also recompiles the project, but it does so first saving the contents of any files open in Studio's editors. This means if another editor has made changes to a file since Studio loaded the file, those external edits will be lost to the Studio save.

Both the save and refresh buttons undeploy the current project. You'll need to use the run button again to redeploy the application before testing the changes against the deployed application in the browser. As test/run also compiles the project, test/run is the easiest to use if you don't have external edits to files open Studio editors.

RuntimeAccess

Working with custom Java services in WaveMaker is not radically different from working with Java in web applications. So far, we've added resources to the classpath and got our project into a proper editor. The last Java topic specific to WaveMaker to be aware of is RuntimeAccess (http://dev.wavemaker.com/docs/javadoc/6.5/com/wavemaker/runtime/RuntimeAccess.html). The com.wavemaker.runtime.RuntimeAccess class is the runtime bean that provides our interface to the session, request/response, and other project services.

To obtain an instance of the runtime bean, use the static method getInstance(). Ensure you've imported RuntimeAccess:

```
import com.wavemaker.runtime.RuntimeAccess;
```

To get an instance of the runtime, use the following line of code:

```
RuntimeAccess runtime = RuntimeAccess.getInstance();
```

Never attempt to renew RuntimeAccess or otherwise attempt to access the session outside of a request. It is not supported and it doesn't work.

From `RuntimeAccess`, we can obtain four useful servlet objects:

- ServletContext (`javax.servlet.ServletContext`)
- HttpSession (`javax.servlet.http.HttpSession`)
- HttpServletRequest (`javax.servlet.http.HttpServletRequest`)
- HttpServletResponse (`javax.servlet.http.HttpServletResponse`)

These objects provide us with access to a number of useful details, such as the IP address of the client from the request object:

```
String remoteAddress = RuntimeAccess.getInstance().getRequest().
getRemoteAddr();
```

As we don't know the location of the application on the server's filesystem, access is best done through `ServletContext`. The `ServletContext` object enables communication with its servlet container including access to resources. All paths are relative to `/webapproot`. Here, we open `InputStream` on the file `Readme.txt` from the `resources` folder:

```
InputStream is = RuntimeAccess.getInstance().getSession().
getServletContext().getResourceAsStream("/resources/Readme.txt");
```

Access other service beans

The other very useful objects we can access via `RuntimeAccess` are other project service beans. The `getServiceBean()` function allows us to get another service bean by its ID. For example, from our `DbOpsSvc` service, we could get an instance of our database service, `CustpurchaseDB`:

```
CustpurchaseDB custpurchaseDb = (CustpurchaseDB)RuntimeAccess.
getInstance().getServiceBean("("custpurchaseDB");");
```

Note that we must cast the return from `getServiceBean()` to the specific service type. The ability to easily access other service beans, including other custom Java services, unlocks many options for developers. A common example is using `createSQLQuery()` to execute SQL queries against the database. Accessing the generated database service enables us to get the database session (`org.hibernate.Session`). With the session in hand, we can call the session object method `createSQLQuery()` when we want to use SQL instead of HQL; visit the following link for detailed examples: `http://dev.wavemaker.com/wiki/bin/wmdoc_6.5/JavaServices#HUsingcreateSQLQuery5C5C`.

Server-side validation

Another use of a custom Java service is to perform server-side validation. In the `updateCustomer()` function from our `DbOpsSvc` service, the length of the `state` field is checked before updating the record. If the length of the string passed is anything but two, a runtime exception is thrown. Let's walk through the function.

First, we perform our validation on the update object. In our example, we throw an exception causing the function to fail if the state's length is not two:

```
public Customer updateCustomer(Customer customer){
Customer updatedCustomer = null;
 log(INFO, "Updating customer: " + customer.getCompany());
 if(customer.getState().length() != 2){
   throw new RuntimeException("Invalid State length
            Must be 2 digits only.");
```

 The exception is thrown outside of a try/catch block to ensure the error message is returned to the client. If we catch our own exception, the error is not returned to the client and its service variable error condition will not be triggered.

Next we get an instance of the runtime service by using the `getServiceBean()` method:

```
 try{
   //Get an instance of the RuntimeService, named runtimeService,
   RuntimeService runtimeService =
 (RuntimeService)RuntimeAccess.getInstance().getServiceBean("runtimeSe
rvice");
```

Finally, we use `runtimeService.update()` to perform the actual update of the customer record. To `update()`, we pass the string constants we defined for the service and table names as well as the updated `customer` object from the client. Note that the update method also requires an index value, which is always zero, for the final parameter:

```
   //Always use zero for index when calling update from java service
   TypedServiceReturn tsrCustomer = runtimeService.update(CUSTPURCHASE_
DB, COM_CUSTPURCHASEDB_DATA_CUSTOMER,customer,0);
   updatedCustomer = (Customer)tsrCustomer.getReturnValue();
   } catch(Exception e) {
   log(ERROR, "There was a problem updating customer");
     e.printStackTrace();
   }
```

The `runtimeService.update()` method returns a `TypedServiceReturn`, which we can cast into a `Customer` object and return to the client:

```
return updatedCustomer;
}
```

Dependency injection

Now that we've seen how useful other service beans can be in our Java code, let's make it easier to get to those services. The best way to get an instance of the runtime bean, or any other project bean, is to "inject" it into the service class using **dependency injection**.

Dependency injection is when the bean declares a dependency and the container (for example, Tomcat and Spring) provides or injects that dependency to the bean as part of its initialization. The benefit is that the property is populated for us by the container. We do not need to fetch an instance of the service in code.

In our example, `DbOpsSvc` from the `JavaServices` project, we also inject `runtimeService` into our service class. The `updateCustomerInjected()` method repeats the `updateCustomer()` example function but using dependency injection.

The runtime service has the bean ID of `runtimeService`. We can confirm the bean ID for any bean by examining that service's `spring.xml` file. In the case of the runtime service, we can find its spring file, `runtimeService.spring.xml`, in\ `WEB-INF\ classes`. In which, we can see the bean's ID is `runtimeService`:

```
<bean class="com.CustpurchaseDBwavemaker.runtime.service.
RuntimeService" scope="singleton"
  lazy-init="true" id="runtimeService">
```

Next, we edit the spring file for our custom Java service to perform the injection. In this example, it is `DbOpsSvc.spring.xml` within the `/services/DbOpsSvc/src` folder that we edit. To the `DbOpsSvc` bean definition we add a property named `custpurchaseDBruntimeSvc` with a reference to the bean ID:

```
<bean class="com.custpurchasedb.DbOpsSvc" scope="singleton"
lazy-init="true" id="DbOpsSvc">
<property name="runtimeSvc"><ref bean="custpurchaseDBruntimeServi
ce"/></property>
 </bean>
```

So far, we've told Spring to provide our `DbOpsSvc` with an instance of `runtimeService`. Next, we've got to give the `custpurchaseDBruntimeService` service instance a home in our class. To do that, we edit the `DbOpsSvc.java` source file. First, we import the service class:

```
import com.CustpurchaseDBwavemaker.runtime.service.RuntimeService;
```

Next, we declare a private instance variable to store our reference to the service. Note that the member variable name must exactly match that of the property value we added to the `spring xml` file:

```
private custpurchaseDBRuntimeService runtimeSvc;
```

Last, we provide a public setter for the container to use to inject the instance. As the method must be public, we hide it from the client by using the @ `HideFromClient` annotation:

```
@HideFromClient
public void setRuntimeSvc(RuntimeService runtimeSvc){
  this.runtimeSvc = runtimeSvc;
}
```

That's it. We can now access `custpurchaseDBruntimeSvc` in our Java service methods.

 Another example and a webinar recording on dependency injection are available at `http://dev.wavemaker.com/wiki/bin/Spring`.

Logging

The built-in logger should be used over `System.out` at all times. Examples of using the log function are included in the sample service operation added to each newly minted service class. If you use the default extension of `JavaServiceSuperClass`, logging is already set up for you, and all you need to do is use `log()` with a log level instead of `System.out.println()`.

Good logging is critical to supporting and debugging any Java service. The `JavaServiceSuperClass` class makes using the logging subsystem so easy there is no good reason to use `System.out.println`; `System.out` simply lacks the controls of log. Using the logger with levels allows you to control the verbosity of logging using `/src/log4j.properties` instead of recompiling sources.

For example, in our `updateCustomer()` example function, we use `INFO` to log the name of the company being updated:

```
log(INFO, "Updating customer: " + customer.getCompany());
```

But, if there is an exception in performing the update, we use `ERROR` to log the condition:

```
log(ERROR, "There was a problem updating customer");
```

By categorizing our logging into levels, we can have many log statements in our code without cluttering the log files. Use the most verbose level, `DEBUG`, for logging details needed when troubleshooting problems. If a particular operation is prone to questions, leave `DEBUG` entries for the appropriate values. The entries will only be logged if the log level is turned up to `DEBUG`.

Further information about logging and controlling log levels is available at `http://dev.wavemaker.com/wiki/bin/wmdoc_6.5/ServerLogs`.

It is relatively easy to add logging and otherwise debug an application in development. Once deployed, troubleshooting can be much more difficult. A quality application has good logging for use in deployment.

Summary

In this chapter, we examined the key aspects of using custom Java services in a project. We started by ensuring we wouldn't get better results from provisioning the functionality as a web service. We then looked at what happens when we add a Java service to the project and how we can add additional classes to the project classpath.

We then opened our projects in STS and NetBeans so we could edit our code in our favorite editor and enjoy the benefits of working in an IDE. We were careful to use the Studio tooling to refresh and recompile our project.

We then explored the many uses of the runtime access bean. From the runtime, we were able to access key objects, such as the servlet and request objects. We also used the runtime bean to access other service beans. This enabled us to build rich Java services with features such as server-side validation.

As the runtime bean is so convenient to have in our Java service, we looked at examples of dependency injection. Using dependency injection, our Java service was provisioned with a service reference during its creation.

Java services are a powerful tool for customizing our application. Next, we'll look at some of the customization tools available to use client-side using JavaScript.

10
Customizing the User Interface with JavaScript

We have seen that the use of JavaScript is not required to develop complete applications. However, the WaveMaker client framework provides a rich palette to work with for those who wish to take advantage of JavaScript. This chapter will introduce using JavaScript to customize the user interface of WaveMaker applications.

We'll review the asynchronous part of the AJAX model as well as the component and DOM events that dictate how and when we invoke functions, from button clicks to service call returns. Once we understand events, we will explore some of the things we can do within those events. We will work with `wm.Variables` and see how they act as instruments for getting and setting data values. Not to be left out, we'll also include the role of JavaScript variables in page code.

We will also cover bindings. We'll show you how you can use simple binding expressions and custom JavaScript to enhance the responsiveness of the user interface.

Finally, we'll review some of the resources available to developers, from the client API reference to the component classes themselves. We'll also demonstrate how the community forums are not the only way to learn new JavaScript tricks.

Important warning for browser-executed code

All JavaScript in WaveMaker is executed in the browser. Unless you are deploying your application to a private, secure network only accessible by highly trusted devices, the client must be considered as untrusted. Even when a username and password is required to access the application, the client host could potentially be under malicious control. Never should secrets or security be entrusted to JavaScript. Any system password, proprietary logic, access restriction, or validation done in JavaScript can be circumvented, modified, extracted, or disabled. Such things must be done on the server-side in order to be secure.

Previously, we used the Chrome Developer Tools JavaScript console in *Chapter 1, Getting Started with WaveMaker*. Malicious users can also use the console to manipulate application components in the very same way. Finally, no matter how secure we could make the client code, any and all logic used in the client can be circumvented by sending a manually crafted XHR request to the server. Therefore, data must be validated on the server side to ensure enforcement of rules.

Client-side customization enables you to deliver a rich, responsive interface to the user. Form validation on the client side is better for the user than server-side validation, but it's not secure. All required data validation must be performed on the server side. You can do some or all of the validation in JavaScript too, but always remember that it is executing on the client side and the client is not to be trusted.

Events

Events are pretty straightforward creatures. We looked at how the binding dialog is really a visually tooled version of `dojo.connect()` in *Chapter 2, Digging into the Architecture*. Binding via connect registers a function to be called when an event occurs; "when X happens, please also do Y". We will look at this in detail in a short while.

Asynchronous events

If events are easy to understand, you'd be forgiven for not expecting asynchronous events to be one of most common sources of trouble. Not understanding the impact of the "A is for asynchronous" part of AJAX is a common cause of frustration in accessing service call results.

When the browser invokes an asynchronous server call, for example using a service variable, the browser sends the request off to the server, but it doesn't wait idle until it receives a response. For example, if you used the following code in your application to invoke a service variable and immediately fetch the results, the `result` variable will be undefined nearly every time, if not always:

```
this.serviceVariable1.update();
var result = this.serviceVariable1.getData();
console.log(result);
```

Every once in a while, if the service call can be completed quickly, you might get a value in `result`. Every other time, `result` will be undefined.

To ensure we access server call results at the correct time, WaveMaker provides callback functions (`https://en.wikipedia.org/wiki/Callback_(computer_programming)`). The callback functions `onSuccess`, `onResult`, and `onError` should always be used when depending on values returned from a service variable. Until these events fire, it cannot be assured that the service variable has returned.

Event handlers

When you choose **JavaScript** from an event menu, such as the **onclick** event of a button, an empty event handler function is created for you:

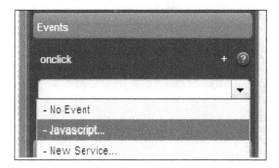

The empty event handler function is as follows:

```
button1Click: function(inSender) {

},
```

Within these functions, you can utilize any valid JavaScript. The function name is added to the widget definition in the page's widgets file; for example, `Main. widgets.js`. This causes the WaveMaker client runtime to connect the custom event handler to the event. For example, `button1` in the following code snippet, when clicked, will invoke the function named `button1Click`:

```
button1: ["wm.Button", {"margin":"4"}, {"onclick":"button1Click"}],
```

This enables the function to be called when the event occurs. This also means that if you change the name of a function and the function name is not updated in the widget definition, the function will not be invoked upon the occurrence of the event.

If you rename the widget using the name editor of the **Properties** panel, Studio will rename the event handler and update the widget definition. However, if you change `button1Click` to `myButtonClickFunction` in the **Source** tab manually, `myButtonClickFunction` will no longer be called when `button1` is clicked. Either use the name editor of the **Properties** panel or manually type the function name into the event.

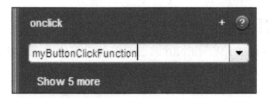

 Entering a function name in events is an easy way to use the same function for multiple event bindings. Instead of repeating the logic in each event handler, define a new function in the page code to perform the common logic and have numerous events call that single function.

For convenience, within page code, `this` always refers to the current page. From a page named `main`, `main` and `this` are the same such that `this===main` is true. That is, `main` and `this` are strictly equal and refer to the same object.

Another convenience of component event handlers is `inSender`. The function argument `inSender` always refers to the sending object; the object on which the event occurred. In the case of our button-click, the button is `inSender`. If our button is named `button1`, `inSender` and `this.button1` are strictly equal, or `inSender===this.button1`.

Other event handler templates have additional parameters that you can utilize. A live form's `onBeforeServiceCall()` function, for example, provides `inSender`, `inOperation`, and `inData`. The following is an example usage of `inData`:

```
customerEditLiveForm1BeforeServiceCall: function(inSender,inOperation,
inData) {
   if(inData.zip.toString().length!=5){
      app.toastError("Zip code must be 5 digits only");
      //Must be error of "Abort" to stop service call
      throw new Error("Abort");
   }
}
```

The value of `inOperation` is the name of the operation about to be performed, such as `update`, and `inData` is the data values that are about to be sent to the server. The function template arguments provide quick access to commonly needed components; however, you are not required to use any of the arguments passed to the event handler function. They are for your convenience.

Binding expressions

Binding expressions are an alternative way to use JavaScript to customize the user experience. Instead of using an event handler function from the **Events** dropdown, binding expressions are accessed using the **Expression** tab of the **Binding** dialog:

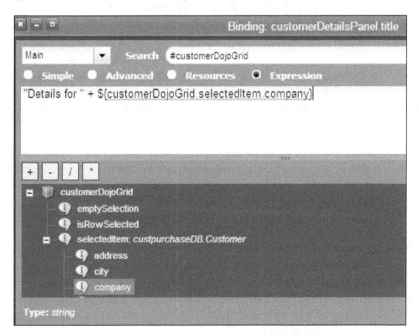

In the preceding screenshot, the title of `customerDetailsPanel` is bound to the following expression:

```
"Details for " + ${customerDojoGrid.selectedItem.company}
```

This causes the panel's title to look like the following:

Studio informs you of the presence of the expression in the **Properties** panel by displaying **expr:** and the beginning of the expression in the bound property:

The same result could be achieved by calling `setTitle()` in a custom event handler for the `customerDojoGrid's onSelect()` event:

```
customerDojoGridSelect: function(inSender) {
    this.customerDetailsPanel.setTitle("Details for " +
    inSender.selectedItem.getData().company);
},
```

 In the case of customizing the panel's title using the grid's `onSelect` event, unless you use the `selectFirstRow` property or otherwise programmatically select a row, the panel title will first be shown with the title property value. The title will be set only upon grid selection. Using   for non-breaking space (`http://en.wikipedia.org/wiki/Non-breaking_space`) is a common trick to set the value as an empty space to reserve space for the value upon selection.

The same result can be achieved using either binding expressions or event handlers; however, there are some distinct differences between the two.

For one, binding expressions are part of the widget definition, not the page code. This moves the expression out of sight. This keeps your page code cleaner and can be desirable, but it also means that setting a breakpoint in an expression is far more complicated. Setting a breakpoint in an event handler is a simple matter of opening the page in the debugger. On the other hand, setting a breakpoint in an expression is much more difficult, even for experienced users.

Another significant difference between page functions and binding expressions is the context in which they are executed. Because of this difference in context, binding expressions use a `${...}` syntax to refer to components. Within the `${...}` syntax, this refers to the window, not the page. As of WaveMaker 6.5, you can use this in an expression to refer to the page outside of the `${...}` syntax. This means that you can access the data value of an editor named `text1` by using `this.text1.getDataValue()` or `${text1.dataValue}`. However, only the `${}` part of the expression is notified of the changes to the evaluated data value. This means that we cannot use the same syntax that we successfully used for the grid's `onSelect` handler as our binding expression:

```
"Details for " + this.customerDojoGrid.selectedItem.
getDataValue().company
```

The preceding code does not work as an expression. The expression will never evaluate and the title will never be set. Only changes to values referenced within the `${...}` parts of an expression result in the expression being re-evaluated. As this expression lacks a `${...}` evaluation, the expression never evaluates. Furthermore, only bindable properties and values are accessible within the `${...}` syntax. If you want to use a value or property that has not been exposed in the binding dialog, you need to get that value outside of the `${...}` syntax or use a page event handler function instead.

For further information on binding expressions, visit the binding expressions page in the advanced topics documentation at `http://dev.wavemaker.com/wiki/bin/wmdoc_6.5/Binding+Expressions+Display+Expressions`.

Setting and getting values

The getting and setting of values is very common in JavaScript page functions. Whether it is to validate user input, assemble input values to service calls, or generate messages and summaries, page code often reads and writes component values. It is best practice to use setters and getters whenever available. Getters and setters are the functions that get and set values on an object. They almost always use `set` and `get` in their name, such as `getDataValue()`, `setCaption()`, and `setDataValue()`. The use of getters, and especially setters, instead of performing an assignment ensures that change notifications and any required refreshing of the component takes place.

Take, for example, a label named `labelTitle`. We might be tempted to assign the caption to a value as shown in the following line of code:

```
this.labelTitle.caption="Welcome";
```

Now, what happens if we use the preceding line of code to assign a new value to a caption via the console? Well, nothing. We will not see a change in the caption displayed on the screen. Yes, `this.labelTitle.caption` now returns `Welcome`. Even calling `this.labelTitle.getValue("caption")` returns `Welcome`. However, in the case of a label caption assignment, we also need to call `renderLabel()`, as in `this.labelTitle.renderLabel()`, before the caption on the screen changes to the value set by the assignment. Calling `this.labelTitle.setCaption("Greetings")`, on the other hand, changes both the caption property value and the displayed caption with the single call. The `setCaption()` function calls `renderLabel()` for us, so we don't need to call it separately.

JavaScript variables

WaveMaker page code is standard JavaScript code executed in a Dojo environment. All the rules of JavaScript apply here. This means you can use JavaScript variables in your page code. JavaScript variables are simply any variable you declare; for example, the following stores the string `Success` in the variable named `result` and then logs the string `Success` to the console:

```
var result = "Success";
console.log(result);
```

JavaScript variables are useful for storing transient values — values that you don't want after the function is complete. For example, consider the following line of code:

```
var State = this.textState.getDataValue();
```

Here we get the text value the user entered into the `textState` editor and store it in a JavaScript variable named `State`. Let's see how even in simple cases there is benefit to using a local variable to store a value. Consider the following code:

```
var State = this.textState.getDataValue();
console.log(State);
```

If nothing further will be done with the `state` data value, it is just as easy and more succinct to perform this in a single line:

```
console.log(this.textState.getDataValue());
```

There is no functional difference between the two versions and readability is not impacted. However, if we check the value first, which is often advisable, the benefit of using a local variable becomes clearer:

```
var State = this.textState.getDataValue();
if(State!=""){
console.log(State);
}
```

The use of the JavaScript variable saves us the cost of having to get the value from the editor multiple times. It is more efficient to get the data value once and store it locally than to repeatedly fetch the data value from the editor. As an added benefit, the multi-line version provides more flexibility for setting debugger breakpoints.

wm.Variable

The other kind of client variable in WaveMaker is wm.Variable. A wm.Variable component is a non-visual component used for storing data values with type information. A key distinction between a JavaScript variable and wm.Variable is that wm.Variable is a component present in the project. This enables wm.Variable to be part of the project component tree and can be bound to other components, unlike a JavaScript variable.

Service variables and many other components contain or use wm.Variable components. Being objects, wm.Variable components have functions, including setData(), getData(), setValue(), and getValue().

To add a wm.Variable component to a project, choose **Variable** from the **Insert** menu:

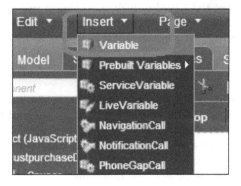

Upon creation, you will want to immediately specify a value for **type**, whether the variable is to be a list, and if we want to save the values in a cookie:

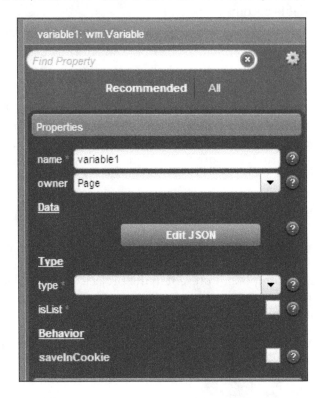

Saving the data in a cookie automatically creates a cookie and stores the variable's value in the cookie. This is ideal for small preference values, such as preferred language or country. Select the **saveInCookie** option to use this feature.

If you intend to store multiple instances of an object, select the **isList** property checkbox.

The **isList** feature lets you specify that the variable will contain a list prior to assigning a value, thus enabling you to bind the variable as an array. If you want to retain the **isList** property of wm.Variable but need to store a single value in the variable, use an array of a single element. For a `NumberData` type, we can set the data value to an array of a single number such as the following:

```
main.varPartNumbers.setValue("dataValue",[1242]);
```

Type mismatches will cause problems, so choose the type carefully. In addition to the project types, such as the database entity types, the type dropdown includes choices for simple types such as **EntryData**, **NumberData**, and **StringData**, as well as **PhoneGap** types such as **Address** and **Contact**:

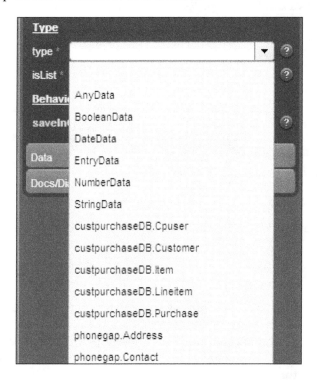

Using a wm.Variable component directly is no different than using wm.Variable embedded in service variables. With that said, direct access gives us "more rope with which we can hang ourselves", notably in the topic of our old friend: types. How one sets the data value of a wm.Variable component from code differs between simple and complex types. Examples of service variables returning primitive types include the security service getUserId() and getUserName() functions. Studio, with tooling such as the binding dialog, mostly absolves us of having to know there is a difference. Let's examine this in detail.

Simple types

Simple types are the "built-in" types including String, Number, and Boolean. In the **type** dropdown, these types are shown as **AnyData**, **BooleanData**, **DateData**, **EntryData**, **NumberData**, and **StringData**. These types lack the service name prefix of complex types.

When using a `wm.Variable` component of a simple type, use the `setValue()` and `getValue()` functions with `dataValue` as the first argument. For `setValue()`, the second argument is the new value. Let's see some examples:

- To get the values from a `wm.Variable` component of a simple type, call `getValue()` on `dataValue`:

  ```
  this.numVar.getValue("dataValue");
  ```

- Set a `wm.Variable` component of type `StringData` to the string `"Hello WaveMaker"`:

  ```
  this.stringVar.setValue("dataValue","Hello WaveMaker");
  ```

- Set a `wm.Variable` component of type `NumberData` that has **isList** checked to an array of integers:

  ```
  this.numVar.setValue("dataValue", [24,27,32,34]);
  ```

- Set a `wm.Variable` of type `DateData` to January 1, 2014:

  ```
  this.dateVar.setValue("dataValue",new Date("01/01/2014").
  getTime());
  ```

EntryData

Of the simple types, `EntryData` is among the shortlist of the most useful candidates. A `wm.Variable` component of type `EntryData` is a really easy way to drive a custom dataset for user choices, most commonly as a select menu. The select menu's `dataSet` property is set to the entry data variable. The entry data of the variable can be set statically at design time or dynamically at runtime, or both.

Of the various use cases, the easiest is setting static values in Studio using the **Edit JSON** button in the variable's **Properties** panel:

This brings up the **Edit JSON** dialog:

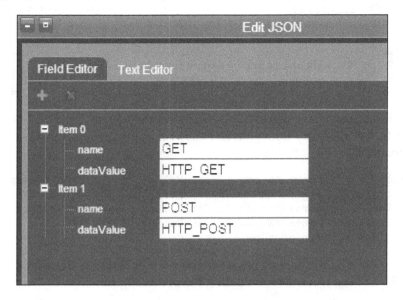

Here, we can add, remove, and edit entries using a simple but effective interface. Use the plus button to add, the cross button to remove, and the editors to edit an entry. It is that simple!

If we use the **Text Editor** tab, we'll have an editor in a dialog revealing the simple formula of EntryData data. The following is what we see for our HTTP method example:

```
[
    {
        "name": "GET",
        "dataValue": "HTTP_GET"
    },
    {
        "name": "POST",
        "dataValue": "HTTP_POST"
    }
]
```

Entry data is an array of objects. Each object in the array has a name and a dataValue value. That's all there is to it, an array of value-pair objects.

Syntactically, we have the outermost brackets of the array: `[ ]`. Within this array, we have objects: `[{},{},{},…]`. Each object has a name and a `dataValue` value: `{"name": "GET", "dataValue": "HTTP_GET"}`.

> The use of quotes around `name` and `dataValue` is optional with `EntryData`.

This is the same pattern we use to dynamically set the values. We simply pass a JSON structure of the entry data pattern to `setData()`. Consider the days of the week for example:

```
var jsonDoW = [{name: "Monday", dataValue: 1},{ name: "Tuesday",
dataValue: 2},{ name: "Wednesday", dataValue: 3},{ name: "Thursday",
dataValue: 4},{ name: "Friday", dataValue: 5},{ name: "Saturday",
dataValue: 6},{ name: "Sunday", dataValue: 7}];
this.varDoW.setData(jsonDoW);
```

If we have a select editor dataset bound to the `varDoW` variable, the select would show the days of the week after executing the preceding functions:

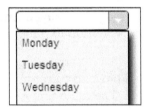

Complex types

Complex types are the entity and service types that comprise the project types. We first discussed project types in *Chapter 2, Digging into the Architecture*. The `Wm.Variable` components of complex types are easy to use. Use `setData()` and `getData()` to access the whole object and `setValue()` and `getValue()` to access individual fields of the object.

Consider a variable of the type `Customer` from the `custpurchase` database data model. We can set the value of the `customer` object variable by passing a JSON object, even a partial object, to `setData()`. In the following line of code, we call `setData()` with a partial `Customer` object:

```
this.varCustomer.setData({"city": "San Francisco","state": "CA"});
```

Or, we can set a single field of the customer type by using `setValue()`:

```
this.varCustomer.setValue("state","CA");
```

To learn more about using variables, see the variables page in the documentation at `http://dev.wavemaker.com/wiki/bin/wmdoc_6.5/Variables`.

Filters

Setting live variable filters using JavaScript can be troublesome for some developers. Filters are nothing more than a member `wm.Variable` named `filter`. This provides us with a few ways to manipulate filters.

The easiest way is to bind the live variable filter to a `wm.Variable` component and manipulate `wm.Variable` as we already have done. The type of `wm.Variable` must match the filter variable type. This means that we can filter on related objects; however, when we create the `wm.Variable` component, it must be for the related type, and we'll bind the related field to the `wm.Variable` component, not to the entire filter object.

Another option is to use `setFilter()`, passing a `wm.Variable` component as the parameter to `setFilter()`. Again, we are setting the desired values of the `wm.Variable` component as any other `wm.Variable`. Just be certain to update the `wm.Variable` values before calling `setFilter()`.

Finally, we can directly manipulate the filter variable using only JavaScript without binding:

```
this.filteredCustomerLiveVar.filter.setValue("company", this.
textCompany.getDataValue());
}
```

However, we choose to manipulate the filter values, as this can provide useful functionality. Consider the following search button click event handler function:

```
buttonSearchClick: function(inSender) {
//clear previous filter data
this.filteredCustomerLiveVar.filter.clearData();

//empty value for editors is empty string
    if(this.textState.getDataValue !== ""){
        this.filteredCustomerLiveVar.filter.setValue("state",
        this.textState.getDataValue());
    }
```

```
    if(this.textCompanyName !== "") {
        this.filteredCustomerLiveVar.filter.setValue("company",
        this.textCompany.getDataValue());
    }

        //AutoUpdate would fire on state if user set
       //both state and name
      //call update() here instead
      this.filteredCustomerLiveVar.update();
},
```

First, we clear the filter to ensure we don't have any leftover values by calling `clearData()` on the filter. Next, we check the editors for values. In this example, we set our editor's `emptyValue` property to an empty string. So, we check if the editor data value is an empty string. If it is not, we set the corresponding value of the filter. We do this for as many fields as we may have input for. Finally, we fire the live variable using `update()`. Note that we do not use auto update, as that would cause the live variable to fire immediately upon setting the first filter field that had a value, even if the user had set both `state` and `company`. This is yet another example of how not using auto update gives us better control over our data access.

For more examples of using and manipulating filters, visit `http://dev.wavemaker.com/wiki/bin/Dev/Filters`.

Resources

We've examined the building blocks of using custom JavaScript page code in a WaveMaker application. Unfortunately, being armed with this knowledge does not preclude you from staring at the flashing cursor of a source editor knowing what you want to do but having no idea of how to achieve it.

Fortunately, there is an array of resources available to us to help guide us to the desired syntax. Let's review our options.

The console

The Chrome Developer Tools console, and others such as Firebug, provides command-line completions. The console displays a dialog of possible completions. As shown in the following screenshot, we've entered `main.varCustomer.setD` and the console is showing us all the members of the main page's `varCustomer` object that start with `setD`:

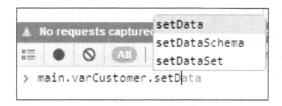

Completions are context-sensitive, meaning that when used in a breakpoint of page code, this refers to the current and inSender refers to the sending object it is the same context as page code. This can be an incredibly useful way to probe some return value or otherwise unknown object. Set a breakpoint or enter the debugger keyword in the function you need to figure out. When you get it working, you can often directly paste the code into the **Source** tab, as the context used for debugging is the same as runtime.

Trees

Open the model and services trees when in the source editor to see names and types when editing code. Expanding entities and operations will show you name and type information. In the following screenshot, we have expanded the **Customer** table so that we can reference its fields:

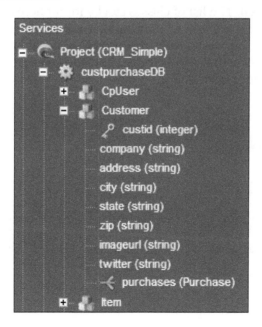

The model tree and the components tree are also useful to remember names, cases, and spelling.

Completions

The script **Source** tab also provides completions. Like the console completions, the **Script** tab filters to match partial entries. Double-click on an entry from the **Completions** list to add to it the cursor point in the code:

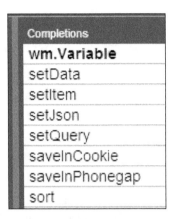

JS reference

We've seen the JavaScript client reference as the in-Studio help system. It can be useful on its own as well. The list of classes can be found here at `http://dev.wavemaker.com/wiki/bin/wmjsref_6.5/WebHome`. Each class has a page with sections for a synopsis, full description, direct methods, and links to parent class methods. Some pages even include examples and code snippets. The client reference is an excellent source for information.

JavaScript toString()

When in the Chrome console, the `toString()` function is a convenient way to view a function's implementation without finding the function in the sources. This works best when in debug mode. Without debug loading, all variables are shown as `_1c3` or other less-than-ideal names due to minification. In debug mode, calling `toString()` on a function displays the implementation of the function. As shown in the following screenshot, we've called `toString()` on a label's `setCaption()` function:

```
> main.label1.setCaption.toString()
  "function (inCaption) {
          if (inCaption == undefined) inCaption = "";
          var innerHTML = this.sizeNode.innerHTML;
          if (inCaption && dojo.isArray(inCaption)) {
              inCaption = inCaption.join(', ');
          } else if (inCaption && dojo.isObject(inCapti
              inCaption = "";
          }
          this.caption = inCaption;
          this.renderLabel();
          if (innerHTML != this.sizeNode.innerHTML && (
```

Source code

"In vino veritas" would be "in vino" and "code veritas" if the Romans had software. The WaveMaker source code is an excellent reference if you are comfortable with code and an ultimate reference for all others.

The most commonly referenced source for JavaScript developers is the WaveMaker classes in `/lib/wm/base` (`https://github.com/SpringSource/wavemaker/tree/master/wavemaker/wavemaker-studio/src/main/webapp/lib/wm/base`). As we first saw in *Chapter 2, Digging into the Architecture*, all the classes for the WaveMaker components are found in `/lib/wm/base`. If a new component lacks documentation, or we just need more information, being able to peek at the source code can be very informative.

Summary

We have just completed our first tour of using JavaScript to customize WaveMaker applications. We started with events. The custom JavaScript we write in our application is invoked in response to events. When working with server response data, we must always wait until the `onSuccess` or `onResult` events to ensure the service call has returned.

We also studied `wm.Variable`, the non-visual variable component. Unlike JavaScript variables, `wm.Variable` can be bound to other components and manipulated via code. We can use `wm.Variable` to customize widget datasets and filter live variables. Finally, we looked at the references available to use. From the API reference to the completions available to us in Studio and the console, there are multiple ways to learn more.

In the next chapter, we will continue our use of JavaScript to customize the user experience. We'll look at some advanced techniques such as creating components at runtime. We will also discuss examples of common operations such as forming display expressions for grid columns and manipulating live form values.

11
Mastering Client Customization

Now that we have a better understanding of the basics of working with JavaScript in the client, let's continue to explore customizing the client-side user interface. In this chapter we will focus on custom client code.

We will begin with formatters, expressions, and validation. These areas all have some tooling that can be used to provide simple customization. When the tooled options do not meet our needs, custom code can be utilized to achieve the desired results. In order to provide more practical examples, we will use examples utilizing labels, grids, and forms.

This does not preclude the application of these examples to other use cases. WaveMaker has done well to keep the number of runtime-specific syntactical patterns, which the users need to know, to a minimum. In the page code, the view is page-centric. The current page can be referenced using the `this` pointer. Other than what has been passed in as a function argument, anything we need is obtainable from the page or the app (which is `app` or `this.app`). In expressions, display, or binding, the context is not the page. Expressions are part of the widget definition, and thus exist in the widgets file, for example, `Main.widgets.js`. In expressions, `this` refers to the window, and we use the dollar-and-braces `${}` syntax to access values. The runtime evaluates the value of the expression and can be used for everything from `${main. nameEditor.getDataValue()}` for the data value of an editor to `${twitter}` for the value of another field in the row data. Being mindful of these two execution contexts reduces the number of "rules" you need to know to a minimum.

No discussion of mastering client customization would be complete without addressing dynamic content. As such, we will conclude this chapter with examples of both adding components to the page and rearranging those components at runtime.

The sample project for this chapter is named MasteringClientCustomization and can be found at https://github.com/edwardcallahan/Easy-Web-Samples/tree/master/projects/MasteringClientCustomization.

Formatters

The graphical tooling provided by Studio for formatting handles the proverbial 80 percent of situations with relative ease. Got a grid column that has currency values such as a price? In the **Grid Designer** section, set the value of the **Format** dropdown to Currency. The editors for **Currency Type**, **Digits**, and **Round** are then made available for configuration:

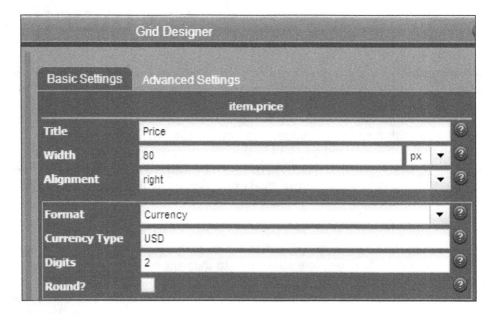

 Unlike dates and numbers, monetary values rarely should be localized. **Currency Type** should be specified to avoid any potential localization of monetary values.

Setting a value for the label's **Format** dropdown to DateTime adds editors for options including data and time patterns in a similar manner. Of particular interest is a checkbox for **useLocalTime**:

useLocalTime

If the component is sending/receiving date and/or time values to the server that could have been written or could be read by clients in other time zones, **useLocalTime** handles time zone conversions for you. Users will see points in time as dates and time using the time zone indicated by the browser, while all values sent to the server will be sent in the time zone of the server's JVM. Use of a single time zone on the server side ensures that clients in differing time zones are given consistent points in time.

WaveMaker transports date, time, and date-time values between the client and the server in UNIX time (http://en.wikipedia.org/wiki/Unix_time). **UNIX time** is the number of seconds that have elapsed since a specific single point in time. Except in special cases, users want to see dates and times expressed as a date and time value, not as a large numeric value. An invitation for September 30th, 2013 at 2 P.M. EDT is far more meaningful to users than 1380564000. The **useLocalTime** feature uses the server's time zone for transporting values in a consistent offset while using the browser's settings for user local display values. Any component reading and writing date and time values should use the local time unless time zone offset conversions are being handled elsewhere.

Custom Function

For the other 20 percent of use cases, we use **Custom Function**:

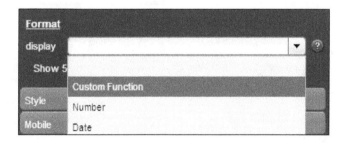

Selecting **Custom Function** inserts an empty format function to the page. From this page function, we return the formatted value however we wish it to be, including the use of HTML tags. We don't even need to use the value passed to us if we don't want to. In the following example, we create a custom message for a label caption using a JavaScript date object:

```
loadTimeLabelReadOnlyNodeFormat: function(inSender, inValue) {
var now = new Date();
return("Application loaded at: " + now.toLocaleTimeString() +    " on
" + now.toLocaleDateString());
},
```

As this particular label's caption is only set during the application's initialization, it is functionally equivalent to setting the label caption from the page start function.

 Studio does not update the format display's function name when the component name changes in the same way JavaScript event functions are updated. If you change the name of the component, the page function name will not be updated. Reselect **Custom Function** from the dropdown and move your code into the new function to keep your function names up-to-date. Don't forget to clean up the old function if you are done with it.

The online documentation for formatters can be found at `http://dev.wavemaker. com/wiki/bin/wmdoc_6.5/Formatting+Data`.

DojoGrid

Grids are an ideal widget for displaying lists of multi-column data. This results in many customization needs. In earlier versions of WaveMaker, advanced grid customization required using page functions that were called when each row of data was rendered. Now, all needs can be obtained using **Grid Designer**, accessed using either the **Edit Columns** button in the grid's properties or **Edit Columns** from the menu brought up by right-clicking in the grid on the canvas, as shown in the following screenshot:

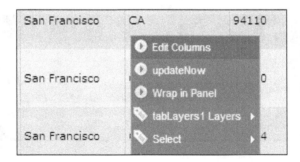

We saw earlier how the **Grid Designer** dialog allowed us to set formatters for columns. The **Grid Designer** dialog is where we control the details of how the contents of the grid are displayed, including display expressions and custom columns.

Display expressions

We first saw display expressions way back in the WaveyWeb Department tab, where we had a label displaying the name of the selected customer:

```
"Viewing " + ${departmentDojoGrid.selectedItem.name}
```

Building a display expression for a grid column also uses the dollar-braces syntax. Other fields of the row data can be accessed using the `${}` syntax on fieldnames. If our grid has a column for `firstName` and another for `lastName`, we could concatenate these two row values into a single-cell entry with a space separator using the `${firstName} + " " +${lastName}` expression.

Further details and examples of using the dollar-brace syntax and binding expressions can be found at `http://dev.wavemaker.com/wiki/bin/wmdoc_6.5/Binding+Expressions+Display+Expressions`.

Custom columns

The left part of the **Grid Designer** dialog lets us control what column is shown where, including the addition of new custom columns with the use of the **Add** button in the lower-left corner of the dialog, as shown in the following screenshot:

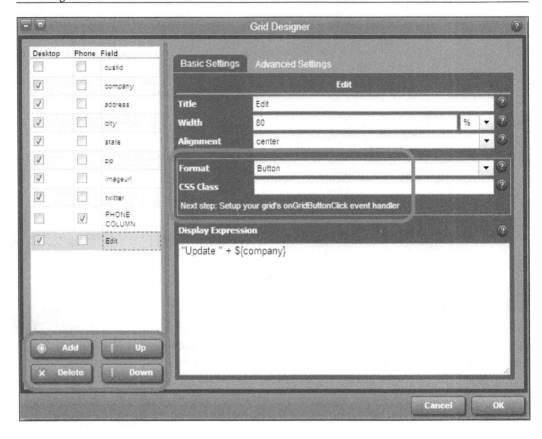

With the custom column added to the layout, we use the right-hand side section of the dialog to set the column properties. In the preceding screenshot, we have added a button column by choosing `Button` for **Format**. We have set a display expression that will be the button's label. It simply prepends `"Update "` to the company name, being certain to leave a space to go before the company name value for the row. This dialog does not handle events, so it reminds us that the button action must be configured using the grid's **onGridButtonClick** event handler.

In our example, the grid button click event navigates the user to the customer-editing layer and sets the form to update the mode by calling `beginDataUpdate()` on the form:

```
customerDojoGrid1GridButtonClick: function(inSender, fieldName,
rowData, rowIndex) {
        inSender.setSelectedRow(rowIndex);
        this.customerEditLiveForm1.beginDataUpdate();
        this.layer3.activate();
},
```

Note that the event must first set the selected row index of the grid, `inSender`, for the `customerEditLiveForm1` binding on the grid-selected item to work. This is because the button DOM node click event does not result in a grid row selection, only the button click.

LiveForm

Live form customization encapsulates all of the formatting, validation, and styling of its child components as well as the events and functions of the resultant data object's interactions with the rest of the application. There are many methods and properties to a live form. The client API reference for live forms (`http://dev.wavemaker.com/wiki/bin/wmjsref_6.5/LiveForm`) is a good reference for live form methods and properties.

There are a few things one should keep in mind when working with live forms. First, they have their own live variables. This is why live forms have their own success and error event handlers. Those are the embedded live variable's events. There is one live variable for a form and its operation is toggled among read, update, insert, and delete operations as needed. Be careful to check the live form operation on your page code if the event is called for multiple operations.

Second, a form's state is controlled by the form, not the **Edit** panel. In our **Update Customer** button in a previous grid example, we used `beingDataUpate()` to save the user from having to press the **Update** button after we navigated them to the customer edit layer:

```
this.customerEditLiveForm1.beginDataUpdate();
```

Use these methods instead of calling the click events of the buttons on the **Edit** panel.

By default, the **Edit** panel of a live form is locked. This prevents Studio from opening the children of the locked components. It reminds us that we generally don't edit the **Edit** buttons directly. There are a few cases were you would want to unlock a component. To do so, clear the **lock** checkbox to inspect the children of a locked component.

Last, but just as important, is that live forms have a `DataOutput` object that contains the data values of all the form's editors. It is the `DataOutput` object that you are nearly always using in bindings, and it is the `DataOutput` object you almost always would want to be working with in code. However, sometimes, when working with `DataOutput` in code, you will need to call `populateDataoutput()` on the form in order to trigger the process of populating the object. If the `DataOutput` object is empty or out-of-date, you just might need to trigger the population with `populateDataOutput()`.

While primarily being a layout widget, panels also provide some consolidation of child states that can be quite handy at times. Live panels inherit these states from the container. One can specify an action for the *Enter* key while the panel has focus by using the `onEnterKeyPress` event. Using the bindable `invalid` and `isDirty` properties of containers are easy ways to know if any component in a panel is invalid or has been modified, respectively.

> Got an invalid container but don't know what widget is invalid? Use the `getInvalidWidget()` container method. It reports out the invalid widgets.

Validation

Validation may best be used at the container level, but it is set on the widget level. The majority of validations can be set using properties. Enabling the required property of a widget is the simplest form of validation; the user must provide a value. Numeric editors, including date and time editors have minimum and maximum properties. User-entered values outside of these ranges will cause the editor and it's container to be invalid.

String editors can use regular expressions (`http://en.wikipedia.org/wiki/Regular_expression`), better known as regexp, to evaluate values. If the regular expression matches, the string is considered valid. In the customer **Edit** tab, the URL editor uses the following simple regexp to ensure the user has entered an HTTP or file URL:

```
^(https?|file)://.+$
```

Volumes have been written about regexp, and almost all common expressions can be looked up.

There are cases were you will need to use events such as onChange to get full custom validation; for example, if you needed to compare a user-entered date and time using a wm.DateTime widget against some restricted, or otherwise, some special date. A good example is of the DateTime widget because its onChange event will be called when the date or the time changes. This means the event handler function can be called before the user has had a chance to set both values.

The select menu widgets have a validation property that no other type of editor possesses—**restrictValues**:

The **restrictValues** property, enabled by default, allows the user to only select among the entries in the editor's dataset. Removing this restriction enables a user to enter a new value into the editor such as a text editor, in addition to choosing a value from the dataset. Such an entry can be used for allowing the user to initiate a new related object when using a related editor, for example. When the user enters an unrestricted value entry, the data value of the editor will be the same as the display value—whatever the user entered. This will be true despite the dataField property setting.

onBeforeServiceCall

The last chance for live form data modification or validation before data is sent to the server is the beforeServiceCall event. From a live form beforeServiceCall page function, you can perform either of the following two operations:

- Throw an "Abort" error
- Let the operation continue to the server

Let's look at the example used on the customer **Edit** tab of the example application:

```
customerEditLiveForm1BeforeServiceCall: function(inSender,
inOperation, inData) {
        if(inData.zip.toString().length!=5){
            //Tell the user what's going on
            app.toastError("Zip code must be 5 digits only");
            //Must be error of "Abort" to stop service call
            throw new Error("Abort");
        }
},
```

In the `customerEditLiveForm1BeforeServiceCall()` function, we use the `inData` parameter to access the members of the data output and check the length of the zip code. If the length is not five, it raises an error toast to tell the user what went wrong and throws an `Abort` error to prevent the server call from occurring. Only an error of `Abort` will stop the server call.

Dynamic page content

Creating new widgets or rearranging the layout of widgets at runtime is the AJAX version of dynamic content. The two key functions to unlock such magic are `createComponent()` and `reflow()`.

Reflow

Reflow tells the layout engine to re-render the specified container. This is required after adding components to the container or adjusting the layout of the components of the container. The `reflowParent()` helper function can be used to reflow the parent container without having to lookup the parent. Consider the example presented on the **Dynamic Content** tab of this chapter's sample application, `MasteringClientCustomization`:

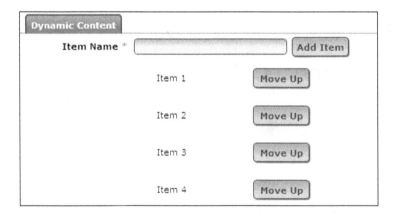

Each **Move Up** button shares the `upButtonClick()` function for its `onClick()` event:

```
upButtonClick: function(inSender) {
  try {
      var thisControl = inSender.parent;
      var newIndex = thisControl.parent.indexOfControl
      (thisControl) - 1;
      if (newIndex >= 0) {
```

```
        thisControl.parent.moveControl(thisControl,(newIndex));
        thisControl.reflowParent();
      }
  } catch(e) {
      console.error('ERROR IN upButtonClick: ' + e);
      }
  },
```

When the user clicks on a **Move Up** button at runtime, the index of the control of the panel, which is also the button's parent, is decremented by one with its parent. If the panel was not already at the top of the list, the new control index, `newIndex`, is at least zero. The `moveControl()` function is used to set the new order. This changes the layout of the children within `itemsListPanel`, but the user does not see this change until the call to `reflowParent()`.

createComponent()

Creating new components at runtime is achieved by using the `createComponent()` component function. The signature for `createComponent()` is:

```
parentWidget.createComponent(inName, inType, inProps, inEvents,
inChildren, inOwner);
```

The simplest use of createComponent() is to specify only a name and a type:

```
this.createComponent("myButton", "wm.Button");
```

This creates a new button named myButton. This call would need to be followed by a call to this.reflowParent() to render the newly minted button.

The `AddItemButtonClick` event handler demonstrates the full use of `createComponent()` by adding a new panel with a label and button inside of it, including event connections. First, we asked the user for the new item name. This name is then used to construct names for the panel, label, button, as well as the label caption. After the call to `createComponent()`, `reflow()` is used to render the new panel and its children:

```
AddItemBttonClick: function(inSender) {
  var name = this.newItemtext.getDataValue();
  //component names will auto increment if duplicated
  var panelName = "panel" + name;
  var labelName = "label" + name;
  var caption = "Item " + name;
```

```
    var buttonName = "button" + name;
    this.ItemListPanel.createComponent(panelName,    "wm.Panel",{"heig
ht":"46px","horizontalAlign":"center","layoutKind":"left-to-right"
,"verticalAlign":"middle","width":"100%"}, {}, {
    labelName: ["wm.Label", {"align":"center","caption":caption,"paddi
ng":"4"}, {}],
    upButtonName: ["wm.Button", {"caption":"Move Up","margin":"4"},
{"onclick":"upButtonClick"}]
    });
    this.ItemListPanel.reflow();
    },
```

Let's quickly dissect the call to the createComponent() function. The first parameter is the name, for which we used our freshly concatenated panelName variable. Next is the type, which is simply wm.Panel, the type of the component we want to create. The properties, events, and the children are copied and pasted from the widgets file except for the custom names. The default owner is used.

As we are duplicating the panels already added by Studio, we can use the definitions Studio used in the widgets file for everything but the component names. This should come as no surprise, as we know that WaveMaker itself uses the widgets definition to render the layout we defined at design time.

Further information about createComponent() is available by visiting the advanced section of the customizing applications with JavaScript page of the documentation: http://dev.wavemaker.com/wiki/bin/wmdoc_6.5/CustomizeAppsWithJS#HCrea tingWidgetsatRuntime28advanced29.

Custom components

It is possible to define your component types within projects. Custom and composite components can be added to the palette for use with `createComponent()`. Custom widgets are single custom widgets and composites are pages turned into widgets.

A simple example of a custom widget can be found in the `common/packages/example` folder of the WaveMaker home folder. It is a button that changes color and cursor during mouse-over movements using pre-connected `mouseout` and `mouseover` events called `myButton.js`. By extending the `wm.Button` type, `myButton` inherits the functionality of a button, so it only needs to add the calls to connect and the page functions that would otherwise go in page code. Information about building custom components can be found at `http://dev.wavemaker.com/wiki/bin/wmdoc_6.5/Custom+Components`.

The composite mechanism available in WaveMaker 6.5 is limiting and will not be covered here. A new mechanism has been introduced with WaveMaker 6.6. For information on 6.5 composites, see `http://dev.wavemaker.com/wiki/bin/wmdoc_6.5/Creating+Composites`; for 6.6 composites, see `http://dev.wavemaker.com/wiki/bin/wmdoc_6.6/Advanced+Composites+Tutorial`.

Summary

In this chapter we have examined advanced topics in client customization with a focus on JavaScript code and expressions. The tooling for formatting and validation can handle many common needs. For anything not achievable with those methods, custom expressions or functions can be used. The good news for developers is that while there are many areas one can specify such creatures, all expressions and all page functions share the same syntax and context.

We discussed functions, events, and properties of significant importance to customization along the way. The `dataOutput` object and `onBeforeServiceCall` event of live forms are of common use in live form validation. We also spent some time with the **Grid Designer** dialog, in which we specify everything about the presentation of the grid contents from display expressions to custom columns.

Finally, we looked at how we can have dynamic page content using `createComponent()` and `reflow()`. `CreateComponent()` allows us to add components to a container at runtime, while `reflow()` re-renders the layout of the container. For even more customization, custom and composite components enable developers to define components with built-in customizations.

In the next chapter, we will discuss securing our application. Readers will gain an understanding of how authentication works in WaveMaker and the authorization features available to developers. We will enable security on a project and examine customizations of the server-side security role filters as well as use Java for additional server-side enforcements.

12
Securing Applications

We have been discussing how to develop rich web applications using WaveMaker Studio. Before we deploy any application out into the wild, we must ensure that our application is secure. The application must not allow users, malicious or otherwise, to gain inappropriate access to data. In this chapter, we will learn how to secure WaveMaker applications.

WaveMaker security tooling provides for both authentication and authorization strategies. Authentication is the process of verifying the authenticity of the user's identity. Authorization is the function of determining what services, components, and capabilities the user is authorized to access. In WaveMaker, authentication is achieved by logging in to the application using a username and password combination. The username and password are compared to the stored values in an authentication source, such as a database or **Lightweight Directory Access Protocol (LDAP)**. Once the user is authenticated, the groups that the user belongs to are mapped into the user's roles. Authorization is done by role, and thus is referred to as **Role Based Access Control (RBAC)**.

We will begin with how security works and how to setup security in WaveMaker applications. We'll examine the security tooling within Studio from which we can configure the demo, database, or LDAP source, as well as user roles and service access control. We'll discuss the security service, its functions, and how to properly use roles to secure access to server resources while customizing the user interface to match the users' permissions. WaveMaker's built-in multitenant isolation feature will also be covered.

With an understanding of the tooled security options, we'll learn how we can edit the `project-security.xml` file to customize our server-side role-based access control. No discussion of security would be complete without discussing the risks introduced by exposing the runtime service as well as techniques for addressing those risks. We'll end the chapter with a few words about troubleshooting security issues.

The example application for this chapter is called `SecureDbAccess` and can be found in the example project repository at `https://github.com/edwardcallahan/Easy-Web-Samples/tree/master/projects/SecureDbAccess`.

Security in WaveMaker

As discussed in *Chapter 10, Customizing the User Interface with JavaScript*, the browser cannot be trusted. Even if we are able to completely lock down the browser, the service endpoints would still require securing against falsified XHR network requests. Therefore, it is the authorization of access to services on the server that is the foundation of security in an application.

WaveMaker uses Acegi Security, which is now Spring Security (`http://static.springsource.org/spring-security/site/`), for request authorization. When security is enabled, every request received by the server is subjected to a chain of filters, or checks, before it is serviced. If an unauthenticated user requests access to a restricted resource, the user is redirected to the login page for authentication. Upon successful authentication, the original request is continued. Other filters may restrict access to service operations by role. If the requesting user has been authenticated but lacks the required group membership needed to access the resource, the request will be returned HTTP 403, access denied.

WaveMaker 6.6 upgrades the security subsystem from Acegi Security 1.0.7 to Spring Security 3.1.x. In this chapter, we will only be discussing the use of the Acegi Security tooled by WaveMaker 6.5.x.

Configuring security

To enable security on a project, choose **Security** from the **Services** menu. Select from **Demo**, **Database**, or **LDAP** from the **Security Provider** dropdown and check the **Enable Security** check-box. Don't forget to save the settings after configuring security.

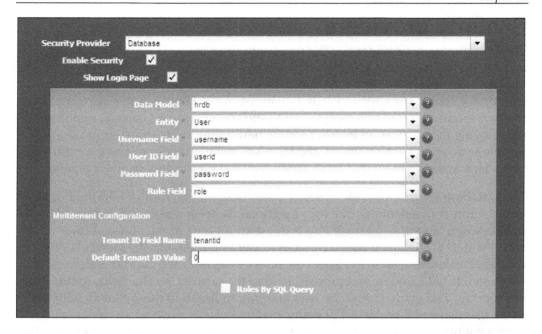

Enabling security copies the default login page into the project. The default login page is fully functional and can be customized by editing the page in Studio. Simply open the page just like any other project page.

When you check the **Show Login Page** checkbox, users will not be able to access the application without having an active login session. If they do not have a session, they are directed to the login page and prompted for credentials. If you do not use the **Show Login Page** option, users will be able to anonymously access the application, but all service calls will fail until authenticated. In this use case, a custom login such as a dialog can be shown to enable the user to authenticate. A pre-built login service variable is available from the **Insert | Advanced** menu in Studio by choosing the **Login Variable** menu item. To disable all security restrictions in a project, clear the **Enable Security** check-box and save the project.

 Both login.html and index.html create new instances of the application. This means variables and all other application data cannot be passed between pages as one can within a single instance of an application. If you want to pass data from the login page to the application, save the data in wm.Variable and use the saveInCookie feature.

Security providers

The **Demo** security provider enables you to specify a static username, password, and roles. The credentials specified here are stored directly in the project's `project-security.xml` file. This makes **Demo** security quick and easy to set up and use for simple situations such as a demonstration. However, this also means that any modification to this configuration, such as a password change, requires redeploying the application in order for the new values in the `project-security.xml` file to be read. For this reason, the **Demo** security provider can be very difficult to manage in deployment and is not recommended for production deployments.

The **Database** security provider utilizes a user entity table from an imported data model entity for credentials. The user **Entity** can be from a user account-specific database or a table of a database also being used for data in the project. Either way, the data model must have been previously imported into the project before configuring database security. Select the data model with the user table from the available data models and proceed to map the security service fields to the appropriate data entity fields. The user account information must contain both the user's username and password in a single table. Roles, however, can be obtained from a column in the user table or from a related table by enabling the **Roles By SQL Query** option.

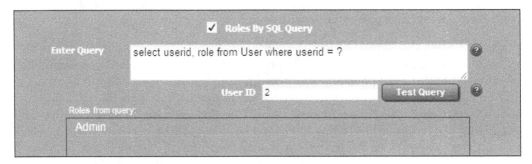

The SQL query used for obtaining roles must return both the user ID and the role based on the user ID, returning the ID first. Remember that this is a SQL query, not HQL.

LDAP is a protocol for accessing directory information services. A variety of LDAP servers, including Microsoft's Active Directory, can be used with the **LDAP** option. Of the three tooled providers, LDAP is the most secure. Stored passwords should always be salted and hashed, which LDAP servers support. The **LDAP URL** should use HTTPs for secure communication between the server and the LDAP server whenever the LDAP server supports SSL. Furthermore, unlike database security, using LDAP as the provider does not expose the user records to possible access via the runtime service, which we will discuss later in this chapter.

For those who are unfamiliar with LDAP, the greatest challenge in using LDAP for security is often due to a lack of knowledge of the LDAP server structure and schema. While there are a few common schemas in use, an LDAP server could be using any one of them, or even a custom schema. If you are unsure of the correct mapping for your LDAP server, a LDAP browsing tool such as the free LDAP Browser by Softerra, `http://www.ldapbrowser.com/download.htm`, can be very helpful in gaining visibility into the LDAP structure. An example of LDAP configuration is shown in the following screenshot:

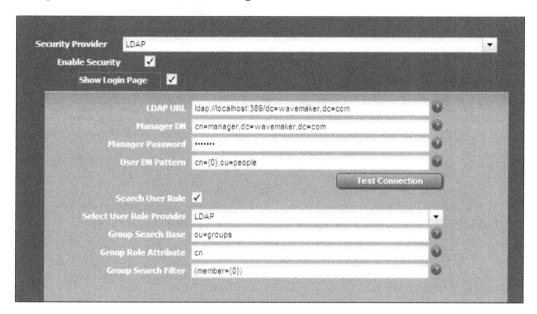

These values are common ones, but may not match any given server. The editor's `helpText` include common values. A sample of a valid **User Distinguished Name (DN)** can also be helpful for determining the correct **User DN Pattern** to use.

The **Manager DN** and **Manager Password** are only used for testing the connection with the **Test Connection** button. You do not need to enter or save manager credentials if you do not wish to.

The LDAP provider option has a special option that allows you to obtain role information from a database instead of using group membership from the LDAP. This is a useful feature when authenticating against a centralized LDAP server, but the application has role membership requirements that cannot be represented in the LDAP groups. To use this option, choose **Database** from the **Select User Role Provider** instead of **LDAP** and perform the same field mapping one would use for database provider configuration.

The tooled LDAP support in WaveMaker 6.5 cannot be used to search multiple branches of a large LDAP structure. The **User DN Pattern** must specify the **Organizational Unit (OU)** relative to the base **LDAP URL** that directly contains the users. Searches for user DNs across multiple OUs can however be obtained by hand editing `project-security.xml`.

> Use the Studio security tooling before you make any manual edits to `project-security.xml`. Use Studio to configure as much of the security configuration as possible first. Studio's security tooling may not retain any manual edits you make to `project-security.xml`.

To enable multi-OU search, first use the **Security** panel to configure the first **User DN Pattern**. Next, open `project-security.xml` in an editor and find the `ldapAuthProvider` bean's `userDNPatterns` property. You will see that it already contains the first OU pattern entered via Studio. As `userDnPatterns` is already a list, we only need to add our additional entries to the list. We have added two additional `userDnPatterns` properties to be searched for a total of three values:

```xml
<bean class="org.acegisecurity.providers.ldap.
LdapAuthenticationProvider" id="ldapAuthProvider">
    <constructor-arg>
    <bean class="org.acegisecurity.providers.ldap.authenticator.
BindAuthenticator">
        <constructor-arg>
            <ref local="initialDirContextFactory"/>
        </constructor-arg>
        <property name="userDnPatterns">
            <list>
                <value>cn={0},ou=Users,ou=Scala</value>
                <value>cn={0},ou=Users,ou=Akka</value>
            <value>cn={0},ou=Users,ou=Play</value>
            </list>
        </property>
    </bean>
    </constructor-arg>
```

> Anytime we edit a project XML configuration file outside of Studio, the application must be redeployed for the changes to take effect. Studio's **Run** button is a simple way to redeploy the app.

Roles

Roles in WaveMaker are determined by group membership. If a user is a member of the `admin` group, that user has the `admin` role. On the **Roles** tab of the security editor, enter the names of all the roles that the application is to use for authorization. All of the user's group memberships from the security source will be returned by the `getUserRoles()` method; however, tooled role-based access can only be performed on roles specified in the security configuration roles list:

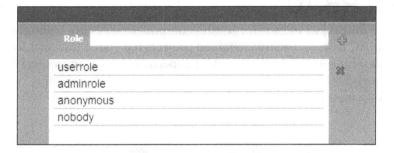

The roles specified in the roles list must match exactly as returned from the security provider in order for users to be successfully authorized. With the project roles defined, you can use these roles to define service access and component visibility.

Setup Services

Project roles are also shown in the **Who can access** drop-down lists of the **Setup Services** tab. When you first enable security in a project, all services are set to require authentication for access. This means any logged-in user can call any service, but you must be logged in.

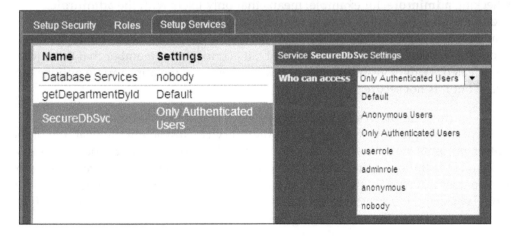

The **Setup Services** tab allows you to customize service accessibility by role. This enables you to quickly open up a service for anonymous access or lock-down access to a service to administrators only. In the example project, a **nobody** role has been added to the project roles. The **nobody** group has been specified for access to **Database Services**. As **nobody** is a dummy group with no members, this disables access to databases via the runtime service.

Widget RBAC

The other use for project roles is for setting component visibility using the client-side RBAC feature. Security-enabled projects have an additional **Roles** property group for each widget in the **All** properties of the **Component Property Inspector** panel. This enables developers to easily control the visibility of a widget based on group membership:

Checking **adminrole**, for example, means that only users with the **adminrole** group membership will be able to see the widget. This is client-side functionality that effectively controls the showing property of a widget based on the logged-in users' roles. Being client-side functionality, it is critical to remember that this can be defeated. Widget visibility is a great way to provide the appropriate options for users, but it is not secure.

Consider the example of a button that navigates a user to an administration page or invokes an operation in an administration service. Restricting the visibility of the button presents the proper interface to the user. The user does not expect to be able to invoke the button as the button has been hidden from view. However, hiding the button does not prevent the user from invoking the button's onClick event directly from JavaScript. It is critical to enforce the role restriction server-side, commonly by restricting access to the service using **Setup Services**.

Multitenancy

Multitenancy is a feature of database security that enables the ability to serve multiple organizational clients, a.k.a. tenants, from a single instance of a web application. Multitenancy reduces deployment overhead by allowing multiple customers to share infrastructure while keeping tenant data segmented.

There are multiple ways to provide multitenancy. The WaveMaker implementation uses the data access layers of the WaveMaker runtime to isolate all data access by the tenant ID stored in a tentant ID column in the user's login table entry.

To use the multitenancy feature, each database table that is to be restricted by tenant ID must have an integer type column for the tenant ID. All tenant column names must be exactly the same throughout the database schema. The tenant ID column name is specified in the database security configuration panel as the **Tenant ID Field Name**:

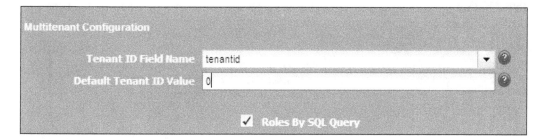

With this enabled, WaveMaker will restrict all database access operations with a `where tenanted = ?` clause, thus preventing users from reading or writing other tenants, data.

To learn more about multitenancy in WaveMaker, visit `http://dev.wavemaker. com/wiki/bin/wmdoc_6.5/Multitenancy`.

The security service

The security service is added to the project upon first enabling security, and it provisions five functions that can be invoked with service variables or from custom Java for additional functionality. Those functions are:

- `getUserId()`
- `getUserName()`
- `getUserRoles()`
- `isAuthenticated()`
- `logout()`

A common use case for `getUserName()` is displaying the returned username as a welcome message. Additional user information, such as additional user table fields or LDAP attributes, is not accessible through the security service. If we need access to such data, `getUserId()` is a good way to obtain the user's ID as a key for further attribute querying.

> If invoking security service functions client-side, be certain to wait until `getUserId()` has returned before using its return value as input to additional queries by using the `onsuccess` event of any service variables.

Customizing the configuration

There are numerous additional customizations that can be made to the security configuration by editing the `project-security.xml` file in an editor outside of Studio.

> The tooling of the security configuration panel is not able to maintain all customizations made by manually editing `project-security.xml`. If you choose to edit `project-security.xml` outside of Studio, subsequent use of the security panel to save changes may overwrite any externally made customizations. It is recommended to keep such customized projects under version control.

URL access

In Studio, we use the **Setup Services** tab to customize access to services. **Setup Services** works by modifying the `objectDefinitionSource` properties of the `filterSecurityInterceptor` bean of the `project-security.xml` file. By manually editing the same `objectDefinitionSource` property, we can restrict access to resources beyond services by role.

The following code gives a full `filterSecurityInterceptor` bean definition:

```
<bean class="com.wavemaker.runtime.security.
WMFilterSecurityInterceptor" id="filterSecurityInterceptor">
        <property name="authenticationManager">
            <ref bean="authenticationManager"/>
        </property>
        <property name="accessDecisionManager">
            <ref bean="accessDecisionManager"/>
        </property>
        <property name="objectDefinitionSource">
            <value>
                CONVERT_URL_TO_LOWERCASE_BEFORE_COMPARISON
                PATTERN_TYPE_APACHE_ANT
                /services/runtimeservice.json=ROLE_nobody
                /services/securedbsvc.json=IS_AUTHENTICATED_FULLY
                /services/custpurchasedb.json=ROLE_nobody
                /services/hrdb.json=ROLE_nobody
                /*.upload=IS_AUTHENTICATED_FULLY
                /*.download=IS_AUTHENTICATED_FULLY
                /index.html=IS_AUTHENTICATED_FULLY
                /=IS_AUTHENTICATED_FULLY
                /securityservice.json=IS_AUTHENTICATED_ANONYMOUSLY
                /pages/login/**=IS_AUTHENTICATED_ANONYMOUSLY
                /pages/**=IS_AUTHENTICATED_FULLY
                /*.json=IS_AUTHENTICATED_FULLY
                /*/*.json=IS_AUTHENTICATED_FULLY
            </value>
        </property>
    </bean>
```

This URL filter list is evaluated from top to bottom. As each request comes in, it is evaluated against the list of rules and the first matching rule is applied. We know from the **Network** tab of the Chrome Developer Tools that requests to the runtime service are sent to `runtimeService.json`. As all requests are relative to `webapproot`, the **Request URL** in the example is `http://localhost:8094/SecureDbAccess/services/runtimeService.json`:

In our example project, we disabled access to the runtime service by restricting access to those in the **nobody** group; a group with no members. By doing so, Studio added to `project-security.xml` the highlighted filter property rule `/services/runtimeservice.json=ROLE_nobody` from the previous code.

In the example of the runtime service, the first rule of the list matches, so the rule is applied and no further URL patterns are evaluated. The rule dictates that only members of the group `nobody` can invoke that URL. As `nobody` is a member of that group, access is denied and with the 403 error, we see the previous results.

Now we start to encounter some of the details that the **Setup Services** tab absolved us from having to be aware of. First, you will notice that the first two directives of the `objectDefinitionSource` properties dictate that URL's will be in lowercase (`CONVERT_URL_TO_LOWERCASE_BEFORE_COMPARISON`) and that an ant pattern will be used (`PATTERN_TYPE_APACHE_ANT`). This requires that all URLs be defined in lowercase only as URLs will be converted to lowercase for matching. Inclusion of a capital letter in the URL will result in the project failing to deploy and an error message will appear in the logfile. For example, if we added a filter rule for `/pages/AdminPage` instead of the lowercase converted `/pages/adminPage`, the project would fail to deploy with the following error:

```
Caused by: java.lang.IllegalArgumentException: You are using
the CONVERT_URL_TO_LOWERCASE_BEFORE_COMPARISON with Ant Paths,
yet you have specified an uppercase character in line: /pages/
AdminPage/**=ROLE_adminrole (character 'A')
```

Additionally, within patterns, ant patterns will be used. Ant patterns for inclusion and exclusion are similar to those used in LINUX and Windows. For example, `*.java` matches all files with the `.java` extension, and `/pages/**/*.html` matches all HTML files anywhere under the pages folder. See the "patterns" section of `https://ant.apache.org/manual/dirtasks.html` for more details and examples of ant patterns.

Finally, the role prefix `ROLE_` is specified further down the configuration file:

```
<property name="rolePrefix">
    <value>ROLE_</value>
</property>
```

This dictates that all roles will be prefixed with `ROLE_` within the configuration. This means that we must prefix the role name with `ROLE_` in the XML meaning we end up with the rule `/services/runtimeservice.json=ROLE_nobody`.

Page access control

Let's apply our understanding of the `filterSecurityInterceptor` bean to restrict access to a page. Our example application includes a page name: `AdminPage`. If this page contained functionality, only administrators should be able to access, we could add a custom rule to `objectDefinitionSource` that prevents anyone but members of the `adminrole` group from seeing this page.

It is important to remember that URLs are evaluated top-down. This means that we need to be careful about the placement of a rule, particularly when working with wildcards. For example, Studio placement of the `*.json` pattern last in the list causes it to be a catch-all rule for when no specific service access rule was specified. Yet putting `*.json` first in the list would cause any subsequent service access rules to be ignored.

In the case of pages, Studio has already nicely grouped the page rules together with rules to make the login page available to anyone anonymously, but all other pages require authentication. If we put our `AdminPage` rule after the all page's `/pages/**` rule, the all page's wildcard rule would match first and our directive would be ignored. We will place our custom rule in-between the login page and all pages:

```
/pages/login/**=IS_AUTHENTICATED_ANONYMOUSLY
/pages/adminpage/**=ROLE_adminrole
/pages/**=IS_AUTHENTICATED_FULLY
```

Now, only users authenticated with `adminrole` group members will be able to load this page from the server.

In the example application, we left the admin menu item visible to everyone. However, attempting to load that page while logged in as a user will put the application into an unexpected state. This is a good example of the case for using the widget RBAC visibility with server-side enforcement. RBAC prevents the honest users from accidently trying to load the admin page, while using a server-side URL filter protects the application from unauthorized use. As we cannot specify RBAC visibility of menu items within a menu, we could use two menus for presentation. One menu contains the admin item and is only visible to admins, while the other menu does not contain the admin item but is shown to all other users.

There are several other ways we can use URL pattern matching to restrict access to server-side resources. Consider the case of the `*.script` files that back the in-memory HSQLDB database engine in the `webapproot/data` folder of a project. If an application were to use HSQLDB in production, unless access to `/data/*` is restricted, any user can download the entire database script file. To close that vulnerability, we can use our `nobody` group again. By adding `/data/*=ROLE_nobody` to the `filterSecurityInterceptor`'s `objectDefinitionSource` value string, authenticated users will no longer be able to download the HSQLDB database if they can determine the database file name. However, that is often as easy as watching a database request in the developer tools **Network** tab. This is another reason HSQLDB is not recommended for production use, and is also an example of how security configuration customization can be useful.

Service operation access

Restricting access to pages can be an effective part of a security strategy. It ensures that any page code or page- owned components are only made available to authorized users. However, services are application-owned components. Even if all service variables for the `admin` service are defined on a restricted admin page, malicious authenticated users could still attempt to access the `admin` service directly.

There are two ways we can secure access to services at the operation or function level: by code or by configuration.

Using code

As we learned in *Chapter 9, Custom Java Services,* custom Java services provide us with unlimited possibility for customization, and security is no exception. From within our Java service, we can perform various validations and checks before executing a task. In the SecureDbAccess example application, the SecureDbSvc service demonstrates how we can use the security service to authorize the invocation of an operation by user role.

The first thing we need to do is get an instance of the security service. This example also uses dependency injection to inject the security service into SecureDbSvc. As before, this is done by editing the SecureDbSvc.spring.xml configuration file where we map the securityService bean into the securitySvc property:

```
<bean class="com.wavemaker.example.SecureDbSvc" scope="singleton"
lazy-init="true" id="SecureDbSvc">
    <property name="runtimeSvc">
        <ref bean="runtimeService"/>
    </property>
    <property name="securitySvc">
        <ref bean="securityService"/>
    </property>
</bean>
```

Then, we need a securitySvc member variable and a setter for the Spring container to use:

```
@HideFromClient
public void setSecuritySvc(SecurityService securitySvc){
    this.securitySvc = securitySvc;
}
```

> The setSecuritySvc() method must be public. Therefore, it has been annotated with @HideFromClient to prevent client use. Due to WM-4704 (http://jira.wavemaker.com/browse/WM-4704), the operation will still be visible in the service SMD file; however, the annotation will prevent this function from being invoked from a service variable even though it is public.

With an instance of the security service secured, we can use `getUserRoles()` to obtain the requester's group membership. In this example, we've separated out the checking of roles into a function that can be reused from multiple client-facing operations called `roleCheck()`:

```
private void roleCheck(String[] requiredRoles){
   List<String> reqRoles = Arrays.asList(requiredRoles);
   List<String> roles = Arrays.asList(securitySvc.getUserRoles());
   for(String role : roles){
       for(String rRole : reqRoles){
          log(DEBUG, "Checking " + role + " for " + rRole);
          if(role.equals(rRole)){
           return;
          }
       }
     }
   }
   log(ERROR, "User is not member of required role");
   throw new WMRuntimeException("Access is Denied");
}
```

The operation takes a string array of required roles. The user's roles are then compared against the required roles. If the user has a required role, the method returns and the caller can continue on its way. If the user does not have the required role, an exception is thrown, aborting the service call.

Using XML

The previous code is a good example of how we can utilize the security service from Java to perform access control. In some cases, we want to combine the user's role information in conjunction with other states to determine how the operation proceeds. However, if we only need to permit or deny the ability to execute an operation by role, we can do so by only modifying the `project-security.xml` file.

Also in the `SecureDbSvc` service is a wrapper operation for deleting customers. In our application, only administrators should be able to delete a customer record. However, there is no call to `roleCheck()` in the `deleteCustomer()` method:

```
public void deleteCustomer(Customer customer){
     log(INFO, "Deleting customer for user: " + securitySvc.
getUserName());
   try {
```

```
        runtimeSvc.delete(CUSTPURCHASE_DB, COM_CUSTPURCHASEDB_DATA_
CUSTOMER, customer);
    } catch (Exception e) {
        e.printStackTrace();
    }
}
```

Access control here is being enforced by Acegi's `securityInterceptor` bean. To use this method, we first need to tell the `autoProxyCreator` bean about the service we want to add method level access control to. To do that, we start with the bean ID of our service from its `spring.xml` file:

```
<bean class="com.wavemaker.example.SecureDbSvc" scope="singleton"
lazy-init="true" id="SecureDbSvc">
```

We then add that bean ID to the `beanNames` property of the `autoProxyCreator` bean, as shown in the highlighted code:

```
<bean class="org.springframework.aop.framework.autoproxy.
BeanNameAutoProxyCreator" id="autoProxyCreator">
        <property name="proxyTargetClass">
            <value>true</value>
        </property>
        <property name="beanNames">
            <list>
                <value>SecureDbSvc</value>
            </list>
</property>
        <property name="interceptorNames">
            <list>
                <value>securityInterceptor</value>
            </list>
        </property>
    </bean>
```

Next we add any operation level restrictions we want to the `securityInterceptor` bean and `objectDefinitionSource` using the same Acegi expression syntaxes we used earlier. Here, we've specified that the `deleteCustomer()` operation from the class `com.wavemaker.example.SecureDbSvc` requires the user to have `adminrole` with the role prefix `ROLE_adminrole`:

```
<bean class="org.acegisecurity.intercept.method.aopalliance.
MethodSecurityInterceptor" id="securityInterceptor">
        <property name="authenticationManager"
ref="authenticationManager"/>
```

```
          <property name="accessDecisionManager"
ref="accessDecisionManager"/>
          <property name="objectDefinitionSource">
               <value>
   com.wavemaker.example.SecureDbSvc.deleteCustomer=ROLE_adminrole
=ROLE_adminrole
               </value>
          </property>
     </bean>
```

 Note that we used the SecureDbSvc fully qualified class name, not the bean ID, when specifying methods in securityInterceptor.

Which technique is best to use depends on the situation. Manually editing the project-security.xml file restricts our ability to use the **Security** tab in Studio. However, for straight deny or allow access by role, it is relatively simple to configure and can be applied to any service operation, as custom Java is not required.

Securing runtime service

WaveMaker's use of service variables insulates applications from SQL injection types of attack (http://owasp.com/index.php/SQL_Injection). However, use of the runtime service exposes a insert(), update(), read(), and delete() method for every imported table. This can create a significant vulnerability, including exposing the user login table when using database security.

For example, using curl (http://curl.haxx.se/), a command-line tool for making HTTP requests, we could perform an update of the customer table by POST'ing directly to the runtime service URL. Here, we update the customer record with customer ID 3 with bogus data

```
> curl -H "Content-type: application/json" -d
'{"params":["custpurchaseDB", "com.custpurchasedb.data.Customer",
{"address":"12 Chump Lane", "city" : "Hackville", "company": "Fools
R Us", "custid" : 3, "imageurl" : "", "state" : "TX", "twitter" :
"ivebeenpawnd", "zip": "3333"}],"method":"update","id":1}' -X POST
http://127.0.0.1:8094/SecureDbAccess/services/runtimeService.json
```

There are a number of things we can do as developers to mitigate this access. First, we can limit the tables imported into the project to only those that authenticated users should be able to fully access. If all users are able to insert, update, read, and delete from all tables, simply enabling security meets our requirements.

Second, we can use a limited authority account for the JDBC connection to the database. If we use an account with no delete privileges in the RDBMS to connect the application to the database, no user of the application will be able to delete from any table.

 The user/password combination used to connect for the initial schema import and for final deployment can be different accounts. Import requires additional privileges to interrogate the RDBMS schema that are not required for runtime use.

For many applications, enabling security and using a limited authority connection to the database may be sufficient security, particularly if not using database-based security. If all imported tables are expected to expose all operations to all users, then requiring authentication to access services by enabling security is sufficient protection. Applications requiring a greater degree of granularity in database access control may want to disable all use of the runtime service outright.

We've already seen that it is simple to disable access to a service. In this chapter's example, we have set access to the role `nobody` to close off all access to the runtime service. That is the easy part. With the runtime service disabled, however, we need to replace the functionality of the service with our own service. The `SecureDbSvc` service of the `SecureDbAccess` project is an example replacement service. The `SecureDbSvc` implements read, update, insert, and delete for the customer entity.

Let's look at the `insertCustomer` operation in `SecureDbSvc.java` (https://github.com/edwardcallahan/Easy-Web-Samples/blob/master/projects/SecureDbAccess/services/SecureDbSvc/src/com/wavemaker/example/SecureDbSvc.java). We define it to take a `Customer` object and return a `Customer` object:

```
public Customer insertCustomer (Customer customer) {
roleCheck(USER_OR_ADMIN_ROLE);
Customer insertedCustomer  = null;
log(INFO, "Inserting customer for user: " + securitySvc.
getUserName());
try {
    TypedServiceReturn tsrCustomer = runtimeSvc.insert(CUSTPURCHASE_
DB, COM_CUSTPURCHASEDB_DATA_CUSTOMER,customer);
    insertedCustomer = (Customer)tsrCustomer.getReturnValue();
    log(INFO, insertedCustomer.getCompany());
} catch(Exception e) {
    log(ERROR, "Error inserting customer", e);
    e.printStackTrace();
}
   return insertedCustomer;
}
```

Our service has been injected with an instance of the runtime service and uses this instance, `runtimeSvc`, to invoke the `insert()` operation, as shown in the preceding highlighted code. The `insert()` operation returns `TypedServiceReturn`, which is cast to a `Customer` for return. Access to the runtime service has been cut-off from the network, but from our Java service, we are still able to invoke the runtime service.

The `update()` operation is noteworthy as it uses a special overloading of the runtime service update operation:

```
TypedServiceReturn tsrCustomer = runtimeSvc.update(CUSTPURCHASE_DB,
COM_CUSTPURCHASEDB_DATA_CUSTOMER,customer,0);
```

This overloading allows us to specify an index value, which is always zero.

 Failure to use the overloaded version will cause the update to fail.

Disabling live saving

With the replacement service implemented, we can restrict access to our service using any of the Java or XML techniques we've discussed. With that done, we will want to convert all live forms in our application to our secure service. We could do that by unlocking the **Edit** panel and reworking all the live form's button actions. However, that is a lot of work and error prone. Instead, we will turn off `liveSaving`.

`liveSaving` is a property of live form that is not exposed via the **Properties** panel, so an easy way to disable it is to set it to `false` directly via the form in the `start()` method of the page. Here, we set `liveSaving` to `false` for `customerLiveForm1`:

```
start: function() {
   this.customerLiveForm1.liveSaving = false;
},
```

With `liveSaving` turned off, rewiring the live form is a simple matter of specifying service variables operating against our service for the `onDeleteData`, `onInsertData`, `onUpdateData`, and `onSuccess` events.

 You will need to use the properties **show more** or the **All** tab of the live form's properties in order to see those events.

With `liveSaving` disabled, the live form will call our service variables instead of the form's built-in live variable while retaining all the read-only management of a live form:

Now we have a fully-functional customer editing form without using any of the runtime service, giving us precise control over all database access.

Troubleshooting

Security errors are generally not helpful by design. If an error provides too much information, that information could be used to further advance an attack. This is fine for security, but makes troubleshooting security issues extra challenging.

XML errors generally prevent the application from deploying. These errors will be logged to the server log file. The exceptions logged are usually helpful and are rarely specific to WaveMaker, meaning that you can often apply search results from other projects to reported errors.

Enabling the debug logger for Acegi in `log4j.properties` is a good first step in troubleshooting any security issue:

```
log4j.logger.org.acegisecurity=debug
```

With this debugger logging enabled, all request processing against the `filterSecurityInterceptor` URL list is logged. This can be very helpful in tracking down why URL rules worked or didn't work as expected.

Finally, you might need to enable logging on another server. When using LDAP security for example, Acegi logging provides little information about why authentication failed. Sometimes it is necessary to enable logging on the LDAP server to fully see why authentication is failing.

Summary

Security is a critical aspect of application design and development. In this chapter, we have examined the Acegi security based-security service provided in WaveMaker 6.5.

We started by using Studio's security tooling. This allows us to easily enable security using a database, LDAP, or a simple store for user credentials. Using the security panel, we can configure if users must login before being able to load the project home page as well as roles to be used for role-based access. We also learned how roles are determined by group membership. Studio's security panel also tools service access restriction by role and a multitenant isolation feature for databases.

We then looked at various ways we can customize the security configuration, generally by editing `project-security.xml` outside of Studio. We also looked at examples of how we can utilize the security service from a custom Java service to provide almost any custom server-side validation or authorization scheme we may need.

We also discussed the vulnerabilities presented by the runtime service and looked at the example project that demonstrates a solution for mitigating that vulnerability. To close our discussion on security, we looked at some of the special considerations of troubleshooting security-related issues.

Additional information about security in WaveMaker including configuring security providers can be found by visiting the security page of the product documentation at `http://dev.wavemaker.com/wiki/bin/wmdoc_6.5/Security`.

This concludes our discussions on project development. In the next chapter, we will deploy our application. There are several items to consider for deployment, with some changes needing to be made before going to the deployment dialog. Readers will also learn about their deployment infrastructure options, from a private server, to Cloud Foundry and Amazon's EC2.

13
Deploying Applications

We have now addressed all of the development topics that we will be covering in this book. You have seen how WaveMaker eases web development, but at the same time, building a quality application requires time and effort. As such, it is common for developers to become a little extra excited when we get close to pushing our application out to the world for its initial deployment. Unfortunately, unless we are deploying the application to a known, good environment, we have more decisions to make and some amount of work to do before we can send out the URL of our new application.

In this chapter, we will discuss the deployment of WaveMaker applications; the generation of the deployment package and our deployment options. We will start with deployment requirements for WaveMaker applications and the process of using Studio to generate the deployment package. This is to include the changes we may need to make to the project prior to generating the deployment archive.

We will then examine the three deployment types tooled by Studio and the common use cases for these options, including cloud options. We will not be providing step-by-step instructions for using each and every deployment option in this book. Take a look at documentation, blog posts, and other platform specific-guides for those. Instead, we will discuss the categories of options available to us while providing suggestions and considerations.

Deployment requirements

The main requirement for the deployment of WaveMaker applications is a Java application server running in a JDK 1.6 or newer JVM. Apache Tomcat is the most commonly used server, but other common application servers are known to work as well, including JBoss, GlassFish, WebSphere, and WebLogic. If an application server can run Spring 3.x applications, a WaveMaker application should also be runnable in that server as well. Issues with application servers generally come in the form of JVM issues such as classpath, or server-specific issues such as missing server-specific configuration entries.

OpenJDK works equally well as Oracle's JDK. OpenJDK does not include a few proprietary fonts that are distributed by Oracle. These fonts can be downloaded separately if needed.

Preparing for deployment

Studio generally does well to present tasks logically and intuitively. Deployment may be the task that can single-handedly do the most damage to that reputation due to the range of possible configuration elements that have not been abstracted out into the deployment dialog.

Some of the project configurations can only be updated outside the Studio or by using the resource manager, akin to the enabling of dependency injection in our examples by editing XML files. The classic example here is if your deployment environment requires a custom entry in the applications' web-app context, it can be added using user-web.xml. However, you must manually edit user-web.xml before generating the archive.

 Spring profiles enable you to have different configurations for different environments so you don't have to change values between environments. An example from the WaveMaker runtime server is how the bean named serviceResponse obtains its connectionTimeout value depending on the environment cloud: cloud-test or default. See springapp.xml for the details at https://github.com/SpringSource/wavemaker/blob/master/wavemaker/wavemaker-runtime/src/main/resources/springapp.xml.

The ability to change a web service endpoint address is an excellent example of a configuration value in transition. Prior to WaveMaker 6.5, changing a web service endpoint from test to production server requires editing the generated service files. With 6.5, the server name can be edited using the **Endpoint Address** editor found by selecting the web service in the project services tree.

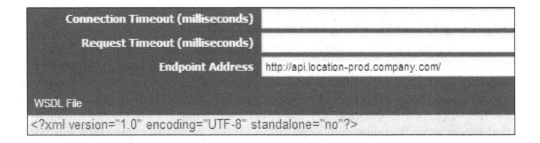

Use this editor to update the URL and save the service prior to deploying the application. While representing a nice improvement over previous releases, developers are still required to toggle the address between environments. Future releases might enable developers to set both test and production addresses using Spring profiles. This would save developers from having to remember to update the hostname prior to generating a WAR file for a different environment.

The deployment dialog

With the configuration items addressed, we are ready to open up the deployment dialog. The **Deploy Project** item from the **File** menu has three subsections:

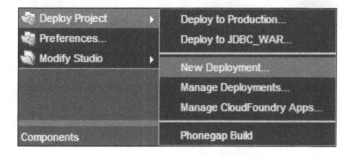

The top section lists previously saved deployments. **Production** and **JDBC_WAR** are the two deployment names in the previous screenshot. The middle section contains two items for creating and managing deployments with a third option for managing Cloud Foundry V1 applications. The bottom section contains the single mobile deployment option for a **Phonegap Build**, which we will cover in the next chapter.

Selecting **New Deployment** brings us to the **Choose Deployment Type** dialog:

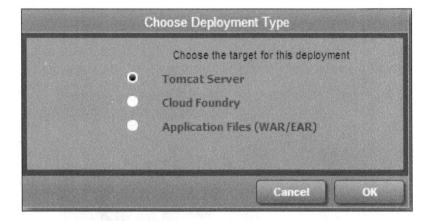

Here we choose from deploying directly to a Tomcat 6 manager application with **Tomcat Server**, direct deployment to **Cloud Foundry**, or generating a WAR or EAR file with **Application Files (WAR/EAR)**.

WAR/EAR

The simplest option for the list is also the most versatile and the recommended. **Application Files (WAR/EAR)** generates a web application archive (WAR) or enterprise archive (EAR) that you can deploy using any deployment method you would like. In short, this is the option to use when you want to deploy to anything other than directly to Cloud Foundry V1 or a Tomcat 6 manager application.

Selection of a deployment type brings us to the deployment dialog, which is customized for our project and our deployment selection. The left-hand side bar of the dialog is a list of saved deployments with **add**, **delete**, and **copy** buttons. These are the same controls shown in the **Manage Deployments** submenu items for managing saved deployments. Selecting an existing deployment, such as **Production** by selecting **Deploy to Production...** from the **Deploy Project** item, opens that deployment configuration.

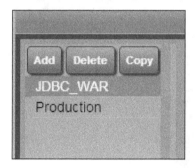

In the **Settings** panel, we can specify a **Deployment name** and select the **Type** of archive we want. If the project has database services, a **Database Connection** panel is shown for each database, excluding HSQLDB databases. HSQLDB databases have no configuration, and instead generate a warning panel to remind us that HSQLDB is not recommended for deployment:

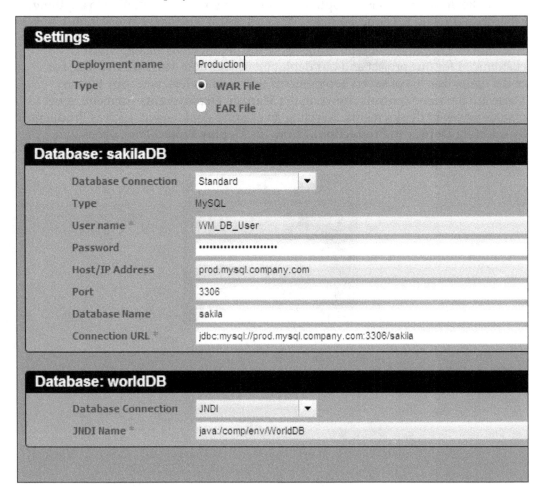

The default database connection type is **Standard** or **JDBC**. The **JDBC** option provides a form for building the URL to be used in the deployment as well as the resultant **Connection URL**. When we import the database originally, we can add parameters directly to the URL. This is also where we would change the **User name** and **Password** to that of the restricted authority user we discussed in the last chapter.

The JNDI connection choice presents a single **JNDI Name** editor. The convention for defining JDBC JNDI resources within an application server is to preface the name with `jdbc`. Our `worldDB` database might be given the resource name `jdbc/WorldDB` in the server configuration by the server administrator. The JNDI resource would be placed into the application's context in the `java:comp/env` namespace, and we thus would use `java:/comp/env/WorldDB` for the **JNDI Name** field. If you are unsure of the JNDI name to use, check the resource definition or ask the server administrator. The Tomcat documentation provides a good JNDI how-to, which can be found at `https://tomcat.apache.org/tomcat-7.0-doc/jndi-resources-howto.html`.

The **Deploy Now** button at the bottom of the panel starts the archive generation process. The process will take some time, even on fast systems. First, the project is copied to a staging area in the Studio server's `temp` folder. This staging folder is provisioned with fresh copies of all the project libraries. The Dojo Toolkit libraries that were loaded from Studio's `webapproot` during test runs are copied into the project's `webapproot` as part of this preparation. Deployment-specific configuration changes are then applied to the staging area: manifests and application descriptions are generated as needed and the contents of `user-web.xml` are merged into `web.xml`. Finally, the `webapproot` of the staging area is packaged up into the requested archive file format and the archive is copied into the project's `dist` folder. The developer is presented with a link to download the freshly assembled archive should they not have easy access to the project filesystem.

Internal changes to WaveMaker for version 6.5 removed the command-line building script used in previous versions. It is still possible to build a WAR file for a project without running Studio, but you'll need to write your own script. A sample Jenkins plugin to help you get started has been shared by the community at `http://dev.wavemaker.com/forums/?q=node/9721#comment-34246`.

Tomcat

The **Tomcat Server** deployment type option presents a deployment dialog with a larger **Settings** section. The additional editors provide the connection parameters to the Tomcat 6 manager required to deploy the archive.

 There must be a Tomcat 6 manager application reachable via the information provided. Studio's deployment service is not compatible with the Tomcat 7 manager application. For Tomcat 7 deployments, use the WAR/EAR target and use the Tomcat 7 manager application directly in a browser. Tomcat 7 is recommended for deployments.

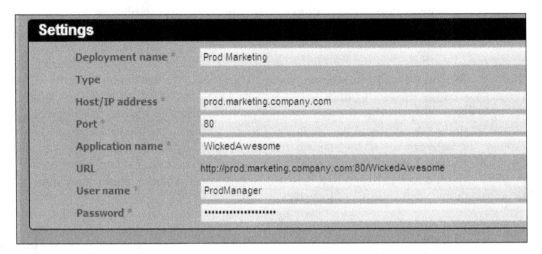

Settings	
Deployment name *	Prod Marketing
Type	
Host/IP address *	prod.marketing.company.com
Port *	80
Application name *	WickedAwesome
URL	http://prod.marketing.company.com:80/WickedAwesome
User name *	ProdManager
Password *	••••••••••••••••••

This time, when we invoke the **Deploy Now** button, Studio starts by generating a WAR file using the same process as the WAR/EAR option. However, upon successfully copying the WAR file to the project `dist` folder, the WAR file is then also deployed to the specified Tomcat server using the information provided. Studio uses the Tomcat manager API to deploy the application. If the Studio server is successfully able to connect and deploy the WAR file, the URL of the newly deployed application will be displayed.

Under the covers, the Tomcat server deployment target is simply a convenience target for generating a WAR and immediately deploying the WAR via the manager application. There are numerous flavours and variations on deploying with and managing Tomcat. Some find exploding the WAR directly into the Tomcat `webapps` folder the easiest way to deploy an application. Others prefer to use enterprise tools such as VMware's Application Director and Hyperic or Mulesoft's Tcat server instead of Tomcat's manager.

JVM configuration

There are many good resources available for further information on configuring Tomcat. The Tomcat Documentation Index (`https://tomcat.apache.org/tomcat-7.0-doc/`) alone could be an adequate reference.

Other than possibly setting up Tomcat as well, configuring the JVM of the application server is the other task you are most likely to need to undertake when deploying WaveMaker applications. WaveMaker applications load many libraries and can require increment in both memory and PermGen space. If you are not using some form of management tool, the easiest way to set these is to set `CATALINA_OPTS` in a file named `setenv.sh`, or `setenv.bat` on Windows, using variable assignment syntax. For example, to set the max memory of the JVM to 1 GB and PermGen space to 256 MB, we would add `CATALINA_OPTS="-Xmx1024m -XX:MaxPermSize=256m` to `setenv.sh`.

> The files `setenv.sh` and `setenv.bat` do not exist by default and must be created in the Tomcat bin folder the first time you wish to set values.

Another common area for making configuration changes on Linux servers is the Tomcat startup script, for example, `/etc/init.d/tomcat7`. Here you may have to set other values, for example, using `TOMCAT6_SECURITY=no` to enable log4j logging on some systems.

Mod_proxy

One commonly used Tomcat feature to be aware of when planning your deployment environment is `mod_proxy`. "The `mod_proxy` feature" (`https://httpd.apache.org/docs/2.2/mod/mod_proxy.html`) is an optional module for Apache HTTP Server. It is best known for enabling virtual hosting. Virtual hosts allow for a single HTTP server host to serve the content of multiple sites. For example, in the WaveMaker community infrastructure, a single virtual machine running a single instance of Apache HTTP Server serves the virtual hosts of `http://www.wavemaker.com`, `http://dev.wavemaker.com`, and `http://community.wavemaker.com`.

For Java applications such as WaveMaker applications, another key feature of `mod_proxy` is AJP support. The **Apache JServ Protocol (AJP)** allows Apache to proxy inbound requests through to a Java application server such as Tomcat. This means we can have static HTML, PHP, and other Apache served content and Tomcat served WaveMaker applications returned Apache on port 80. We do this by mapping requests to our application to an AJP worker. The AJP worker communicates with Tomcat and returns the result to Apache. The result is that the end user sees the site as a single Apache server on a single port and never gets redirected to port 8080 in order to run the application. The Tomcat 7 `mod_proxy` "how-to" can be viewed by visiting `https://tomcat.apache.org/tomcat-7.0-doc/proxy-howto.html`.

Cloud deployment

The other deployment type to choose is Cloud Foundry. Cloud Foundry is the only cloud deployment target tooled by Studio, but is hardly the only cloud deployment option available to WaveMaker developers. Cloud Foundry is a Platform-as-a-Service, or PaaS. A PaaS aims to free developers from the complexity of configuring and managing the hosting environment. Other examples of PaaS clouds include Engine Yard, Cloud Jee, and Open Shift.

Amazon Elastic Compute Cloud (Amazon EC2) on the other hand is considered as an Infrastructure-as-a-service (IaaS). IaaS is the 'do it yourself' version of cloud compared to PaaS. The provider, Amazon in this case, provides the virtual machines, disk storage, and firewalls. That's it. Unless using Amazon's Beanstalk PaaS service, users must install and configure operating systems, services, and everything that goes with it. While there are many ways to simplify much of that build up, some of which we will cover soon, ultimately that configuration is the user's responsibility and not that of the IaaS vendor. Other IaaS cloud vendors include Rackspace Cloud, Linode, and Joyent.

Cloud Foundry

The Cloud Foundry deployment target and the **Manage Cloud Foundry Apps** feature of Studio are specific to the V1 version of Cloud Foundry, which was suspended in June 2013. These features do not function against the V2 version of Cloud Foundry being used today. These features will not be discussed as they are no longer usable.

Amazon EC2

No discussion of the cloud is complete without addressing Amazon EC2 specifically. WaveMaker 6.5 does not directly tool deployment to EC2, so we use the WAR/EAR deployment option to produce the deployment archive for deployment to our EC2 server(s).

Unless you are using Amazon's Elastic Beanstalk PaaS, you will need to build your instance up to support the serving of your application. Starting with the right AMI can save you a lot of time and effort. If you are looking for an easy to use Linux to get started with, many suggest Ubuntu. Alestic (`http://alestic.com/`) maintains Ubuntu AMIs (Amazon Machine Images) in each region to help you get started.

If you would rather an instance that is more pre-assembled and requires less effort to configure, BitNami (`http://bitnami.com/`) maintains AMIs for numerous stacks. Their Tomcat stack is a ready-to-run Tomcat 7 stack in which the Apache Server is already connected to Tomcat via AJP with MySQL Server also pre-installed.

Finally, if you are looking for something more specific, there are a growing number of AMI catalog sites such as the Cloud Market, `http://thecloudmarket.com/`. These sites allow you to search across thousands of listed AMIs to find the AMI that is just right for you.

Summary

In this chapter, we have addressed the deployment of WaveMaker applications. We have examined both the process of generating the deployment archive as well as our options for a deployment environment.

WaveMaker applications require a JDK 1.6 or newer Java application server. Studio tools the generation of archives and direct deployment to Cloud Foundry and Tomcat 6. The WAR/EAR generation option is used to generate an archive for deployment to any target not tooled or for deployment using any other tool we may prefer. Use of Tomcat 7 for deployment is recommended. We also learned that some configuration changes must be made prior to using the deployment dialog to generate the archive.

We have also discussed various aspects and considerations of common deployment environments. In particular, we looked at the Amazon EC2 IaaS cloud environments. We also addressed configuring the Tomcat JVM and using AJP to front Tomcat with Apache Server.

In the next chapter, we will look at the PhoneGap deployment feature that packages our application into a native mobile application.

14
Mobile Deployment

We first discussed WaveMaker's PhoneGap feature for Apache Cordova in *Chapter 2, Digging into the Architecture*. In *Chapter 4, Designing a Well-performing Application*, we explored the considerations for designing applications to be used on the smaller screens of a mobile device. In this chapter, we shall package, build, and deploy our application to a mobile device.

Deploying an application to a mobile device is quite different than deploying it to a Java application server. In both cases, Studio generates an archive package of the application, but that is where the similarities end. An HTML application on a mobile device is also a different creature than native applications, lacking their look and feel for example. JavaScript may be king in the browser, but on mobile devices, native Objective-C for iOS and Java for Android still reign supreme. However, the ability to access native hardware combined with cross-device support make frameworks such as PhoneGap rather advantageous. Likewise, the HTML and JavaScript require the use of additional Cordova native libraries in order to be executed as an installed application.

This chapter will address the steps needed to take our browser-based application and build it into a native application for installation on Android and iOS mobile devices.

The mobile hybrid

WaveMaker builds HTML5 applications. We could deploy our application to a server as we normally do and provide users with an 'm' site URL, as in `http://m.mysite.com`, for a mobile layout. This is a fine solution, but it is not the only way to run your application on a mobile device. Users have come to expect the features of installed applications; namely applications that can access their device's hardware, such as taking pictures with the camera or obtaining geolocation information. Installed applications also load relatively quickly, even when network data is slow or unavailable. Unless we use a mobile operating system with built-in HTML5 support such as Mozilla's Firefox OS (`http://www.mozilla.org/firefoxos/`), our HTML-based application requires helper or wrapper libraries in order to run as an installed application. To do this, we assemble what is referred to as an HTML or hybrid application for mobile devices. In short, the PhoneGap build process embeds our HTML application inside of what is known as a WebView component.

We know that the client side of our application is actually HTML, JavaScript, and CSS. It is important to note that only the client-side components are used on the mobile device. The server-side Java components are not included in the Cordova package. We can continue to use Java services such as databases from our mobile applications by making network calls to a remote system, or we can have no server-side components at all. If we do use the WaveMaker server, service calls will be remote XHR calls from the device to a designated server, just like when we run the application in a browser. Unlike the browser version of the application, however, the mobile application is loaded from the device's local storage and not from a server. This frees developers from the constraints of the same origin policy (`https://en.wikipedia.org/wiki/Same_origin_policy`), allowing them to call services from multiple domains directly.

Before you begin

There are a few prerequisites that need to be addressed before you build a Cordova application. First, you'll need to apply Studio patches using the **Upload Studio Patches...** item from the **Modify Studio** menu to ensure you've got the latest updates:

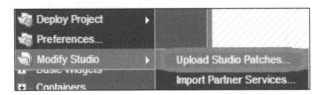

Changes to the PhoneGap namespace are addressed by a post-WaveMaker 6.5.3 release patch that can be applied using the built-in Studio patching system. If you do not apply the latest Studio post-installation updates, your PhoneGap application will fail.

You will also need to fulfill any requirements of the mobile platform(s) you wish to target. Apple requires that, in order to build an iOS application to be installed on an iOS device, you must be a member of the iOS Developer Program (`https://developer.apple.com/programs/ios/`), currently 99 USD per year for individuals. Membership includes a key that is compiled into the application. Android devices also require a signing key for submission to the Play store; visit `http://developer.android.com/tools/publishing/app-signing.html`. However, unlike iOS applications, Android applications can be built and installed without a key by enabling the installation of non-market applications on your test device or in your user's device settings.

> Not all platforms are supported directly by the Studio-generated ZIP file. Some platforms require modification. See *Customizing the ZIP file*.

Cordova API

PhoneGap provides an API for accessing device-specific functionality such as obtaining the user's location using geolocation, reading and writing to the device's contact list, and capturing video and audio. Studio tools a subset of the PhoneGap API for you. From the **Insert** menu, choose **PhoneGap Call** to insert a `PhoneGapCall` component. The `PhoneGapCall` component has functions similar to a service call. It has an `onError` and `onSuccess` event, for example. Unlike a service call, a PhoneGap call never calls a `remote` server, and instead calls only into the local device. APIs not tooled by `PhoneGapCall` can still be used, but you'll have to call it from code, following the examples from PhoneGap.

The other PhoneGap-specific feature available to the application is the **saveInPhonegap** property found in `wm.Variable` and its subclasses, `wm.ServiceVariable` and `wm.LiveVariable`.

When enabled, variable data is written to the device's local storage. This saves `autoStart` service variables from firing if cached data is available to the application when started. This enables developers to customize applications for mobile usage, such as caching data for offline use.

PhoneGap build

There are two ways we can generate a hybrid mobile application from our HTML5 application using PhoneGap: locally or online in the cloud. We will be using the cloud build option; the easier of the two.

Local build

Local builds require significant effort to set up and configure. Requirements include an appropriate build device, SDKs, and compilers, as well as the PhoneGap binaries. In the case of iOS, this means developers need a Mac OS X system with both Xcode and the iOS SDK installed, as well as the Cordova libraries from `http://phonegap. com/download/`. Android local build requirements are similar, but requiring Eclipse and the Android SDK instead. In both cases, developers must manually manage `wm.xhrPath` for final deployment.

The setup of the build environment can be time consuming. However, once successfully configured, the build/test cycles with the local build are much faster, providing a more productive development environment. The emulators in the development kits provide a convenient testing environment, avoiding the need to install/uninstall a new version on the device to test. Local builds also enable developers to take advantage of the plugins available from `https://github.com/ phonegap/phonegap-plugins/`. Cordova plugins enable developers to access additional functionality from JavaScript; examples of plugins include a barcode scanner, a native volume slider, and access to Bluetooth and NFC hardware. See the getting started guides in the PhoneGap documentation for instructions on setting up a local build environment by visiting `http://docs.phonegap.com/guide_getting-started_index.md.html`.

Cloud build

Using the cloud build option requires significantly less setup than local builds. Developers will need to set up an account with the Adobe build service `https://build.phonegap.com/` and upload to their account any of the aforementioned certificates or keys required by some platforms.

To start the generation process, choose **Deploy Project** from the **File** menu and select the **Phonegap Build** submenu item:

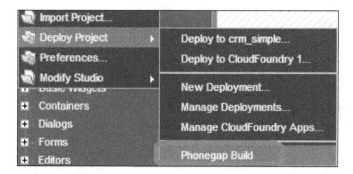

Configuring the build

This will bring up the **Phonegap Build Config** dialog, in which we set the values used in the project's `config.xml` file. The `config.xml` file is used by PhoneGap Build to set project options. A sample `config.xml` file can be seen in the PhoneGap start example application at `https://github.com/phonegap/phonegap-start/blob/master/www/config.xml`.

The first tab of the dialog is **Required Info**, in which we set the **Application Name** and the **Server Path**. The **Application Name** is simply the name users see for the application. The **Server Path** is the path to the WaveMaker server, if used, and is the same URL of the deployed application that you would use to load the application in a browser. This value is applicable only if the application uses any WaveMaker services, databases, Java, and so on. If so, it is important that this path be correct and reachable. Generally, this should be a public URL and not the IP address from a local network:

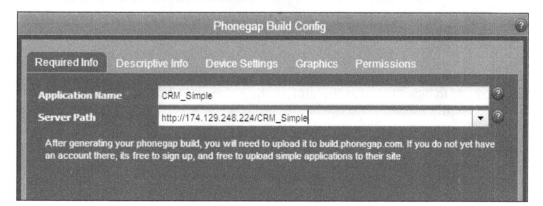

If the application only uses XHR/JSON web services, calls to those web services will be sent directly to the service as the installed application is not bound by the single origin rule; in which case, no **Server Path** is required.

 When an application with XHR/JSON web service calls is loaded in a browser from a server and is subject to the same origin policy, WaveMaker uses the WaveMaker Service to proxy the XHR/JSON calls.

The next tab is the **Descriptive Info** layer, in which we set information such as **Description**, **Developer Name**, and **Developer Email**.

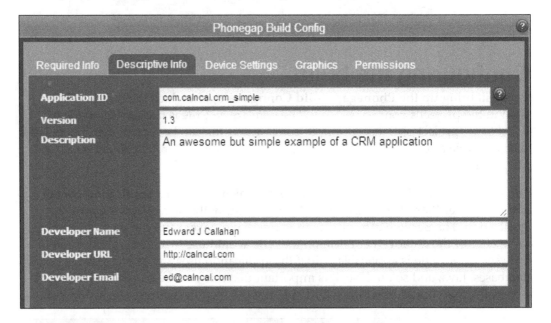

Of the **Descriptive Info** fields, only the **Application ID** has a restriction. It must end in the **Application Name**.

Next is the **Device Settings** layer, in which we can set an **Orientation**, enable **Full screen** mode to hide the status bar, and set the iOS specific **IOS: prerendered-icon** and **IOS: Status Bar Style** settings.

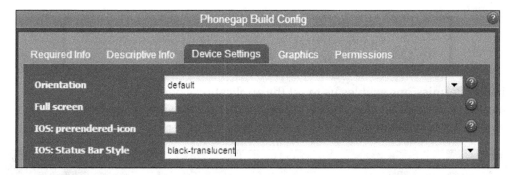

The next layer is the **Graphics** layer. Here we can set image files used for icons and splash screens for **IOS**, **Android**, and all **Other** platforms. For best results, use a nine-patch image to ensure the image scales properly when rotated.

iOS builds require the use of the Portable Network Graphics format, or PNG. Your build for iOS will fail if you do not use PNG files for images.

Finally, **Permissions** enables us to set the application's permissions. Selecting a permission checkbox will request that permission group from the user upon installation.

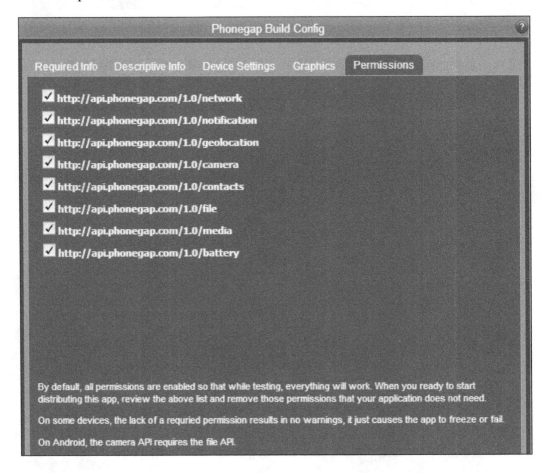

Phonegap Build Config

| Required Info | Descriptive Info | Device Settings | Graphics | Permissions |

☑ http://api.phonegap.com/1.0/network

☑ http://api.phonegap.com/1.0/notification

☑ http://api.phonegap.com/1.0/geolocation

☑ http://api.phonegap.com/1.0/camera

☑ http://api.phonegap.com/1.0/contacts

☑ http://api.phonegap.com/1.0/file

☑ http://api.phonegap.com/1.0/media

☑ http://api.phonegap.com/1.0/battery

By default, all permissions are enabled so that while testing, everything will work. When you ready to start distributing this app, review the above list and remove those permissions that your application does not need.

On some devices, the lack of a requried permission results in no warnings, it just causes the app to freeze or fail.

On Android, the camera API requires the file API.

 As noted in the dialog, the lack of a needed permission can have unpredictable results. Applications executing with insufficient permissions can fail with no indication of a permissions problem. For this reason, all permissions are checked by default. If your application fails after removing permissions, try re-enabling the removed permission(s).

Uploading the ZIP

With the build configuration set, press **OK** and Studio will create a `phonegap` folder in the top level of the project. In this folder, Studio will stage the project for the PhoneGap build service. A project `config.xml` file will be created using specified values and copied into the workspace, the Dojo libraries will be copied to the `lib` folder, and so on. When complete, a ZIP file will be made available for download.

This ZIP file can be directly uploaded to `https://build.phonegap.com` using the **Upload a .zip file** button on the PhoneGap site:

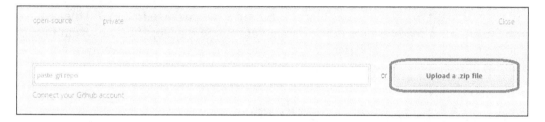

Once uploaded, PhoneGap will begin to build the application into native device installation packages.

If the build is successful, an installation URL and QR code for each successfully built package will be presented.

The application can be installed by scanning the QR code or otherwise downloading the application package, such as from the platform's application store.

If the build failed, an error message will be shown instead of a download link for the failed platform:

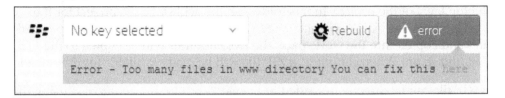

Some errors, such as the too many files error for Blackberry shown previously, are very difficult to overcome, as Blackberry limits the package to 200-250 files and Studio has already removed the debug versions of the Dojo libraries from the package. The PhoneGap documentation includes a reference for common build failures at `https://build.phonegap.com/docs/build-failed`.

Customizing the ZIP file

In some cases, it can be advantageous to customize the contents of the `phonegap` folder and create your own ZIP file to upload. For example, you might want to add additional entries to the `config.xml` file or add/remove additional files. Some platforms may require such customization in order to successfully build as they are not supported directly by the Studio-produced ZIP file, such as Blackberry. Likewise, future enhancements and new features could be introduced that Studio is unaware of.

Whatever the cause, preparing a custom ZIP file is as simple as modifying the contents of the `phonegap` folder and re-zipping up the archive. Remember that any customizations to the `phonegap` folder will be lost when you re-run Studio's PhoneGap build process to update the project contents.

For additional notes and information about using the PhoneGap feature, visit the PhoneGap page in the WaveMaker documentation at `http://dev.wavemaker.com/wiki/bin/wmdoc_6.5/PhoneGap`. For further information about using the PhoneGap build service, visit the PhoneGap build documentation site at `https://build.phonegap.com/docs`.

Summary

WaveMaker makes mobile development easy with its PhoneGap feature. The PhoneGap feature produces a ZIP file of the application's `webapproot` configured for the PhoneGap build service by Adobe at `https://build.phonegap.com/`. The build service compiles our application into a hybrid application that can be run natively on common mobile devices such as Android and iOS.

In this chapter, we discussed how to produce a mobile application using this feature. We examined the differences between the cloud build service and performing our own local builds of mobile installation packages. We also took a peek inside the `phonegap` staging folder and looked at how we can use this folder to customize the application.

This completes the deployment section of our journey. In the next and final chapter, we will take a comprehensive look at application debugging in WaveMaker. In debugging our applications, we will bring everything we have learned together and learn how to tackle any problem we encounter throughout the lifecycle of our applications.

15
Debugging

If at this point you have successfully deployed your project and everything is working to your satisfaction, then bravo! If instead some things are not working, if there is an error, or three, or if you want to investigate how something works in order to understand it better, then I encourage you to stick around for this, the final chapter of our journey together.

In this chapter, we will cover diagnostics and debugging. We shall start at the beginning with logging and some items to be generally aware of. After that, we will apply our knowledge of WaveMaker's XHR client/server communications to use the **Network** tab as a way to determine when problems are client- or server-side issues.

Next, we'll focus on the client. We'll look at the tooling available to us when working with JavaScript across browsers. We'll be certain to address mobile development too. With our client tools in place, we'll provide some tips on using the console. We'll look at the most useful diagnostic features as implemented in the Chrome DevTools and the WaveMaker built-in debugger.

Shifting to the server side, we'll show how working with the WaveMaker server is just another Java process. We'll do this by attaching to a server Java process using Eclipse and JPDA. And that, dear reader, will be the end of this journey. At that time, we shall say our goodbyes and part ways. But let's not get sentimental just yet; there's still some fun remaining. Let's get to it!

General troubleshooting

Before getting into debuggers and breakpoints, let's start with some first-response troubleshooting steps. These are the fundamentals. In time, many of them will become second nature to you, if they are not already. In short, these are the things that you need to do at the first sign of even a minor problem, or even just to understand test results in the development cycle.

Logging output

Good logging remains essential to good software. When things go wrong, one of the first things to do is to check for errors, messages, and warnings that may have been logged in the process of things going wrong. These messages should provide you with at least a starting point for your investigation. Good logging will reduce the scope of investigation and can sometimes tell you exactly what the problem is.

Your own code should also utilize logging to provide appropriate information to users, developers, and system administrators. It should utilize the logging levels so that the levels can be changed without redeployment. This is the key to providing variability of verbosity in deployment. At the same time, logging alone is not a replacement for a debugger. Excessive logging of state and variable values make it more difficult to find the relevant information in the logfile.

Server messages, from Java's `System.out.println()` to log4j's `log()`, are streamed as part of the Java server output streams. For applications deployed to Tomcat, this is primarily `catalina.out`. For applications that run from Studio's embedded Tomcat, such as when using the run button, this is `wm.log`. `wm.log` is the redirection of `catalina.out` for Studio's Tomcat. `wm.log` can be found in the `logs` folder of the WaveMaker folder, right next to the `projects` and `common` folder.

The log level for classes is determined by the `log4j.properties` file discussed in *Chapter 9, Custom Java Services*. Always edit only the `/src/log4j.properties` file as it is copied into the `WEB-INF` folder. Edits made to `WEB-INF/log4j.properties` will be lost when `/src/log4j.properties` is copied in preparation for deployment.

Client runtime messages are shown as toast messages within the application, with additional messages being logged to the browser console. Messages that end users may need to see, which are mostly errors, are generally shown using toasts. Alerts can be used if the user should be made to acknowledge the error, but multiple alerts quickly become a burden to dismiss. As such, alerts should be reserved for grave conditions. More detailed or diagnostic logging intended for developers on the other hand will generally only be logged to the console. As a result, it can be advantageous to keep the console open when developing an application, even if you are not actively debugging it, as these messages can often help identify problems.

> In some cases, client messages for server-side errors can be of limited value beyond indicating that a problem occurred. For this reason, keep an eye on the server log as well as the client console. A common technique is to use a utility such as tail to follow the `wm.log` file in a separate window.

Clearing the cache

"Clear the cache" may very well be the most often provided advice to WaveMaker developers. With time, some may develop a love/hate relationship with browser caching. We enjoy the loading speed and reduced server load that caching can enable, but we curse it when it loads an outdated version of a file.

Browser caching is not as straightforward as we can be led to believe. To complicate matters further, the aggressiveness of browser caching varies across browsers. Even within a single browser family, how the browser responds to caching directives can vary across versions as standards and practices evolve. The reality is that caching is much less of an issue today than it was just a few years ago. However, it only takes a single session of cache-induced frustration to jade even the most experienced developer. The bottom line is that applications cannot directly and fully control browser cache. Yes, we can set headers, and WaveMaker sets `cache-control`, `pragma`, and `expires` in the headers. However, applications cannot tell a browser to clear its cache without browser-specific code and elevated permissions, such as a browser add-on. Even with headers set, experience tells us that some browsers will sometimes still get it wrong, particularly during development with a single URL being repeatedly updated.

To address this, WaveMaker adds a **dojo.preventCache** parameter to page request URLs. We can see this in the **Network** tab. Here we see a page named **Main** being loaded in debug mode:

```
Main.js?dojo.preventCache=1355541711064
/CRM_Simple/pages/Main

Main.css?dojo.preventCache=1355541711064
/CRM_Simple/pages/Main

Main.html?dojo.preventCache=1355541711064
/CRM_Simple/pages/Main

Main.widgets.js?dojo.preventCache=1355541711064
/CRM_Simple/pages/Main
```

Each of the requests shown append a **dojo.preventCache=135541711064** to the path. The **dojo.preventCache** value used comes from `/webapproot/timestamp.txt`, which is updated each time the project is saved. This URL parameter ensures a unique path for every saved version of the project. This technique generally works well. Note that this is only done for project artifacts, such as pages, and not the runtime, such as `dojo_build.js`, which are only changed when upgrading WaveMaker. This is specific to the development process, and whenever updating to a newer version of Studio, it is highly recommended to clear the browser cache to ensure you are loading the new version of the runtime.

Browser add-ons, such as the Clear Cache (`https://chrome.google.com/webstore/detail/clear-cache/cppjkneekbjaeellbfkmgnhonkkjfpdn`) add-on for Chrome from Benjamin Bojiko, provide quick and easy cache-busting buttons for the browser of your choice.

Resetting WEB-INF

Sometimes the contents of `WEB-INF` can get into a bad state. Getting into this state is usually the result of some form of jiggery-pokery on the part of the developer, and is not common. However, when a project does get into such a state for any reason, it can be a maddening experience as the rules of Java seem defied.

Fortunately, there is a simple way to completely reset a project's `WEB-INF` folder: export and re-import the project. We know that exporting the project provides the minimal set of files needed to recreate the project. When we import the project into Studio, all the Java classes are recompiled and fresh copies of runtime libraries are copied in. Therefore, the act of exporting and importing a project is an easy way to reset the `WEB-INF` folder of a project.

Restarting the server

Early in our adventure, we looked at how Studio is itself a WaveMaker application. With that said, Studio can be a rather demanding client. Some of the Studio tool services can require significant amounts of resources, particularly when run across larger sets of classes. Should the Studio server throw an exception due to limited resources (PermGen space is an easy example in Java today), the server must be restarted. The server will often continue to operate, but Studio may not operate correctly. If the server throws an out of memory exception, increase the memory setting as needed and restart the server. Getting a job to complete, such as importing a very large database schema, may require significantly increasing the constrained resource, at least temporarily. Once imported, the memory settings can be restored to more normal levels.

Undeploying old applications

If you are building WaveMaker from source or otherwise running Studio in your own Tomcat, you'll want to occasionally monitor your Tomcat's deployments. We know that when we test deploy our applications from Studio, they are deployed to Studio's Tomcat. Studio automatically undeploys the application when you close the project in Studio. If you always close your project in Studio before stopping Tomcat, you will not accumulate deployments. However, if you forcibly close or kill Tomcat, the application will remain deployed. This cycle, if repeated, can lead to Tomcat being burdened with unused deployments, which will reduce performance. Many deployed applications can significantly reduce responsiveness.

Clear out these deployments to lighten Tomcat's load. Simply use Tomcat's manager application to undeploy any old applications. For Studio's embedded Tomcat running on port 8094 of a local host, use `http://localhost:8094/manager/html` with the username `manager` and password `manager`. Use the appropriate port and manager account, usually `8080` and `manager/manager`, to access your own Tomcat manager.

Watching the network

As we have seen throughout our development effort, watching the network traffic of our application can be extremely insightful. The **Network** console tab can help us understand everything from an application that fails to load to service call failures. The **Network** tab can often help us determine if the problem is in the client or on the server.

A simple example is database reads using the runtime service. Take the example of a grid that does not populate with the expected results. The **Network** tab, which we first used in *Chapter 4, Designing a Well-performing Application* for page loading, is a simple way to learn what happened. If the XHR service call does not return the expected results to the client, it is impossible for our grid to display them. This is a server-side issue, and we would look to the server for further information about the failure. On the other hand, if the service call did return the correct results, we know our problem is in the client. In the following screenshot, we see the **Request Payload** from a company search in the CRM_Simple example application:

```
▼ Request Payload      view source
  ▼ {params:[custpurchaseDB, com.custpurchasedb.data.Customer, null,…], method:read, id:836650}
      id: 836650
      method: "read"
    ▼ params: [custpurchaseDB, com.custpurchasedb.data.Customer, null,…]
        0: "custpurchaseDB"
        1: "com.custpurchasedb.data.Customer"
        2: null
      ▼ 3: {properties:[], filters:[company=Foo], matchMode:anywhere, ignoreCase:true}
        ▶ filters: [company=Foo]
          ignoreCase: true
          matchMode: "anywhere"
          properties: []
      ▶ 4: {maxResults:500, firstResult:0}
```

The user has entered Foo as the company name, which we see in the filters parameter. This search returns no results and the response is an empty result set, shown in the following screenshot:

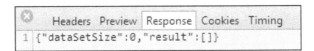

As our database contains no companies with Foo anywhere in its name, this is the correct result. If instead the read operation had failed with some error or exception, the response would contain an error. The response message alone may be insufficient to determine the exact problem. Only the final exception message is returned to the client, for example. However, the **Network** tab does quickly provide us with the service call's inputs and result's so we can quickly narrow down our search. If the response contains an error message, we immediately know the service call failed.

Client

The **Network** tab may help us determine that the issue is in the client, but it cannot help us to be more specific than that. In order to do that, we'll want to use our browser tools again.

As we have learned, running the application in debug mode (using `?debug` on the URL) loads the original JavaScript source files instead of compressed and minified packages of the client library. It is still possible to debug an application without running the client in debug mode, but it is definitely easier to do it in debug mode. As we have seen, we can use the console to invoke components in order to determine state and values. The debug mode is not required to invoke components from the console. If viewing a variable value, updating a value, or some simple task enables you to better understand an issue, then you don't need to reload the project in debug mode. Otherwise, reloading the project in debug mode before investigating an issue is almost always worth the wait. Whenever the WaveMaker runtime or Dojo Toolkit is involved in the investigation, reloading in debug mode should be conducted before starting.

Logging

From within JavaScript, we can use `console.log()` to send string messages to the browser console. Sending messages using `app.alert()` works, but requires the user to dismiss every message. Toast messages by contrast provide a means to notify a user without forcing them to dismiss the message. For more detailed messages, `console.log()` allows us to log as many lines as we need that the user will not see unless they open the console. If that is not reason enough to avoid `alert()`, there is a whole family of console functions to go with `console.log()`. For example, `console.error()` will log the entry as an error. For a nice listing of other common console functions, visit the logging page on the getfirebug site: `https://getfirebug.com/logging`. As always, support can vary across browsers.

As we saw in the `WaveyWeb` project's `waveytools.js` shared function example, we can use `console.log()` in our custom functions to customize logging. If we don't want to define custom shared functions, there are a number of open source projects that we can use to enhance our logging. One example is Ben Alman's JavaScript Debug (`http://benalman.com/projects/javascript-debug-console-log/`), which provides a simple but effective wrapper around `console.log()`.

Built-in debugger

When you run a project in debug mode, the bottom left corner of the project will contain a button to open the **WM Debugger**, WaveMaker's built-in debugger:

The WaveMaker Debugger is not a full debugger, and is not a replacement for Chrome Developer Tools, Firebug, and similar others. It cannot set breakpoints for example. Instead, it compliments browser tools by providing a WaveMaker-friendly debugging tool.

Upon opening the WM Debugger window, we see the **Services** tab. The **Services** tab lists all service variables and their status:

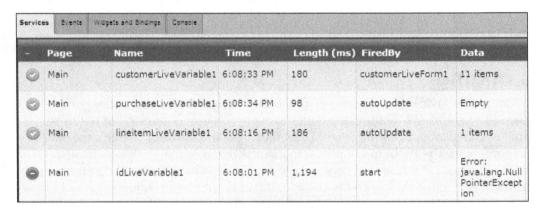

Here we see three successful and one failed service variables along with the time of their last invocation, how long the call took, what triggered the call, and the size of the result. All of this information is available in the console **Network** tab; the WM Debugger just made it easier to consume the information, such as providing the red and green icons for success and failure.

One of my favorite features of the WM Debugger is the **Event Details** tab. By selecting a service variable, we can see the chain of events that caused the service variable to be triggered:

Event Details	Properties	Bindings	Data	Request

The grid below shows the chain of events that led to the selected event occuring

Order	Type	Cause of Action
1	autoUpdate	An input has changed
2	Event	main.textSearch.onchange() has been called
3	Service	main.customerLiveVariable1.update()

Here we see that a bound input of `main.customerLiveVariable1` changed, causing the live variable to fire by `autoUpdate`. These event details help us understand why an event occurred, and can be a very helpful tool for improving performance as well as debugging.

The WM Debugger provides the ability to set data values for variables. Here we've set the `company` name filter input to `Fog` by editing the **Request** tab JSON data:

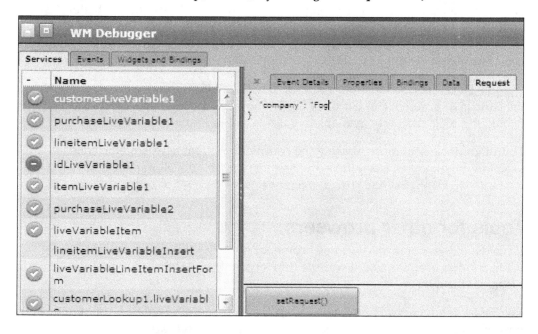

The **setRequest()** button sets the value and invokes the operation. Again, this is easily possible by calling `setData()` on the variable from the console; the WM Debugger simply provides a friendly interface to this functionality.

Other features of the WM Debugger include the displaying of application events, such as binding events. To learn more about the WM Debugger, visit the WM Debugger page in the product documentation: `http://dev.wavemaker.com/wiki/bin/wmdoc_6.5/WM+Debugger`.

Developer tools

JavaScript developers now have a range of tools to choose from when testing and debugging browser applications. We will now review the browser debuggers most commonly used by WaveMaker developers.

Closure Compiler

We saw in *Chapter 3, Using Studio,* how Studio provides JavaScript validation on the **Source** tab using Google's Closure Compiler. If you have JavaScript files you are editing outside of Studio or have pages that fail to load into Studio, the Closure Compiler is still available to you. Simply load the code into the online compiler http://closure-compiler.appspot.com/home.

Chrome Developer Tools for WebKit

We have been using Chrome Developer Tools throughout this book to better understand both WaveMaker and our application. When we need to debug the client portion of our application, Chrome Developer Tools is currently the "go to" choice for many developers.

Chrome Developer Tools offers a full set of tools, all built into the browser. If the issue is reproducible in Chrome, the Chrome Developer Tools are the fastest debugging tools currently available.

Thorough documentation on using the console tool, from accessing the console to setting breakpoints, is available by visiting Google's developer site at https://developers.google.com/chrome-developer-tools/docs/console.

Tools for other browsers

If the issue does not reproduce in Chrome, or if you just prefer to develop using another browser, you'll want to find a console and debugging tool for the target browser.

The Safari debugger can be accessed from the **Page** menu's **Develop** submenu. Safari now includes iOS-specific extensions for debugging mobile applications.

Firefox's Firebug, http://getfirebug.com/, is the original browser debugger. At the time, Firebug was a huge step forward for JavaScript development. Since Firefox 10, Mozilla has developed built-in developer tools accessible from the **Tools** menu in Firefox.

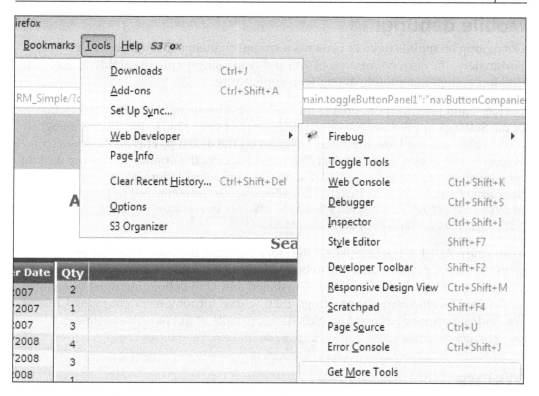

Like the Chrome Developer Tools, Firefox and the built-in Firebug tools allow you to watch network traffic, interact with the application's components, and inspect the page's elements and nodes. Firefox also provides a few unique features, such as tilt (https://blog.mozilla.org/tilt/). All this makes Firefox an excellent alternative to Chrome for development and debugging.

A feature unique to Firebug is its availability for other browsers in the form of Firebug Lite, http://getfirebug.com/firebuglite. Although quite limited, if you must work with older browsers, Firebug Lite can be the only useful console tool available to you. The best part about Firebug Lite is that it can be installed to any page with a bookmarklet, available at http://getfirebug.com/firebuglite#Install. However, it is limited and remains a tool of last resort.

Even Microsoft's Internet Explorer now includes built-in tools accessible from the **Tools** menu in MSIE or by using the *F12* shortcut key. Unfortunately, even as of MSIE 10, Internet Explorer's built-in developer tools are simply not as good as Firebug or Chrome's Developer Tools. However, when debugging MSIE-specific issues, MSIE's built-in tools are sufficient to avoid reverting to alert statements.

Mobile debugging

Debugging on mobile devices presents a special challenge for developers. Fortunately, the current versions of iOS and Android provide the ability to use your desktop system to remotely debug web applications.

On iOS 6 and later, you can enable the Web Inspector using the **Advanced** section of the **Settings** application. Once enabled, connect your Mac to the iPhone using a USB cable and the **Develop** menu of Safari on the desktop. This enables you to inspect, view, debug, and edit, just like when running the application on the desktop. Step-by-step instructions are available on the Apple developer site at `https://developer.apple.com/library/iOS/#documentation/AppleApplications/Reference/SafariWebContent/DebuggingSafarioniPhoneContent/DebuggingSafarioniPhoneContent.html`.

With Android 4.1, Google replaced the stock Android browser with Chrome. Devices with Chrome for Android can be debugged via a USB cable from a desktop. The desktop must have the Android SDK installed and USB debugging must be enabled under the **Developer options** settings. Instructions for remotely debugging Chrome for Android are available on Google's developer site at `https://developers.google.com/chrome-developer-tools/docs/remote-debugging`.

Weinre

WEb INspector REmote (**weinre**) enables remote debugging for mobile devices that do not support the aforementioned remote method. Weinre is the debugger used by the PhoneGap debugging page at `http://debug.phonegap.com/`. Access to weinre has even been built into `http://build.phonegap.com` via the **debug** button:

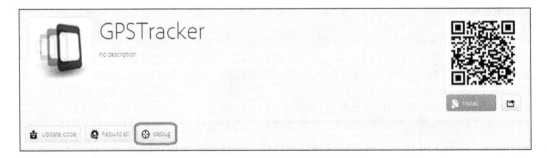

Instructional videos, documentation, issue tracking, and discussion groups can all be found by visiting the weinre home page at `https://search.apache.org/~pmuellr/weinre/docs/latest/Home.html`.

At the console

Now that we've gained console access to our application, let's cover some of the key aspects to debugging with the browser developer tools. If you are familiar with debugging compiled languages such as Java but are new to JavaScript, you'll appreciate the ability to easily evaluate functions from the console.

No this keyword

The syntax you use at the console is the same as the one you use inside page code with one major exception: there is no `this`. Unless you are in a breakpoint within a page function, `this` does not refer to the current page. Instead, the page must be referenced by name. So, instead of addressing `customerDojoGrid` as `this`. `customerDojoGrid` as we would in page code of `Main.js`, we would use the page name explicitly; that is, `main.customerDojoGrid`.

This is simple enough when the component is a direct child of the current page. However, when using page containers, navigation must be done from the top-most page. Consider the `CustpuchaseNavigation` example project. Say we wish to invoke the `onClick` event of the button labeled **Loading Dialog** on the `PageDialogs` page. We could navigate our way through the various page containers starting from the parent page. A simpler solution is to use `wm.getPage()` to get the page. `wm.getPage()` returns the specified page, if found:

```
wm.getPage("PageDialogs").buttonLoading.click();
```

Once we have the page, we can access its components as normal.

That gets us access to the desired component, but if we are going to be spending any amount of time working with this page in the debugger, we will want to reduce the volume of syntax required accessing the page. To do that, we can save a reference to the page as a variable in our console:

```
var pageDialogs = wm.getPage("PageDialogs");
```

Now we can reference the page's components using our variable:

```
pageDialogs.buttonLoading.click();
```

Debugger

Debugger is a useful JavaScript keyword. Of all the JavaScript reserved words, `https://developer.mozilla.org/en-US/docs/JavaScript/Reference/Reserved_Words`, debugger is the only one of particular interest for debugging. Simply drop `debugger;` into any function, and if a console is open, it will break upon reaching that statement. This can be useful in a few cases.

One use-case is to aid the development process. Debugger lets you see the world from the function in question at the point of the `debugger` statement. Having trouble understanding something such as the exact location of something in the DOM at some point in a function? Drop `debugger` in there and have a look. When execution is interrupted in a page function such as this, `this` refers to the page whose function we are in. This is a great place to start exploring from. Use the console to "feel" around if it helps. The console's auto completion provides assistance in real time. Code tested from here can generally be copied and pasted into the function body as it is.

Another use for the `debugger` statement is for debugging situations that should never happen. Got a particularly nasty situation that needs far more than logging to debug? Keep the console open, and if that error occurs, execution will stop then and there.

Finally, some breakpoints can be difficult to find and/or set. For one reason or another, sometimes it is just easier to modify the source file to insert a `debugger` statement and run in debug mode if needed. Inserting a `debugger` statement absolves us of having to find the class we need in the browser's tool to set the breakpoint. If we are unable to use a tool we know well enough to set a breakpoint for any reason, a `debugger` statement is a quick way to set one. For conditional breakpoints, surround the keyword with an `if` statement:

```
if (someCondition == true) {
    debugger;
}
```

 Debugger should be used in development only. Don't forget to remove all `debugger` statements before deployment.

Useful tool features

Browser tools in general, and the Chrome Developer Tools in particular, offer a number of useful features. Some are more useful to WaveMaker developers than others.

Click on the "preserve log upon navigation" button in the network toolbar, as shown in the following screenshot:

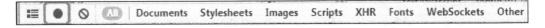

When enabled, the button turns red, and the **Network** tab retains its output across navigations. This is extremely useful when you need to see what happened before loading the application, such as between the user's login button press and the loading of the actual application. Without this enabled, the login page traffic is removed when the navigation to the application begins.

Right next door is the "clear" button:

As we might expect, this clears the network output. This button is perfect to use just before initiating a sequence of network traffic you want to observe. By removing all the previous traffic, you can focus in on just the area of concern.

Finishing up the network row are the filters:

Pause on all exceptions in the **Sources** tab can also be extremely useful:

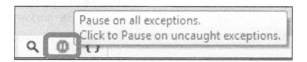

When enabled, execution will pause on all exceptions or any uncaught exception, accordingly.

Server

In a nutshell, the server side of WaveMaker applications are debugged like any other Java application. We use logging, log4j more specifically, and Eclipse, InteliJ IDEA, or otherwise our preferred tool to attach to the server with a debugger. Most often, we use Java Platform Debugger Architecture (JPDA) to establish the connection between debugger and debugee.

Logging

Logging in WaveMaker uses the Apache log4j 1.2, `http://logging.apache.org/log4j/1.2/`, for logging. We have seen that we generate log entries from Java and how log levels are set using the `log4j.properties` file in the `/src` folder. The log levels are in order of increasing verbosity: FATAL, ERROR, WARN, INFO, and DEBUG.

A common mistake made when reading WaveMaker log files occurs when the project fails to start due to some XML error, such as in a bean configuration. The project will most likely fail to start with a `BeanCreationException` error. However, the last error logged is from `testrunstart`, which only knows that that the application failed to start from the manager interface. It does not know why the application failed to start:

```
testrunstart:
      [echo] tomcat.manager.url=http://localhost:8094/manager
      [echo] tomcat.port=8094
  [undeploy] FAIL - No context exists for path /Project_Name
    [deploy] FAIL - Deployed application at context path /Project_Name
Abut context failed to start
```

An informative error message about why the project failed to start can be seen just a few lines above this generic `failed to start` message. In the case of a `BeanCreationException` error, the message will include the name of the bean that could not be created, what file that bean is defined in, and some message about why the bean could not be created.

Those uncomfortable with Java can miss out on useful information by thinking of stack traces as black boxes. Consider the case of a network connection problem to MySQL Server with the error `Connection refused`. In the server logs, we would see a stack that begins as follows:

```
com.wavemaker.common.WMRuntimeException: ConnectException: Connection
refused: connect
    at com.wavemaker.runtime.server.ServerUtils.invokeMethodWithEvents(S
erverUtils.java:412)
    at com.wavemaker.runtime.server.ControllerBase.
reflectionInvoke(ControllerBase.java:219)
    at com.wavemaker.runtime.server.JSONRPCController.executeRequest(JSO
NRPCController.java:182)
    at com.wavemaker.runtime.server.ControllerBase.handleRequestInternal
(ControllerBase.java:89)
    at org.springframework.web.servlet.mvc.AbstractController.handleRequ
est(AbstractController.java:153)
```

The top presents the `Connection refused` message while showing us how it got to calling `connect`. From the function names, we can see that the Spring MVC framework handled a request that was routed to the WaveMaker runtime, which lead to invoking a method that resulted in `WMRuntimeException` being thrown. If we continued through the omitted parts, we'd get to `java.lang.Thread.run` when the thread was started.

This stack is immediately followed by another stack that starts with `Caused by`. This tells us more about what happened to cause the `WMRuntimeException` error:

```
Caused by: java.net.ConnectException: Connection refused: connect
   at java.net.PlainSocketImpl.socketConnect(Native Method)
   at java.net.PlainSocketImpl.doConnect(PlainSocketImpl.java:333)
   at java.net.PlainSocketImpl.connectToAddress(PlainSocketImpl.
java:195)
   at java.net.PlainSocketImpl.connect(PlainSocketImpl.java:182)
   at java.net.SocksSocketImpl.connect(SocksSocketImpl.java:366)
   at java.net.Socket.connect(Socket.java:519)
```

In this second stack trace, it becomes clear that we are seeing the failure of `java.net.Socket.connect`, the `connect` that resulted in a `Connection refused` error.

If we continue physically down that second stack trace to move up the chain of execution, we can see this particular connection failure is from a method called `testConnection()` from Studio's `DataService`. This stack originates from the `invokeMethodWithEvents()` function at which the first stack left off:

```
com.wavemaker.tools.data.BaseDataModelSetup.testConnection(BaseDataMod
elSetup.java:945)
   at com.wavemaker.tools.data.TestDBConnection.
customRun(TestDBConnection.java:36)
   at com.wavemaker.tools.data.BaseDataModelSetup.
run(BaseDataModelSetup.java:424)
   at com.wavemaker.Studio.data.DataService.testConnection(DataService.
java:255)
   at sun.reflect.NativeMethodAccessorImpl.invoke0(Native Method)
   at sun.reflect.NativeMethodAccessorImpl.
invoke(NativeMethodAccessorImpl.java:39)
   at sun.reflect.DelegatingMethodAccessorImpl.invoke(DelegatingMethodA
ccessorImpl.java:25)
   at java.lang.reflect.Method.invoke(Method.java:585)
   at com.wavemaker.runtime.server.ServerUtils.
invokeMethod(ServerUtils.java:345)
   at com.wavemaker.runtime.server.ServerUtils.invokeMethodWithEvents(S
erverUtils.java:389)
   ... 33 more
```

From the preceding stack, you need only be a user of Studio to be able to guess that this came from the database import test connection button. This is a simple example, but it illustrates how we can learn a lot from stack traces if we take the time to let them tell us their stories.

Starting with JPDA

To debug your Java Service code or any WaveMaker Server code, start the Tomcat server under JPDA. Any Java process, including Tomcat, can be started under JPDA by passing the Xdebug flag to the Java command with the Xrun flag, which is used to configure the debugee, such as setting the listening address. To use 8000, the conventional listening port, we would add the following to our Java command:

```
-Xdebug -Xrunjdwp:transport=dt_socket,address=8000,server=y,suspend=n
```

On OS X and Linux, the debug flags can be added to a copy of the wavemaker.sh start-up script. This is the file used to start WaveMaker. It is a text script file that can be viewed. On Windows, the flags can be added to a copy of the WaveMaker startup shortcut. For Tomcat, add the flags to the Tomcat startup-up script.

For example, if we are on Windows using a JDK installed at C:\Java\jdk1.6.0_45\ to launch a WaveMaker installed in C:\program files, we might have a Java command line as follows:

```
c:\Java\jdk1.6.0_45\bin\javaw.exe -Xms256m -Xmx512m -XX:MaxPermSize=256m
-jar "C:\Program Files\WaveMaker\6.5.3.Release\launcher\launcher.jar"
```

Adding the debug flags to the preceding command yields the full Java debug command line:

```
c:\Java\jdk1.6.0_45\bin\javaw.exe -Xdebug -Xrunjdwp:transport=dt_
socket,address=8000,server=y, suspend=n -Xms256m -Xmx512m
-XX:MaxPermSize=256m  -jar "C:\Program Files\WaveMaker\6.5.3.Release\
launcher\launcher.jar"
```

If using a shortcut on Windows, add the flags to the **Target** field of the shortcut's properties.

With the server started with JPDA enabled, we can use a debugging client to attach to the server. We will use Eclipse from `http://eclipse.org/`.

Javaw has no console to report errors to. Changing `javaw` to `java` and running the Java start-up command in a console lets you see some startup errors without attaching with a debugger.

Attaching with Eclipse

Before attaching, we will want to import the project into Eclipse. As before, create a new Java project from an existing source. Clear the **Use default location** checkbox and select the `project` folder. Here we will be using the `SecureDbAccess` example project:

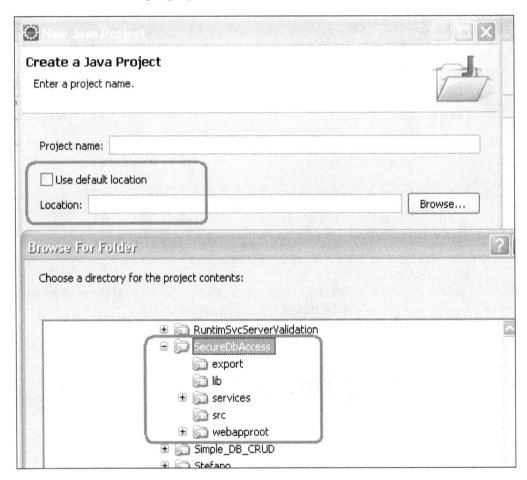

If you also import the WaveMaker sources, you can step between your service code and WaveMaker code as needed.

From the **Run** menu, use the **Debug Configurations** item to bring up the **Debug Configurations** dialog. Configure the **Remote Java Application** using the correct port number and hostname:

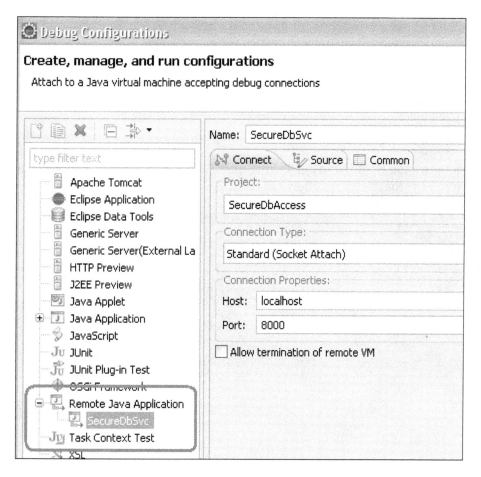

You can now set breakpoints and have the debugger break when it encounters the breakpoint. Here we've broken into the `readCustomer()` function from the `SecureDbSvc` example project of the `SecureDbAccess` project:

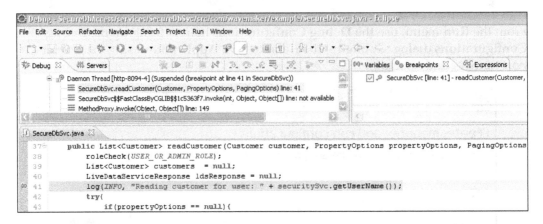

The configuration is added to our **Debug** menu and we can quickly connect again in the future now that the connection has been configured:

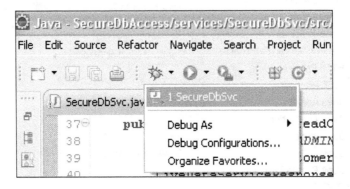

Summary

Debugging is an important part of the development process. A good logging foundation upon which to work makes the debugging process much easier. Even when not chasing down errors or defects, debugging tools can help developers understand the inner workings of their applications.

In this chapter, we looked at debugging and diagnostics. We started with some general troubleshooting tactics, including the classic "clear the cache" issue. We then used the **Network** tab to help diagnose client from server-side problems.

Next we looked at the client side of things, such as the tools available to use in the various browsers and some of the considerations for working in the console. We concluded the chapter by using Eclipse to attach to a server started with JPDA.

This concludes our WaveMaker journey together. I trust that by now you agree that WaveMaker enables non-professional developers to participate in web application development. I hope you also have seen how much fun development can be. If you have not already, may you experience the joys of deploying a real application to the Web soon.

One of the best parts of using open source software is the people and communities that surround the project. The WaveMaker community is a great group of diverse people. If you choose to use WaveMaker in any capacity, I encourage you to participate in its community.

It has been a pleasure. Enjoy the journey.

Index

Symbols

@HideFromClient annotation 221
!important property 111-113
.wmproject.properties file 40

A

Ace editor 10
Acegi Security. *See* Spring Security
addHistory() function 100
alert 87-89
Alestic
  URL 241
Amazon Elastic Compute Cloud
    (Amazon EC2) 240, 241
Apache JServ Protocol (AJP) 240
Apache log4j 1.2 269
app.alert() method 261
Apple 245
application
  planning 65, 66
asynchronous events 174, 175
Atom services 145
authentication 207
authorization 207
autoDataSet property 81
autoUpdate option 77, 78

B

back button feature 99
beginDataUpdate() function 198
binding dialog, Hello WaveyWeb
    project 62, 63
binding expressions 177-179

bindings 25, 26
BitNami
  URL 241
browser-executed code
  warning 174

C

cache
  clearing 257, 258
canvas, Hello WaveyWeb project
  about 49, 50
  working 50, 51
cascading stylesheets. *See* CSS
Chrome Developer Tools console 188
Chrome Developer Tools for WebKit 264
classes
  defining 110, 111
classes folder 37
class files 160
classpath
  about 159
  class files 160
  JAR files 160
  Java source files 160, 161
class rule
  testing, with dojo.query() 114
Clear Cache
  URL 258
client
  about 261
  console access 267
  Developer tools 264
  logging 261

Closure Compiler 264
mobile debugging 266
tools, for other browsers 264, 265
Weinre 266
dialogs
about 92
designable dialog 94, 95
generic dialog 93
loading dialog 93
page dialog 95
Distinguished Name (DN) 211
dojo.connect() 174
Dojo.connect() 25
Dojo framework 24
DojoGrid
about 196
expressions, displaying 197
dojo.query()
class rules, testing with 114
Dojo Toolkit 7, 22-24
drop table statement 125
dynamic page content
about 202
createComponent() 203, 204
reflow 202, 203

E

Easy-Web-Samples repository
URL 121
Eclipse
project, attaching with 274-276
URL 273
Eclipse/STS
about 163
WaveMaker project, importing
  into 163, 164
editor
extracting, from template 117
Engine Yard 240
EntryData, wm.Variable component 184-186
event handlers 175, 176
events
about 26, 174
asynchronous events 174, 175
event handlers 175, 176

external editor
using 161
external edits
compiling 164, 165

F

feed
binding 145, 146
FeedService.Feed object 146
feed services 145
filters 187, 188
FireBird 123
Firebug
URL 264
Firebug Lite
URL 265
Firefox OS
URL 244
form
creating, database objects used 130-132
formatters
about 194
Custom Function 195, 196
URL, for online documentation 196
useLocalTime 195

G

General Public License (GPL) 10
general troubleshooting
about 255
cache, clearing 257, 258
logging output 256
old applications, undeploying 259
server, restarting 259
WEB-INF, resetting 258
generic dialog 93
getDataValue() function 179
getFeed method 145
getFeedWithHttpConfig method 145
getfirebug site
URL 261
getInvalidWidget() method 200
getServiceBean() method 29, 167
getUserId() method 216
getUserName() method 216
getUserRoles() method 213, 222

Properties panel, Hello WaveyWeb project
about 56-61
page properties 61, 62
project properties 61, 62
published page properties 95, 96

Q

Query By Example (QBE) 137, 138
query() method 138

R

RBAC 214
reflow 202, 203
reflowParent() function 202
related editors 81
relational databases 121
resource manager 55
resources 188
REST
about 147
JSON, returning 150-152
XML, returning 148, 149
restrictValues property 201
return merchandise authorization
(RMA) 66
reusability 83
Rich Site Summary (RSS) 145
Role Based Access Control. *See* RBAC
roleCheck() method 222
roles 213
RuntimeAccess
about 165, 166
server-side validation 167, 168
service beans, accessing 166
runtime service
about 130
live saving, disabling 226, 227
securing 224-226

S

sample application
exploring, in Studio 16, 17
saveInCookie feature 209
schema, data model generation
creating 125

exporting 125
screen-sizing strategies
about 68
hybrid approach 70, 71
multiple versions, of application 69
one page, for all devices 69
page per device 70
script tab 52-54
SecureDbAccess
about 208
URL 208
security configuration
about 208, 209
customizing 216
roles 213
security providers 210-212
Setup Services tab 213, 214
security providers
Database security provider 210
Demo security provider 210
LDAP 210, 211
security service 216
security, WaveMaker
about 208
configuring 208, 209
security providers 210
selectFirstRow property 178
server
about 269
logging 269-271
restarting 259
service beans
accessing 166
service calls
optimizing 76, 77
service calls optimization
autoUpdate option 77, 78
client-side querying, of variable results 79
live views 80
related editors 81
result set size, controlling 78
service, data model generation
examining 126, 128
Service Method Definition (SMD) 36
service operation access
about 220
code, using 221, 222

Thank you for buying
Easy Web Development with WaveMaker

About Packt Publishing

Packt, pronounced 'packed', published its first book "*Mastering phpMyAdmin for Effective MySQL Management*" in April 2004 and subsequently continued to specialize in publishing highly focused books on specific technologies and solutions.

Our books and publications share the experiences of your fellow IT professionals in adapting and customizing today's systems, applications, and frameworks. Our solution based books give you the knowledge and power to customize the software and technologies you're using to get the job done. Packt books are more specific and less general than the IT books you have seen in the past. Our unique business model allows us to bring you more focused information, giving you more of what you need to know, and less of what you don't.

Packt is a modern, yet unique publishing company, which focuses on producing quality, cutting-edge books for communities of developers, administrators, and newbies alike. For more information, please visit our website: www.packtpub.com.

About Packt Open Source

In 2010, Packt launched two new brands, Packt Open Source and Packt Enterprise, in order to continue its focus on specialization. This book is part of the Packt Open Source brand, home to books published on software built around Open Source licences, and offering information to anybody from advanced developers to budding web designers. The Open Source brand also runs Packt's Open Source Royalty Scheme, by which Packt gives a royalty to each Open Source project about whose software a book is sold.

Writing for Packt

We welcome all inquiries from people who are interested in authoring. Book proposals should be sent to author@packtpub.com. If your book idea is still at an early stage and you would like to discuss it first before writing a formal book proposal, contact us; one of our commissioning editors will get in touch with you.

We're not just looking for published authors; if you have strong technical skills but no writing experience, our experienced editors can help you develop a writing career, or simply get some additional reward for your expertise.

Learning Kendo UI Web Development

ISBN: 978-1-849694-34-6   Paperback: 288 pages

An easy-to-follow practical tutorial to add exciting features to your web page without being a JavaScript expert

1. Learn from clear and specific examples on how to utilize the full range of the Kendo UI tool set for the web

2. Add powerful tools to your website supported by a familiar and trusted name in innovative technology

3. Learn how to add amazing features with clear examples and make your website more interactive without being a JavaScript expert

Python 3 Web Development Beginner's Guide

ISBN: 978-1-849513-74-6   Paperback: 336 pages

Use Python to create, theme, and deploy unique web applications

1. Build your own Python web applications from scratch

2. Follow the examples to create a number of different Python-based web applications, including a task list, book database, and wiki application

3. Have the freedom to make your site your own without having to learn another framework

Please check **www.PacktPub.com** for information on our titles

CouchDB and PHP Web Development Beginner's Guide

ISBN: 978-1-849513-58-6   Paperback: 304 pages

Get your PHP application from conception to deployment by leveraging CouchDB's robust features

1. Build and deploy a flexible Social Networking application using PHP and leveraging key features of CouchDB to do the heavy lifting

2. Explore the features and functionality of CouchDB, by taking a deep look into Documents, Views, Replication, and much more.

3. Conceptualize a lightweight PHP framework from scratch and write code that can easily port to other frameworks

Drupal 7 Mobile Web Development Beginner's Guide

ISBN: 978-1-849515-62-7   Paperback: 338 pages

Transform your existing Drupal site into one that is completely compatible with mobile and tablet devices

1. Follow the example of a 'Mom & Pop' restaurant site to make the transition to a mobile site easier

2. Prototype a distributed team workflow with GIT version control

4. Implement audio, video, charting and mapping solutions that work on Mobile, Tablet, and Desktop browsers

Please check **www.PacktPub.com** for information on our titles

www.ingramcontent.com/pod-product-compliance
Lightning Source LLC
Chambersburg PA
CBHW062110050326

40690CB00016B/3274